UNOFFICIAL SELVES

UNOFFICIAL SELVES

*Character in the Novel
from Dickens to the
Present Day*

PATRICK SWINDEN

BARNES & NOBLE
BOOKS·
10 East 53d St., New York 10022
(a division of Harper & Row Publishers, Inc.)

First published in the United Kingdom 1973 by
The Macmillan Press Ltd

Published in the U.S.A. 1973 by
HARPER & ROW PUBLISHERS, INC.
BARNES & NOBLE IMPORT DIVISION

ISBN 06 – 496672 – 0

Printed in Great Britain

for
Frank Anderson

Contents

Acknowledgements   ix

1   NOTHING BUT THE TRUTH   I
    Some modern theories of fiction. Kermode. Josipovici.

2   DEATHS AND ENTRANCES   27
    Dickens.   Other Victorians.

3   DETACHMENT   62
    European realism.   Flaubert.   Robbe-Grillet and the
    nouveau roman.   Turgenev and Tolstoy.

4   REGISTRATION   100
    Henry James.

5   TIME AND MOTION   120
    English realism.   Ford.   Bennett.   V. S. Naipaul.

6   GROWING PAINS   158
    Romanticism and the novel.   D. H. Lawrence.
    Richard Hughes.

7   PLOTS   203
    The Concept of Nature.   Bayley.   Iris Murdoch.
    Dan Jacobson.   Muriel Spark.

Bibliography   259

Index   267

Acknowledgements

The genesis of this book lies in the work I completed as a research student at Cambridge. The subject was the English and European influences on the novels of Ford Madox Ford. By the time I had submitted my dissertation, I was dissatisfied with my account of the theory of realism which lay at the centre of the argument. I was also dissatisfied with realist theory itself. Some of the grounds for my dissatisfaction became clearer to me in conversation with Malcolm Bradbury and Tony Tanner, to whom I am grateful for making me re-think the issues involved. I am also grateful to my supervisors at Cambridge, John Beer and Alison Fairlie. My debt to John Bayley, whose books on narrative fiction I have read with great pleasure, will be obvious.

I have benefited from the advice and encouragement of several people during the preparation and actual writing of this book. To my colleagues at Manchester I owe a debt, especially to Professor C. B. Cox and Mrs Felicity Currie. Most of all I am indebted to my wife, Serena, for her continuing contribution to the ideas expressed here, and to the teacher to whom this book is dedicated.

Finally I should like to thank Mrs Nancy Walsh for her labours, both typographical and diplomatic, in the preparation of the book for publication.

P. S.

The author and publishers wish to thank the following, who have kindly given permission for the use of copyright material: Mrs Dorothy Cheston Bennet, Hodder & Stoughton Ltd, and Doubleday for the extract from *The Old Wives' Tale* by Arnold Bennett; Calder and Boyars Ltd and Grove Press Inc. for extracts from *La Jalousie* from *Two Novels*, copyright © 1959 by Grove Press Inc., and *Pour un nouveau roman* from *For A New Novel:*

Essays on Fiction, copyright © 1965 by Grove Press Inc., both by Alain Robbe-Grillet; Chatto & Windus Ltd and Harper & Row, Publishers, Inc., for extracts from *In Hazard* and *The Fox in the Attic* by Richard Hughes; André Deutsch Ltd and Curtis Brown Ltd for the extract from *A House For Mr. Biswas* by V. S. Naipaul; Éditions du Seuil and Farrar, Straus & Giroux Inc., for the extract from *Le dégré Zéro de l'écriture* by Roland Barthes; The Hogarth Press Ltd, the author's Literary Estate and Harcourt Brace Jovanovich Inc., for the extract from *The Common Reader* by Virginia Woolf, copyright 1925 by Harcourt Brace Jovanovich Inc., copyright 1953 by Leonard Woolf; Laurence Pollinger Ltd and the Estate of the late Mrs Frieda Lawrence and The Viking Press Inc., for the extracts from *Sons and Lovers* by D. H. Lawrence and *The Collected Letters of D. H. Lawrence.*

> *'Official sentiments are one thing*
> *We are extra-official.'*

Wemmick to Pip in *Great Expectations*

I

Nothing but the Truth

'We invent man because we do not know how to observe him.'
Gérard de Nerval

How hard it was to describe things. How hard it was to *see* things. He wondered if, since he had completely given up drinking, he had actually been able to see more. . . . Any departure from total sobriety seemed to damage his perception. Even yet he was not sober enough, not quite enough, to take in the marvels that surrounded him. The ecstatic flight of a pigeon, the communion of two discarded shoes, the pattern on a piece of processed cheese. His *Notebook of Particulars* was in its third volume, and still he was simply learning to look. He knew that this, for the present, was all of his task. The great things would happen later when he was ready for them.

Miles Greensleave is the poet of *Bruno's Dream*. Stricken by the death of his first wife, and cut off from the real world by the life he lives with his second, he is discovered from time to time at his work-table, adding item after item to his *Notebook of Particulars*. Of what can I be certain? How can I write down what I see? How can I close the gap between what I see and my description of what I see? These are the questions to which the notebook is intended to provide tangible answers. In his description of a bowl of red and purple anemones, which his wife has placed on the table, he had wanted 'to catch in words the peculiar watery pallor of reflections in polished wood'. He had begun his description of these the night before, and had been successful in realising the strength of the stems, which had struck him so forcefully. But today everything is changed. His contact with a less certain though more complicated reality of friends and relations, that has intervened between the two attempts to describe the anemones, has left him dazed, unable to work. 'He could not see them properly any more. They were not worth looking at anyway.' Miles is living two lives which appear to take place on two different levels. His work on the notebook represents a strenuous attempt to discover the truth by disciplining his powers of perception. What can be known here is severely limited, and each known particular is not related to any other known particular. The world is a chaos of discrete objects, but each of these can be known – by the cultivation of a disciplined method of seeing and of describing what is seen. On the other hand not merely objects, but people, actions, events, 'what happens', come together and fall apart in ways that produce effects and provoke reciprocal actions. Unlike the objects described in the *Notebook of Particulars* these cannot be vouched for, their reality cannot be established. But Miles lives in the world where things happen as well as, and at the same time as, he lives in the world he is 'making true'. He is wrong when he thinks that the great things will happen later, 'when he was ready for them'. They do not wait upon the validation and support of what is not great. Whilst not being certainly true, therefore, they are effective, and part of their effectiveness lies in their power to disrupt the process of knowing what is really true.

Most modern poets and novelists have their notebooks of particulars. The part of the bowl of anemones has been played by a sparrow pecking at gravel outside the poet's window, or a simple table and a chair. We have only to read Keats's letters, Hopkins's notebooks, Ponge's poems to collect items for our own composite notebooks. But they have also had lives that have got entangled with what lies outside the objects their descriptions have verified. Keats's cultivation of negative capability encompassed the sparrow but fell far short of Fanny Brawne. In what sense, then, did he 'know' her? If he did not 'know' her, what justification could he find for including in his work what she 'meant' to him, let alone what she 'was'? Little is certain. Must the writer then restrict his activity to a debilitatingly narrow field? Or should he find ways of including in his fiction events like those Miles could not begin to describe, and of which Keats, with all his humility before the facts, did not live to attempt the description?

Later in *Bruno's Dream* we discover that Miles's preoccupation with his notebook is not at all what it appears to be, or what Miles thinks it is. This modest act of concentration on the particular is an evasion of the truth. It is Miles's way of forgetting his first wife, Parvati, and of closing his eyes to his feelings for his sister-in-law, Lisa. It is a form of consolation, therefore of self-deception. What he does is dictated by what he wants. The contact with reality it affords him, modest though it is, is therefore placed in a perspective that deprives it of its value. The reality Miles has discovered and added to his world through his description of it in the notebook does not stop being real. But that part of his world which is not understood, not made real to himself, is revealed to be vastly more extensive. What is more, it is so by virtue of those trivial, compact realities being discovered. Miles's situation pays him diminishing returns. The more he adds to his notebook, the further away he gets from all that is most urgent in the life that surrounds the notebook. Whether what is most urgent is most real is a question that has considerable bearing on contemporary critical debate. All I propose to say at the moment is that realities of the kind Miles commits to his notebook are discoverable by virtue of the fact that they make no claims: there is no temptation to diminish their reality by placing them in the service of the passions and requirements of a life that is lived outside them. The fact that the descriptions are true may be very much less interesting than the fact that it doesn't matter that they are true. There is no temptation to falsify them.

So far as we can ascertain, the entries in Miles's notebook do not extend to the provision of relations between one thing described and another. This is important, because it is in the relating of one thing to another that interference with reality becomes apparent. What goes on around Miles is entirely a matter of such interference, as must occur when an individual is precipitated into the world as an environment to be experienced rather than a sequence of discrete objects to be observed. It would be possible to go further and to argue that, quite apart from the pressures which have driven Miles to his descriptive exercises, the act of selection that must have preceded those exercises is itself evidence of a personal interference which must relate the objects selected to the subjective requirements of the person who is doing the selecting. Then this argument could be extended to the situation we find in the novel, where Miles's decision to try to describe the flowers which have been assembled by his wife and placed by her on the table is seen as a selfish act bestowing on the flowers, or their reflection in the wood, a significance they do not possess.

I shall discuss Iris Murdoch's views about how we are to think about selves in fact and fiction in my last chapter. For the moment I offer Miles's composition of his *Notebook of Particulars* as a model of the situation in which the contemporary writer finds himself trapped. Aware of his partiality and aware also of his responsibility to the truth, of his duty to respect what is real, he turns away from the mimetic deceptions of the earlier novels and restricts his attention to that area of what is presumed to be real, which he can cleanse of presumption. That area grows smaller with each new attempt upon it, as the area into which it debouches, the area occupied by the writer's stock of interests and presumptions, grows larger. As explanations become less and less total, then give way to relations, which in turn give way to mere selections, all the time diminishing in range and status, the outcome of the process slowly discloses itself. It is a picture of the writer alone, the futility of his ambition laid bare, as his only proper subject.

This is the situation in which many modern novelists have found themselves and are still finding themselves. I have described it as a trap, and I shall have to go on to explain how the trap has been set – by the unavoidable conditions the modern world and our ways of thinking about it impose on the novelist, or by the novelist's wilful self-subjection to delusions about what his responsibility to his art entails. Before I do this, however, I must guard against possible misconceptions of what I have been saying. I am not making the familiar claim that all post-Romantic literature is autobiography. On the contrary, there is nothing a writer is more likely to be more deluded about than what constitutes his own identity. Miles's preoccupation with what he supposes lies outside the circumference of his self is typical of the modern escape from self-concern. But as I have shown, this escape from the self into what is not the self must result in the imposition of personal pressures on what is other than self, and the consequent absorption of the other in the self. This absorption may range from the imposition of a personal symbolism on to the object, to the placing of the object in a position from which it is to be looked at, separated from or related to other objects of the writer's own choosing. Once perceived, the object is no longer free of the self that perceives, and all the intentions, desires, demands of that self. It follows that, if only by virtue of the amount of potential falsehood – fiction, if you like – that is excluded, the less description there is of what lies outside the self of the writer, the less distortion of the truth there will be. But, of course, what most importantly lies outside the self of the writer are the descriptions and interpretations of his own personality, his character. When all other temptations have been thrust outside the circle of self-hood, this last temptation must not be allowed to remain. The writer is left, not with the substance of a spiritual autobiography, but with his situation *as a writer*. He is a man who puts pen to paper with no confidence in his powers to transcribe reality, a stern distrust of the imagination which is the inventor of fictions, i.e. lies, and an impulsion to write. He has therefore to find a way of living with his fictions, or of getting them to destroy themselves in the interests of truth, or at least in the interests of lack of untruth – which is silence. These are the alternatives I want to examine now. On the one hand, fiction is offered us as a consolatory distraction in a world which, with or without it, is meaningless. On the other, fiction destroys itself in order that a silence, which cannot otherwise be articulated, may be articulated.

Professor Frank Kermode is the most celebrated apologist for the first of these views, though I have to reserve judgement as to how far he would agree that the world is meaningless. Certainly he is much concerned with the ways we confer provisional meanings on the world. His book about this, *The Sense of an Ending*, is carefully sub-titled 'Studies in the Theory of Fiction', fiction being understood not merely, though primarily, in its literary manifestation, but also in the sense in which we talk about legal fictions, fictive zero-cases in mathematics, etc. – in other words, all those useful untruths that fall into the category of 'the consciously false'. The phrase is used by Hans Vaihinger in *The Philosophy of As If*, a book Kermode depends upon a good deal to support a philosophy of knowledge that lies just far enough beneath the surface of his theory of fiction to prevent our scrutinising it with the thoroughness it may occur to us is required. By relating literary fictions to other kinds of fictions, Kermode would claim to have shifted the ground of our discussion of the novel significantly in the direction of a more philosophical approach, from which the writing and reading of novels can be seen to be a way of engaging with or even creating a reality which would otherwise be denied us. It is my view that the connections he discovers between one fiction and another are often suspect, and more a tribute to the theoretician's ingenuity than a description of relationships that actually exist. The complementary connection between the fiction and the world, fiction as a means of knowing about the world, strikes me as being very puzzling. I shall try to explain why.

There can be little argument with Kermode's preliminary statement about fiction that it is a way of making sense of life. Fictions, literary and otherwise, do confer a form and organisation on materials that are not themselves necessarily formed and organised. Further, since we cannot conceive of a life being lived outside a time-scale of some kind, we find that we have to relate what is now to its beginning and its end. But we cannot remember our beginnings, where they are private; nor does any one beginning certainly originate all that follows, where they are public; and our ends, private or public, are not known. Beginnings and ends therefore have to be imagined, they have to be created as fictions; and the relationship of beginning and end, thus imagined, to what *is*, 'in the middest', confers organisation on the life of an individual, a civilisation, and what binds an individual to a civilisation. This imagined harmony between beginning, middle and end – the middle of which alone is known – Kermode calls a 'concord fiction'. Since the nature of the relationship between the three points in time changes from one period of literary history to another (as it does, presumably, in the life of an individual), the models of harmony, the concord fictions, are in a continuous process of change. Kermode then goes on to demonstrate this process by providing an account of one important variant of concord fictions in general, which he calls fictions of the End.

Fictions of the End, or of Apocalypse, are concords of an imaginatively recorded past and an imaginatively predicted future, as these are viewed 'from the middest'. The most important fact about apocalypses is that they never happen. By arousing the expectation that they will happen, at a predicted time, the rest of history or narrative that moves towards that time acquires a design, is made sense of. There is a consonance between beginning and middle that is dependent on the prediction of an end. The fact that the end never comes at the appointed time does not invalidate the fiction in general. Only the detail is found wanting. So, adjustments have to be made in the detail to make the pattern of relationships between past, present and future (end) conform with reality. The word 'fiction' now refers to two things which may or may not be identified with each other (depending on whether you are looking forward to the future as future, or backwards to what *was* the future as past). One of these, the general pattern dependent on the prediction of an end event (e.g. the movement of the Christian universe towards the second coming and apocalypse), Kermode called the 'paradigm'. The other, the same pattern dependent on the prediction of an end event *the timing of which is disclosed* (e.g. the movement of the Christian universe towards the second coming and apocalypse *in the year* A.D. *1000*), is not given a name of its own; it remains an apocalyptic fiction, or fiction of the End, just as it can be in its more generalised paradigmatic form. Naturally, the detail of the fiction is subject to a continuing process of revision. Equally naturally, the paradigmatic form stays the same.

The application of this crucial part of a general theory of fictions to literary fictions is now apparent. For literature has its own peculiar type of apocalyptic consonance, i.e. that which relates fictional realities to paradigmatic expectations. It is a function of the plot which Aristotle called *peripeteia*, and as such it is a part of all fictions, not merely the tragedies with which Aristotle was principally concerned. *Peripeteia* is an apparent reversal of expectations which is followed by those same expectations being met in a way that was unforeseen when they were first aroused. In Kermode's terms, it is a disconfirmation, or a series of disconfirmations, followed by a consonance. In this way the literary paradigm is preserved, though the fiction which incorporates the 'real' actions and events that give it present substance undergoes a number of imaginative reconstructions. The intrusion of reality (in this case the events the writer selects to propel the plot towards its conclusion) is for ever falsifying the nature of the fictions we use to explain it. Therefore we keep having to change the fictions, the detail of the paradigms, to keep up the state of our knowledge of reality. In literary terms, we have to keep on revising our expectations about 'what will happen' by testing them against 'what does happen', always ensuring that by doing so we preserve the consonance of beginning and middle. There are therefore always two plots or actions in the reading of a book: there is the plot which the novelist intends, and which gradually materialises as we read his book; and there is the plot which the reader predicts at each stage of his reading of the book. The second plot is made up of a series of plots which undergo revision after revision until, at the end of the book, the final expectation is satisfied and the writer's and the reader's plots come together as a single paradigm, beginning, middle and end identical in each case.

I would accept that in this very loose sense *peripeteia* is common to all actions and that the experience of reading a novel or responding to any kind of literary or theatrical fiction is as Kermode describes it. Indeed, so far there is nothing very extraordinary in what he is saying, in spite of the apparatus of a new technical terminology – of concord fictions, paradigms, consonances and disconfirmations – which appears to have been made necessary by the context of the argument about fictions in general. Though I shall not be using Kermode's terminology, I shall have something to say about disconfirmed expectations and delayed consonances in my discussion of several novels in later pages of this book. The difference lies in the status I accord them as 'ways of making sense of the world'. I shall now return to *The Sense of an Ending* and address myself to the issue Kermode takes up after his description of the fictions of the End, which is that of the status of such fictions and their relationship to the world they help to make sense of.

Fictions have this in common with scientific hypotheses and myths – that they work on the principle of 'as if'. Kermode is fond of quoting Wallace Stevens on this, from a late poem in which the theory of poetry is held to be 'the theory of life/As it is in the intricate evasions of as'. But the evasions of poetic (and all literary) fictions are different from those of science and myth because the 'as if' of science is susceptible to proof and refutation (by experiment) and the 'as if' of myth is a commitment to belief. Both have a claim to permanence or, in the case of the scientific hypothesis, 'as if' can be transformed into 'is the case' where the evidence supports it. But fictions, including literary fictions, are automatically dropped when the finding-out process is completed. As soon as they lose their operational effectiveness they are doomed to neglect. Now we must ask, in terms of what is their operational effectiveness said to function? Kermode's answer, not surprisingly or controversially, is: in terms of their usefulness in bringing us into contact with reality and awakening us to the significance of that reality. The question then arises as to where the significance resides. It is at this point, about half-way through his second chapter and continuing at least until the end of his third, that Kermode becomes, to my kind, impenetrably, though elegantly, obscure.

The argument revolves around a description of fictions of time. Time, says Kermode, can be experienced in one of two ways, as mere successiveness or as plot. Where it is experienced as plot, we shall find that the fictional devices have been used to impose or to discover a pattern upon or within the successive flow of time. The problem lies in the presentation of the alternatives of imposing or discovering. Do we have to choose between them or can they both be held to be appropriate in some way? At first it looks as if Kermode is going to get round the problem, somewhat ingeniously, by using what I can only describe as a half-metaphor. Time, he says, is like the ticking of a clock. We describe this with little real justification as 'tick-tock'. But why not 'tock-tick'? Because 'tick-tock' is the sound a clock makes when we become humanly attentive to it. 'Tock-tick' is mere successiveness. Now since books are 'fictive models of the temporal world', it is the business of those who write them to ensure that 'tick-tock' is the right way round. The imposition of an End, with all the lively expectation – and therefore plot, pattern – that it arouses, is the traditional form this insurance takes. The events that occur between the beginning and end, whilst manifesting their fair share of successiveness ('tock-tick'), are wrought into significance by the paradigm of beginning, middle, end ('tick-tock'), that invisibly binds together the events throughout the fiction. These events, then, become 'historical moments of intemporal significance'. So, continuing the argument about fictions of time, with the line between the passage of time and the experience of the passage of time blurred to such an extent (that is what 'tick-tock' does), it looks as if it is impossible to distinguish discovering and imposing a pattern upon temporal sequence. But at this juncture Kermode re-focuses his point of view, and finds the line drawn clearly between the two. The realism of modern fictions, he says, is a result of the discovery that patterns found in historical time are the products of anthropocentric activity. This throws into dispute all over again the status of those significances to which Kermode attaches so much importance. The question arises as to how far the modern writer is justified in cultivating fictional patterns, paradigms, when the historical excuse for them has disappeared. The result of this, he says, is the novelist's fabrication of a work which, whilst recognising mere successiveness, is not itself merely successive. At this point, clinging to the paradigms whilst being uneasily aware of their 'real' futility, Kermode's argument bears interesting comparison with that of Gabriel Josipovici, whose book *The World and the Book* I shall be looking at shortly. Both point to the dilemma of the modern novelist or composer of fictions in a world which no longer exhibits those real formal arrangements that the techniques he has inherited were evolved to express. What excuse can he find for going on writing at all, and how can he build it into a structure of his own fictions?

Kermode's response to this question is to jolt his readers into a novel way of approaching the issue of what constitutes reality and how fictions are related to it. In effect, he re-blurs the line between the discovery and the imposition of meanings, i.e. reality and fiction, that modern thinking had drawn too clearly. This he does by using another method, or at any rate a surprising and whimsical comparison. The time-order of novels is what the medieval Church fathers called *aevum*, a term that Kermode takes several pages to explain and the meaning of which remains somewhat mysterious in spite of his exertions. As I understand it, the term, and the concept it denotes, originated in the attempts of Aquinas and his followers to bring into line, as far as was possible, the Aristotelian view that the world was eternal, because *ex nihilo nihil fit* (nothing can come of nothing), with the Christian view that God had brought the world into being out of nothing in the six days of creation. This was done in a manner which failed to account for the composition of angels, for Aquinas's achievement had been to distinguish between two kinds of being – matter, which was potential, and substance, which was actual – and angels could not be composed of either of these, nor could they be pure being, since if they were of any of these things they would be God, man, or something less than either. Separated as the angels had become from both time, which is of man, and eternity, which is of God, they were accommodated in a third order of duration, somewhere between the two. This was what Aquinas called *aevum*. Kermode now proceeds to relate *aevum* to literary fictions. The interdependence of beginnings, middles and ends allows what happens in a novel to co-exist with, at the same time as it is now subjected to, time in its character as a successive flow. It therefore partakes of the same order of existence as that which the angels were held to partake of by Aquinas. '*Aevum*, you might say, is the time-order of novels. Characters in novels are independent of time and succession, but may and usually do seem to operate in time and succession; the *aevum* co-exists with temporal events at the moment of occurrence, being . . . like a stick in a river.' Or, we might say, like the pattern of 'tick-tock' that co-exists with the successiveness of 'tock-tick' in the ticking of a clock. And so, like the angels, the contents of novels are real, but in a different way from the way in which we customarily think of things as being real. 'The concords of past, present and future to which the soul extends itself are out of time, and belong to the duration which was invented for angels when it seemed difficult to deny that the world in which men suffer their ends is dissonant in being eternal. To close that great gap we use fictions of complementarity. They may now be novels or philosophical poems, as they were once tragedies, and before that, angels.'

This explanation of how angels, and fictions in general, relate to or fit in with the reality of the world outside them, closes the first half of Kermode's book. I shall summarise much more briefly what follows, which is an account of how modern thinkers and writers have used the traditional paradigms, how they have performed the continuing task of relating these to an accelerated series of changes in their sense of reality. The problem is that most of these writers do not share the confidence of Kermode, Stevens and Vaihinger in the status of concord fictions. Their sophistication of mind seldom extends to being able to endorse the way these three writers and theorists play fast and loose with reality. They are altogether more suspicious of fiction. Novels are not like life because all that seems fortuitous and contingent in them is 'reserved for a later benefaction of significance in some concordant structure'. Living no longer seems to have anything to do with concordant structures. The nineteenth century experienced a breakdown in the relationship between the time of a life

and the time of the world which, far from having been overcome, has only increased in the modern age. There is no longer
a pattern in the world outside, which will serve to suggest how a
pattern can be achieved for the worlds we create – in our personal
lives and in the novels we write. Thus we are suspicious of inherited paradigms, which beckon us, or so we suppose, towards
these discredited patterns. We have made the transition from a
literature which assumed it was imitating an order that lay outside itself, to a literature which assumes that it has to create an
order which is entirely self-sustaining and which can be achieved
only after a breaking-down of all our inherited assumptions about
order. At last we have returned to Miles's situation in *Bruno's
Dream*, in which we see pictured, in Kermode's words, 'the knowledge that our inherited ways of echoing the structure of the
world have no concord with it, but only . . . with the desires of
our own minds'.

As you will gather from my account of his theory of fictions,
this is not a prospect Kermode finds at all daunting. He maintains, and justifies, a faith and indeed an enjoyment of the imagination as a power which can make good whatever deficiencies
our changed sense of reality has brought about. The arguments
he advances, drawing on sources as remote both from ourselves
and from each other as relativity theory and medieval angelology,
place him in what might appear to be an unassailable position
from which he can blur and sharpen the line between reality
and fiction, successiveness and significance, at will and with invigorating effect. Before I go on to look at the way another critic
addresses himself to similar issues, I should like to draw attention
to two facts about Kermode's approach to literary fictions, one
about method and the other about consequences. Firstly, he has
attained the position from which he can live with his fictions by
an argument that proceeds always from a judgement about what
is psychologically convenient, about how we can believe something
to be true, or real, or whatever it is convenient for us to believe.
It is interesting that the argument about 'tick-tock' is conducted
by recourse to what I called half-metaphors, i.e. images which are
taken from the field of study they are being used to investigate, with the result that it is sometimes difficult to know what
we are to take them for: the tools that are being used in the
investigation or the objects that are being investigated? Kermode's

theory of fiction is comprehensive in the scope of its operations, but the method he uses to conduct these operations is defective at several points. These include the starting-point, that if we know what we wish to be the case, then we can find ways of ensuring that it is the case – even if we have to go back to Aquinas's eschatology to provide a rationale, i.e. a convenient metaphor, for it. Secondly, the position he occupies prevents him from observing any clear relationship, not between a particular fiction – a novel, play, poem – and a concept of reality in general, but between a particular fiction and the particular phase in the history of the world that it might appear to have some bearing on. The shape of fiction may, in a somewhat equivocal sense, have something to do with the shape of reality. But as soon as the content of a fiction, in whatever shape it is discovered, is allowed to affect one's attitudes to particular aspects of the world outside it, a damage has been done to our appreciation of both the world and fiction. Fiction has lost its fictiveness, and been misread as a myth. On this view a gap is opened up between the world we commonly observe, or think we observe, and both the world of the book and the most general description of the world that we can articulate. Between these two most particular and most general entities, the ordinary world has been spirited away. Kermode does not appear to regret its passing.

Yet for some readers, and writers, it is regrettable. Many of those who have lost confidence in patterns of history have struggled to find a way of reconciling the absence of such patterns with the presence of their mirror-images, plots, in fiction. And because fabricating plots is what the novelist's gifts and expertise equip him to do, plots have a habit of cropping up in the most unlikely places, bringing with them characters who behave suspiciously like their incredible forefathers in the old-fashioned nineteenth-century novel. There is, even in some of the most uncompromising experiments of the French *nouveaux romanciers*, an imaginative commitment to what, on their own admission, ought to be a manifest absurdity – namely the play of motive, examination of the link between cause and consequence, detailed scrutiny of behaviour which can make sense only on the assumption that character and plot are something more than the pretences of an age we have outgrown. It is often the case that these things are indeed pretences, and the novelist who created them is very much aware of the fact that this is what they are. All he has to do is to pull the carpet from under their feet and they will all fall down. The carpet in the figure is the novelist's relationship to his fiction, which discloses itself in an elegant gesture of contempt for the properties he has assembled to take us in. But as I point out below, in Chapter 3, all too often we refuse not to go on being taken in. The gesture is elegant but futile. The properties never looked more like plots, patterns and characters.

Gabriel Josipovici has produced the most provocative and intelligent statement of what I suppose must be called the structuralist point of view, which is the point of view that places the emphasis on the dismissive gesture rather than the things it dismisses. In his recent *The World and the Book* he draws attention to the same state of affairs Kermode discussed towards the end of his book: namely, the discovery by modern artists that there is no pattern or significance which is 'given' by the world we have to live in; and that the equipment we have inherited for the purpose of describing the world is therefore unsatisfactory. Unlike Kermode, though, he believes that this lack of inherent 'plot' goes back far beyond the late nineteenth century. So also does the fact that writers, and thoughtful people generally, noticed it. What happened during the early phases of modernism was that for the first time those men who were in the vanguard of the most important artistic movements of the period addressed themselves to the task of coming to terms with the situation. It is for this reason that so much modern art is anti-representational. This is conspicuously the case in the novel, which, of all the literary arts, has made the greatest claim to representation, or verisimilitude. Indeed, it is difficult to envisage a novel that is not first and foremost concerned with the representation of what we we feel we know the world is like. But, says Josipovici, this is not so, and the existence of numerous works of literary fiction on the fringe of what we take to be the central tradition of novel-writing in the past two hundred and fifty years show that it is not so. Our expectation of verisimilitude is simply evidence of an enslavement to convention, to habit. We see the world through 'the spectacles of habit', and what we see is governed by the assumptions we bring with us, unconsciously, to the act of seeing. So the best modern writing is that which persuades us, or shocks us, into removing the spectacles and confronting the world that really exists beneath the fictions we have all too self-indulgently allowed to obscure it. And the criticism which can best show us how to do this is one which directs our attention beyond the origins of *modernism*, where for the first time the problem was systematically incorporated in fiction, to the origins of the *problem*, where people first grew conscious of the fact that the world was no longer intelligible to them in the way it had been to their forefathers. Hence Josipovici begins the historical argument of his book with an account of the breakdown of the medieval world order as he finds it expressed in Dante, and its replacement with what Kermode would call new concord fictions in the work of late medieval and Renaissance writers.

A succinct description of the medieval world order is given in the words of Hugh of St Victor, writing in the twelfth century: 'For this whole visible world is a book written by the finger of God, that is, created by divine power; and individual creatures are as figures therein devised by human will but instituted by divine authority to show forth the wisdom of the invisible things of God.' Of course, the ability of individual creatures to show forth that wisdom was compromised by the Fall. By creating individuality, the Fall obscured the image of God, in which all men were made. Therefore the more a man insists upon his individuality, the more he distinguishes himself from other men, in the development of what is pecular to himself, the further he sinks into the sin of pride, which caused even the angels to fall. The medieval view was that a man fulfils himself most completely when he insists least upon what is peculiar to himself, because by doing this he comes closer and closer to the image of God within him, which constitutes his true identity. Now since the world is a book and men and women are figures in it, created by divine power, it follows that to see the world is not only to register an appearance but to educe a meaning. A world created by God for a visible and disclosed purpose provides that meaning and appearance will correspond with each other, so long as we look aright at what is in the world. For the world is a structure of symbolic relations, and man must make what he makes according to what they prescribe.

A book is not an imitation or representation of a part of the visible universe, but 'a model or analogue of the universe itself'.

'Because the universe is seen in terms not of essences but of structures it is possible for the human craftman to imitate the *shape* of
reality itself.' He does this by looking outward to the world rather
than inward to the self as a private and idiosyncratic interpreter
of the world. This is what Dante does in *The Divine Comedy*.
He is a copyist, not an inventor. But he was not always so. The
journey through Hell to Paradise is at the same time a journey
from ignorance to knowledge – the ignorance of the private self,
knowledge of the world beyond the self. To read the *Comedy*
is to share in a growing knowledge of the unimportance of privacy, an emptying-out of our subjective nature as we understand
more and more the structure of the universe and the place of
our own lives in that structure. This was the world view that de-
cayed in the centuries after Dante. The fourteenth and fifteenth
centuries witnessed a breakdown of the 'analogical synthesis'.
Christ became a person whose moral goodness was to be admired
and imitated, rather than Incarnate God whose 'action' was to
be symbolically re-enacted in man, who is created in the image
of God. In art, this brought about the preoccupation with verisimilitude, the presentation of a thing, cut away from the total
world in which and from which it derived its meaning, rather
than of an action which constituted an understanding of the
structure of that world. Meaning and appearance no longer
corresponded. The artist no longer enacted, by seeing, his understanding of the world. Instead he drew attention to his individual
judgement by inquiring into the meaning of the world, which
was no longer 'given' to the seeing eye.

The history of post-medieval literature, properly studied, thus
becomes a history of how writers refused to accept, for the purposes of their art, this breakdown in the system of analogies.
Either they went on writing as if the structure of their fictions
was still validated by a transcendent order which, for other purposes, they did not take seriously; or they assumed they could
convince their readers that what they personally believed to be
true was universally true. The first alternative was stupid, the
second arrogant and presumptuous. But there were and are two
other possibilities which are less reprehensible than these. A writer
can accept the absence of essential meaning in the universe, and
the consequent fallibility of fictions which themselves laid claim
to meaning. He can then proceed to make his fiction out of a

representation of these conflicting and competing false interpretations. Acknowledgement of the relativity of understanding, and
the way in which separate understandings fall short of a truth
which the author cannot himself set down, is thus built into the
structure of the fiction. The other thing a writer can do is to
trap the reader into supposing he has been liberated into understanding, by bringing his interpretation of the world into line
with that of one or more of the characters in his book. Then the
writer pulls back from the character, placing him and his view
of the world in a perspective which, whilst laying no claim to
ultimate wisdom, does triumphantly demonstrate that the character, and the reader who has been manoeuvred into sharing his
responses, is not in possession of ultimate wisdom either. Chaucer
avails himself of the first alternative, Rabelais of the second. In
both cases the writer has demonstrated his distrust of fiction,
whilst providing fictions which are entertaining and self-validat-
ing. Most writers measure their success by the extent to which
they are able to make the reader forget that their worlds are false,
mere fictions. But 'Rabelais like Chaucer is troubled by this freedom, this lack of responsibility to any reality'. As the centuries
pass and those elements of literature (like genre, rhetoric, the
'forms') which testify to its own reality fall into disuse, the
irresponsibility increases, reaching its apogee with the rise of
the novel in the eighteenth and nineteenth centuries. Naturally
enough, Josipovici's comments on this phenomenon, and on the
corrective measures that have been taken from time to time to
reduce its pretensions, occupy the centre of his treatment of the
theme.

The primal error of the traditional novelist can be traced back
to the allegorical fable out of which the novel developed. The
most celebrated example of this is Bunyan's *The Pilgrim's Progress*, which provides a convenient contrast with *The Divine
Comedy* since both fictions describe a journey which in some sense
is to be interpreted symbolically. The principal difference lies in
the relationship between the narrator and his fiction. For in Dante
the speaker is the hero, and his journey both is and represents
an awakening into understanding in which the reader participates.
But in Bunyan the speaker merely reports his dream about
another person's (Christian's) journey. The meaning of that journey one presumes has been there from the start, inherent in its

beginning as much as in its end, with the result that Bunyan does not have to make sense of the world by seeing it more clearly. He flees from it to a better place. In *The Pilgrim's Progress*, then, meaning exists independently of the writer's struggle to know it. It can be embodied in the allegory which is experienced as a dream, i.e. something passively taken in, and therefore disengaged altogether from an active, questing process of finding out. Yet we know very well that neither the meaning nor its allegorical covering is truly independent of the writer. He made it up, and then pretended it was something separate from him, which he dreamed some time in the past, rather than that he is creating now, in the present, as he is writing. This is what all 'naïve realist' fiction does. It fails to get behind the duplicity of the impulse to form, which is a characteristic of consciousness. The novelist implicitly assumes that 'the world and the world as we are made conscious of it are one'. And so he pays the final penalty for the demise of the notion of analogy. A private imagination functions merely on behalf of itself, endeavouring to hide the fact that it is doing so by hiding itself behind what appears to be a free fiction. This is the essentialist fallacy, the supposition that we can be persuaded to believe that somehow or other the marks on the page secrete in themselves a hidden meaning and permanence, whereas in fact their authors have only 'fallen back into a private world where their imagination roams unchecked because it acknowledges no authority outside itself, and thus transforms the real world into an image of their own desire'.

Romanticism paved the way for the collapse of this fallacy, in spite of its early, optimistic reverence of the imagination. For the respect the Romantics felt for uniqueness in nature and in their own sensations brought them up hard against the constriction of language – which must function at a certain level of abstraction and universality, and must take basic social agreements among its users for granted. Not only language, but consciousness itself, became an obstacle to the true understanding of the self, in all its particularity, its quintessential difference from other selves. At first it was believed that language could be manipulated in such a way as to articulate this difference. But the movement from Romanticism to Symbolism to silence demonstrated the increasing strain to which this belief was subjected. Along with this went the collapse of another basic Romantic belief: that what is real is not, but somehow transcends, what is apparent. For the modern writer what is real and what is apparent are the same, though unlike the medieval writer he has no right to suppose they are significant. Habit, however, against all the evidence, convinces us that they are. Therefore it is the business of the writer to get rid of habit, and the only way he can do this is by having his novel or poem or other fiction insist upon its identity as just that: 'an object in its own right, *an irreducible single presence*'. This will force the reader to re-enact the writer's discovery for himself and rescue him from the illusory world created by an imagination which seeks to deprive him of his sense of reality. In this way the double error of post-medieval art – self-expression and imitation – is transcended. As with the medievals, 'art is not the expression of inner feeling or an imitation of part of the world'. It is 'the creation of a structure that will allow us to understand what it means to perceive, and will thus . . . give us back the world'.

How does it do this? Primarily by drawing attention to the fact, as it draws attention to itself, that its meaning lies in its relation to the author who has created it. He has to be seen to be emptying language of all its hidden presumptions – order, consequence and clarity which it suggests correspond with what is in nature. The evacuation of these presumptions reveals a silence, which it becomes the writer's job to articulate. Roland Barthes has said that this is what happens in Camus's *L'Etranger* ('La façon d'exister d'un silence'), and Josipovici draws up an impressive list of other important modern works – Mann's *Death in Venice*, Robbe-Grillet's *Dans le labyrinthe*, for example – in which the same thing happens: 'in the course of each of their works we are made to move from the context of the fiction to the maker of the book, and to recognise that the final meaning of the work is one that it is powerless itself to say, and this is *that it has been made*'. Thus the activity of reading becomes the subject-matter of the novel as in a sense it was the subject-matter of Dante's *Comedy* – with the sole, important difference that in medieval work the reading is revealed at the close to correspond with a reality which is *out there*, in the book of God, which is the world. The aim of the novelist becomes the deception of the reader, not as an end in itself, but as a necessary preliminary to the act of removing the deception. And since what he is deceived by is something that is shown to answer to his own assumptions about what the world is like, the removal of the deception also removes his confidence – which has been acquired by habit – in the picture of the world he brought with him to the reading of the novel. This is why the modern novel must be an anti-novel. 'It enlists the help of the novel to lull the reader into a false sense of security [i.e. familiarity], and then, by pointing to its own premises, pitches him into reality. . . . The modern novel draws attention to the rules which govern its own creation in order to force the reader into recognising that it is not the world.'

What the writer is doing by all this is recognising that he is the limits of his world. His fictions are nothing but the creations of his irresponsible imagination. But their structure acknowledges this fact about them, and thereby 'places' them in a world which is evidently not of them. Kafka's fable of 'The Truth about Don Quixote' summarises the situation beautifully. In it, the knight is revealed as the demon of Sancho Panza, the irresponsible fiction released by Sancho's vigorous imagination. Sancho is the type of the modern artist, who stands outside the activities of his own fancy, removing their power to harm by the very terms in which he brings to the reader's attention the relationship between the fiction that is created and the man who creates it. This is immensely invigorating for writer and reader alike. For the act of reading a book is analogous to the act of writing it. It is not the discovery *of* another world, but an activity *in* this one, an activity which is gradually understood to be converting itself into a meaning. This meaning lasts only as long as the reading lasts. It takes the form of a realisation of the limits of the writer's, and hence the reader's, world; and this allows him to stand for a while outside that world, looking in at it. He experiences himself 'not as an object in the world but as the limits of his world. And, mysteriously, to recognise this is to be freed of these limits and to experience a joy. . . .'

Kermode and Josipovici are in some respects very different kinds of critic. Although their tastes converge in their appreciation of Dante in the Middle Ages and Wallace Stevens in the modern period, elsewhere they betray very different temperaments and preferences. Josipovici more or less writes off the nineteenth-century English novel, whereas Kermode has written warmly, if idiosyncratically, on George Eliot. Conversely, Kermode displays little interest in the *nouveau roman*, and is distinctly lukewarm about Samuel Beckett, whereas for Josipovici writers like Robbe-Grillet, Claude Simon and Beckett himself are very much to be admired. Nevertheless they have important attitudes in common, and none more so than their highly developed awareness of fiction *as* fiction. Kermode values this awareness, some would say excessively – so much so that he has some difficulty disentangling it from reality; indeed, he appears to wonder if this can be done. Josipovici, on the contrary, deplores fiction. The only reason it is important that we should be aware of it is so that we can get rid of it; or, if that should prove impossible, to ensure that it is deprived of a status bestowed on it by nothing more admirable than our laziness and subjection to habit. So for Kermode a novel like *Middlemarch* is appreciated as a 'type' of historical crisis. Its success depends on the way it brings historical and psychological fact into relationship with a secularised version of an apocalytic paradigm. For Josipovici it is a transparent fabrication. He would recognise Kermode's paradigm as just another consoling fiction, encouraging the reader in his attachment to bad habits, just as the 'facts' that are created to test and confirm it are no more than props to shore up the artifice. But both critics are very much aware of the fact that they are reading a fiction. At no moment do they relinquish their grasp of this. At no moment do they surrender entirely to the illusion that most writers assiduously cultivate, that this is a real, not a fictional, world. Sancho Panza will not get out of the way. He is there to ensure that the reader, unlike Don Quixote, does not go tilting at imaginary windmills.

As a critic of altogether different inclinations from either Kermode or Josipovici, I find myself in the intellectually inferior position of Dr Johnson confronted with Bishop Berkeley's stone, which, you will remember, he kicked to prove that it was there. Logically, what they are saying might be irrefutable. In the end, our reading eye must draw back from the world that is created, to the shaping imagination that created it; and this is to recognise it as a fiction. As such it may have its uses, very impressive uses: in administering to our need for order, or in liberating us from false orders of the imagination for which the imagination is itself responsible. But uses are converted into misuses the moment we fail to see the fiction for what it is, an invention *of* the mind created to free us from servitude *to* the mind. It is the way the mind goes beyond itself and celebrates its own creative power, or draws attention to the unreality of what that power has created. Kermode is the optimist, Josipovici the pessimist, of the imagination. In their different ways they are representative of a modernist approach to the novel which develops the thinking of an earlier period. What I propose to do in the pages that follow is to look at the genesis of this thinking, and see how it issued in different kinds of fiction as it became more refined and more extreme. And all the time I shall go on kicking that stone – I mean, testing the strength of the illusion the novelist has created. My own view is that the harder it feels, the better the novel tends to be. Since this is an old-fashioned prejudice, in direct contradiction to the views I have been summarising, I must proceed to justify it, and explain what new things I believe remain to be said about novels by accepting it as a working hypothesis.

Basically, what I think is unsatisfactory in the modernist approach to literature is the altogether exceptional respect in which it holds the truth. So great is its hunger for truth, and its attendant compulsion to confess what is not true, that it fails to interest itself in the enormous area of human life that is accepted as neither true nor untrue but simply *there*. This is the area that was comfortably appropriated, and settled, by the novel in the eighteenth and nineteenth centuries. I recognise that novelists have often been uneasy about doing this – in the early stages producing bundles of letters to vouch for the truth of what appeared in their novels, or drawing attention to the air of parody and joke that surrounded them. Taking the view he does, Josipovici sees these devices as being of extreme importance, revealing the author's awareness of the artificiality of what he is doing. Those novelists who are not only aware of, but also get behind, the artificiality of the fictions they have constructed – Swift, Sterne, Hawthorne in *The Scarlet Letter* – are the novelists he admires. Those who, like myself, prefer Defoe, are forced to accept that their preferences are not justified by any claim they can advance, on behalf of *The Journal of the Plague Year* or *Robinson Crusoe*, that these novels are more truthful. In both the popular and the philosophical senses of that word they most certainly are not. But, coming back to the opening sentence of Kermode's book, can it not be said that they help us, not so much to find out the truth of the world, as to make sense of the world? Certainly they do not do this – or at any rate it does not immediately come into the forefront of my mind that they do this – by bringing the details of the world they describe into relationship with any but the most carelessly inherited paradigms of ends, epochs and apocalypses. They do it by enveloping us in its substance. Far from the novelist standing back from his world and seeing it always as a work, a fiction, he has himself succumbed to the illusion and failed to extricate himself from its power. For Defoe, the gap between the author and his work has ceased to be real. It has been closed as he enters the world that his imagination has so irresponsibly created.

This would be unforgivable if what we, and the novelist, were in search of was the truth. But it is not. What we are in search of is a way of making sense of the world; and to *make* sense is not necessarily the same thing as to *find* it. By stressing the fictiveness of the fiction, the modernist critic sacrifices his ability to make sense of the world as an environment that can be taken for granted, and unthinkingly, unambitiously, occupied. He might discover a great deal about the imagination, and he might also discover something about the world that exists apart from it – though, as I understand Josipovici, he is not likely to discover much more than the fact *that* it exists. But he will discover very little about the world most of us are in the habit of supposing we live in.

I should go so far as to bring into very close contact with each other 'making sense' and 'what our senses make'. There are grounds for admiring novelists whose senses are most fully able to respond to the stuff of which the world is made, or appears to be made. There is no reason why novelists, unlike philosophers and theologians, should be afraid of appearances. They are the most interesting things in the world. Indeed, they may be the only things in the world. Since they include the most delicate nuances of feeling and the most extravagant projections of personality, as well as more tangible properties of things and persons, no one who is not abnormally concerned with the truth is going to worry about this. It is only when our responses to appearances and our ways of making sense of them are conceived as habits, that we grow dissatisfied with them. Most of the novelists we admire have been so close to them, so much involved in them, that the fact that they might be unreal, untruthful, could seldom have occurred to them. When it did, as it did perhaps with Flaubert, the consequences were peculiar. I shall try to show how the tension between respect for the truth and fascination with the appearances was resolved, or how it failed to be resolved, in some novelists who did take the matter very seriously, and very hard.

Many very considerable writers, from Flaubert's time to our own, did not concern themselves with the matter at all. Take William Golding, for example, since he is a contemporary author much admired by both Kermode and Josipovici. On the face of it he conforms in a most obvious way to the requirements Kermode makes of a fiction. The paradigmatic forms that are tested and changed by the contact the book makes with reality are there in the shape of myths or fictions Golding is interested in. The genesis of the early novels in his reading of *The Coral Island*, 'The Grisly Folk' and *Robinson Crusoe* is well known. But is it really of much importance? Does it help us much to understand what these books are saying? Do we, in fact, continue to bear the comparison in mind as we move forward in our reading of the books? If not, in what way does Kermode's general theory of fiction help to explain the specific virtues of each of them? Josipovici uses Golding to show how an English novelist, working in a climate of opinion in no way favourable to the theories of the *nouveaux romanciers*, has evolved a similar view about the function of art, in so far as he too is aware of the errors of fiction and our lack of any firm grasp of reality. At the end of *The Inheritors* and *Pincher Martin*, he writes, 'We are left swinging between the two consciousnesses [of Lok and the new men, Martin and Mr Davidson], suddenly aware of the fact that neither is the "reality" and both are only . . . ways of looking at the world.' And, he goes on, 'these examples reveal how unwilling we are to give up the single viewpoint, how painful it is for us to acknowledge that "our universe" is not *the* universe.' I disagree with this entirely. It seems to me beyond doubt that Golding is not using his switch in the point of view to dismantle any illusions we might have about the real existence of the universe. He is putting us in possession of both points of view to bring us closer to what he believes to be the truth, and that is not by any means a matter of one view being just as good or as bad as any other. Simply, neither of these particular views represents the whole truth. Taken together, however, they provide the reader with all the material he needs to arrive at the truth. So far as I can see, it is important to Golding that he should make use of this and not be left to flounder in a world where all truths are relative. Kermode and Josipovici have allowed their preoccupation with fiction to obscure Golding's concern with substance. Their interest in structure has led them to underestimate the amount of matter that, far from being brushed aside in an uncompromising quest for reality, has been carefully and not at all disrespectfully incorporated in the fiction in an effort to save as much of appearance as is consistent with the author's respect for the truth. I mention Golding because he is one of very few English novelists who do give the impression that they want to find, and tell, the truth. But there is no indication, to my mind, that he draws attention to any radical discrepancy between what, properly seen, *appears* to be true and what *is* true.

We are creatures of a world which, of itself, is neither ordered nor certainly real. Therefore we assume its reality and cultivate our feeling for its appearances. We read into it the order we had wanted to find in it. And in time, this order, and what might have been the real order, become scarcely distinguishable the one from the other – which is to say that we are creatures of habit and we have selective memories. Also, we evolve conventions and traditions, whereby we regulate what appear to be our selves with what appears to be the world. The world of Kermode's paradigms, tested as it is by the facts of appearance, is an elegant skeleton, and the world Josipovici would give back to us at the end of a reading of Borges or Beckett is so inconceivably ethereal as not to be evident to me at all. I prefer to be in the position of the ideal reader of Flann O'Brien's *At Swim-Two-Birds*, a proleptic and hilarious spoof of this approach to fiction, who was 'outwitted in a shabby fashion and caused to experience a real concern for the fortunes of illusory characters'. They are the unofficial selves of my title. They are utterly unashamed of their questionable reality and willing to step out of a paradigm or a frame of perception with as brisk a step as Wemmick stepped out of Jaggers's office into the freedom of the Castle at Walworth, where, he was pleased to say, 'Official sentiments are one thing. We are extra-official.' But they have to justify themselves, not in terms of real identity, but of vivid and convincing appearance. The rest of this book is an attempt to help them do so.

2

Deaths and Entrances

'Will Nelly die? I think she ought.'
Lady Stanley on *The Old Curiosity Shop*

As editor of *Household Words* and *All the Year Round*, Dickens needed to be a sound critic of other people's novels. His criticism, however, was unsophisticated. He knew what he liked but had scarcely any idea why he liked it. 'It is all working machinery, and the people are not alive' he wrote of an unsatisfactory manuscript that had been submitted to him for publication, 'it is very difficult to explain how this is, because it is a matter of intuitive perception and feeling.' It is equally difficult to explain why it is *not* true of Dickens himself, for there is plenty of visible, working machinery in his novels, yet the people are very much alive. And then, as soon as we have said this, we find ourselves in difficulties. Alive, yes. But in what sense? How are the appearances kept up and the machinery, even where it is conspicuously present, made to seem of so little account? I think it has a great deal to do with what I must call the inconsistency of the writer's methods, the way we are made to feel that different characters respond to the world, and are in turn responded to, in very different ways. The variety of the characters in a Dickens novel is matched only by the variety of the demands we make on them and the variety of the uses to which they are put. This, more than anything else, I shall try to show, explains the characteristic density, solidity and interest of the Dickens world.

The deaths of some fictional characters are of much greater interest than their lives, so much so, indeed, that it may be said of them that their lives were little more than the unavoidable preliminaries to their deaths – indifferent spans of time their deaths could not do without. Such a character is Krook, in *Bleak House*. What his life means to himself we are not to know, for on every occasion we have to do with him on behalf of somebody

else. Krook and his rag and bottle shop attract the other characters like flies. At some time, most of the major characters and
many of the minor ones converge upon him; and we do so with
them. On many occasions during a reading of the novel we find
ourselves intimately involved with one group of characters or
another (Ada, Rick and Esther; Guppy, Jobling and Chick Smallweed) before moving with them to Krook's Court and, often, confronting Krook as a visitor – from outside. We never move out
from Krook's Court to meet others, nor do we 'accept' visitors
with Krook. Consequently Krook is a totally opaque character.
Two things are known about him: the physical circumstances of
his existence – the chaos of books and papers within which he
lives; and his inability to read or to allow himself to be taught
to read. These two things are all we need to know or want to
know. Our curiosity about Krook's person is aborted at conception.

His death, however, arouses a great deal of curiosity. Its circumstances are mysterious and its manner – by Spontaneous
Combustion – appalling. But the reason we are curious has nothing
to do with what we have known hitherto of Krook as a person.
How could it? We have known nothing. Instead, it has to do
with what we know of him as that centre to which all lives turn
in the course of the story: to Krook as the proprietor of whatever
Guppy and Smallweed are after; to Krook as Miss Flite's landlord; to Krook as Captain Nemo's landlord; to Krook as the
man whom Jobling cannot teach to read. His role and position
have usurped his claims to self-sufficiency as a person, and it is
as a linchpin of the plot and a receptacle of thematic symbolism
that he explodes. No one cares about his having died. Everyone
cares about his death.

So Krook's attributes are significant primarily in relation to
their ending. The peculiar violence of that ending alerts us to the
nature of the attributes that are destroyed and to the significance
of their being destroyed like that. We cannot say that it is by his
death that we know him, but we can say that it is only *so* that we
can understand why Dickens created him at all – as something
more than a personage rendered necessary by the demands of
the plot. He is the mock Lord Chancellor, who can be exploded
with impunity because nothing follows from that act which could
make any impression on the society Dickens abhors but insists on

putting up with. The real Lord Chancellor is unharmed, and the
need Dickens feels to harm him is sublimated in an act of parodic
violence. The will to destroy and the inclination to uphold the
institution of the law co-exist in a literary trick. That is why
Krook is there. He is a device through which Dickens can intervene and kill the law without getting hurt – and without the law
getting hurt. It is only by virtue of his living somewhere and
being talked at by people that we can call him a character at all.

That is not quite true. It is also by virtue of the position he
occupies in the lives of the characters who are attracted to him.
We, the readers, do not witness Krook's death. In fact none of
the characters witness it either. But Guppy and Jobling come
nearest to doing so, since they are in the house at the time and,
puzzled by a queer smell, make their way down to Krook's room.
When they get there, strange things happen – in respect of what
they see, and *we* see:

> 'What's the matter with the cat?' says Mr. Guppy. 'Look at her!'
> 'Mad, I think. And no wonder in this evil place.'
> They advance slowly, looking at all these things. The cat
> remains where they found her, still snarling at the something
> on the ground, before the fire and between the two chairs.
> What is it? Hold up the light.
> Here is a small burnt patch of flooring; here is the tinder
> from a little bundle of burnt paper, but not so light as usual,
> seeming to be steeped in something; and here is – is it the
> cinder of a small charred and broken log of wood sprinkled
> with white ashes, or is it coal? O Horror, he is here! and this
> from which we run away, striking out the light and over-
> turning one another into the street, is all that represents him.
> Help, help, help! come into this house for Heaven's sake!

The exclamation marks proclaim the presence of what used to be
brusquely thrust aside as Dickensian melodrama. So it is, but it
is skilfully arranged melodrama, emphasising as it does the climactic nature of the act and the indirect way we apprehend it.
The ubiquity of the present tense, combined with the gradual assi-
milation of the fictional to the real – '*They*', 'Here', '*we* run
away' – has the double effect of familiarising us simultaneously
with the characters and with other readers. The sense of belonging to an audience is one more aspect of the theatricality of some

of Dickens's techniques and it is encouraged by the knowledge that thousands of other readers are reading the same instalment at the same time. But familiarity with the characters has another side to it which does not have to be theatrical. We have been *with* Guppy and Jobling before, in circumstances that were not melodramatic at all.

The ability to surprise us into sharing in their lives accounts in large part for the success of these characters. Most readers agree that it is because she tries so hard to do this that Esther fails badly. That is to say, she fails to make us intimate with herself and with the protagonists of her story. Her family circle is so intolerably cosy that we are forced to a distance from which we cannot help but see through it, question motives, disbelieve the evidence. Nothing in the Guppy–Jobling–Smallweed story strikes us as 'evidence'. Elsewhere, in his dealings with Esther, Guppy is not very interesting, whether as lovelorn suitor or as timorous jilt. It is only when he enters into the company of Jobling and Smallweed that he achieves the life which we feel is appropriate to him. These changes in our reactions to Guppy led the late W. J. Harvey to class him with Sir Leicester Dedlock in the same novel as a 'discontinuous character', one to whom we impute a complexity and development that isn't actually there. I doubt whether many readers ever thought that Guppy was a complex character. It seems to me rather that his discontinuity is of the same kind as Toots's in *Dombey and Son*, who fails utterly to be of much interest in relation to the main characters – Florence in particular – but who comes to life within a limited circle of others – with Paul and Mr Feeder in Feeder's room at the Blimber Academy. Animation of course has nothing to do with complexity. Guppy, Jobling, Toots and Mr Feeder are not complex. The word, and others related to it, has no relevance. Characters are complex when they are looked at as characters, when they are brought forth to provide evidence of themselves. Dickens usually manages to avoid this. He prefers us to take up positions among his characters rather than speculate objectively about them. To search out evidence of complexity or simplicity is a waste of time. Complicity becomes a more important matter than complexity – but the *extent* to which we are accomplices is hidden from us. Being involved, we are unlikely to be aware, at the same time, of our involvement, our complicity.

Those who doubt the relevance of this distinction between two ways of apprehending characters, and these characters especially, should re-read chap. 20 of *Bleak House*. Here Jobling arrives on the scene – Kenge and Carboy's office – and, in Richard's absence, is taken out for a meal by Chick Smallweed and Guppy. The balance between observation and involvement is finely but unobtrusively held. Briefly, in the first page or so, we are acquainted with the attitudes Guppy and Chick have taken up towards each other. So when Jobling comes along, hoping to secure a job with the firm, we are close enough to the two clerks to find ourselves in the position of appraising him from something like their point of view. A sense of familiarity made fresh by the arrival of an interested absentee (longing for the security of a stale 'position', just like the one we are placed in) is conveyed by a nice distribution of dialogue and gesture:

'Will you come and dine with me?' says Mr. Guppy, throw-ing out the coin, which Mr. Jobling catches neatly.

'How long should I have to hold out?' says Jobling.

'Not half an hour. I am only waiting here till the enemy goes,' returns Mr. Guppy, butting inward with his head.

'What enemy?'

'A new one. Going to be articled. Will you wait?'

It looks easy, and if we are to be at ease with the characters then it *has* to look easy. But in fact the casually inserted 'butting in-ward with his head' is not at all easy, combining as it does a pointer to where we stand in relation to Guppy and Jobling, an indication of the sort of gesture Guppy likes to make – and keep-ing things moving, as things usually do when we experience them from within, instead of watching them from without. Later, at the chop-house, our involvement becomes even more dynamic as Chick alternates with Jobling as the odd man out, the object, rather than co-subject, of attention. His dubious familiarity with Polly, 'a bouncing young female of forty' who takes the order, brings him into a focus that only a minimally involved scrutiny can account for, and therefore our point of contact shifts from time to time to a position closer to Guppy–Jobling than to Guppy–Smallweed. This change in our way of experiencing the situation corresponds with the reintegration of Jobling into the Kenge and Carboy circle. Third-person generalisations contribute to the

sense of intimacy. They do not remove us, with the author, to a
distance from the scene – as is conventionally held to be the effect
of such generalisations. This is because they are generalisations
from the event, arising out of the likely response of the partici-
pants, not those of the writer or reader looking for 'evidence'.
The 'very popular trust in flat things coming round!', inserted
in the third person as a response to Jobling's forlorn hopefulness,
is the smug sagacity of Guppy and Chick, not of a philosophic
intruder. As such it brings us nearer to the sense of life being
lived; it does not thrust us further away from it.

Even so, Harvey's concept of the discontinuous character
('changing by fits and starts throughout the novel'), is a useful
one, and one that I should apply to more important characters
than Sir Leicester Dedlock and Guppy. Much recent Dickens
criticism has suffered from an unduly sentimental approach to the
circumstances in which the novels were published. The facts, as
presented in Butt and Tillotson's *Dickens at Work*, make it clear
that the intimate relationship Dickens was able to form with his
readers created many opportunities for gratifying unreasonable
claims on behalf of favourite characters, and that he was not the
man to let his readers down. Hence such trifles as Miss Mowcher's
abrupt transformation in chap. 32 of *David Copperfield* in response to a letter from a kindly dwarf. But not only trifles. Edith
Dombey undergoes a similar process of change at Dijon, where
she repudiates Carker and refuses to be his mistress. In this case
the evasions and uncertainties, which are the invariable trappings
of Dickens's presentation of women in what may be presumed
to be their sexual role, make it difficult to be certain whether or
not Carker's inexplicable plan had any chance of success. Dickens,
however, thought it had. A blurred capitulation had been in the
offing until three weeks before the relevant instalment went to
press. Then Dickens informed Forster that his friend Jeffrey
'won't believe (positively refuses) that Edith is Carker's mistress'.
Hence Carker's 'undeceiving' and ours. We are given to know
that 'she never meant that'. What did she mean? We are not
told, and neither is Carker, staggering under the blows of outraged
discontinuity. Walter Gay suffers from the same sort of change
of plan, though this time on Dickens's own impulse, and before
he has time to acquire a character at all. He never does acquire a
character, not even an operatic one like Edith's. But his actions

turn out to be 'good' ones (he makes a modest fortune 'off-stage') rather than bad ones (he doesn't make an immodest fortune or no fortune at all off-stage) which they were intended to be in the first place.

The circumstances of serial publication, along with other more personal difficulties, usually made it impossible for Dickens to convince a sophisticated audience of the credibility of a developing character. Urbane nineteenth-century critics objected to his 'eccentrics' as much as they did to his colourless heroes and heroines. Trollope thought his characters were not human beings. 'There is no real life in Smike', whatever that means. For James he had created nothing but 'figures', adding nothing to our understanding of human character. And though Trollope is being silly, James may be right if we restrict ourselves to the main characters – with the exceptions of Mr Dorrit and Pip in *Great Expectations*. The others are no more than collections of stock attributes which always interlock at the same points with the same other attributes. Good little boys always have impeccable standard English accents – in defiance of the laws of heredity and environment. They always try hard to get on, and when they have done so, buy the same honeysuckle-covered cottage in the Home Counties (one dreads coming across it one day, bursting to the mock-Tudor rafters with its incestuous progeny). Good young girls always wait for the hero to see the error of his ways (the Mistaken Preference), but above all to see his way to buying that cottage and providing her with a liberal supply of offspring – like Mr Toodle 'never out of children, but always kept a good supply on hand'. Radical critics, sensible about most other aspects of Dickens's social criticism, still cannot find it in their hearts to treat this kind of thing with the contempt it deserves. It is not here that we shall discover the life of Dickens's characters.

It is best to forget about a character's ability to change convincingly with the passage of time. The only notion of change Dickens entertains, outside *Great Expectations*, is the change from childhood to maturity, and invariably the mature adult who has to carry the burden of the narrative is nothing like so lively or entertaining as the child. The saving grace of good children is that they don't need to be good all the time to be recognised as good by the most naïve of readers. David Copperfield as a boy is permitted to dramatise his grief at his mother's death, even to the point of being intrigued by his red eyes when he sees them in the mirror: 'I am sensible of having felt that a dignity attached to me . . . and that I was important in my affliction.' No such convincing thought is permitted to the adult husband in the face of Dora's afflictive presence. David bears all with an impossible talent for self-sacrifice – and indeed, he does sacrifice what remains of his self from those childhood scenes.

Fortunately, much of adult life does not change, and so Dickens is not prevented from saving appearances time and time again in the way he describes the behaviour of many of his characters. But the protagonist is often frustrated by the abnormal condition of changelessness that has been imposed on him. He is required to experience, at close range, some of the most traumatic shocks – fire, shipwreck, becoming a writer – which are bound to change him, but mysteriously do not. There are perfunctory changes of detail, but the broad outline remains the same. So it is to the less central characters we turn to find personality undistorted by the author's insistence on meeting his audience's naïve moral requirements, and unhampered by the sketchy consistency in virtue or vice thought proper to the heroes and villains of the tale.

One impressive discovery Dickens hit upon, and made discriminating use of in *Bleak House*, was the fact that, though characters don't change, our attitudes towards them do. It can be a fascinating experience to discover that what you thought a character was like, on a first meeting or even several later meetings, is quite mistaken; provided good reason is given for your having made the mistake in the first place. One reason for this is that in a roundabout way the premise of unchangeability is undermined. The attitudes of the onlooker change, even if those of the person he looks on do not; and the onlooker may be a character in the fiction as well as the reader. The reader may make the discovery through the discovering being made by one character about another.

A comparison of Uriah Heep and Harold Skimpole will make plain what I mean. They are by no means similar characters, but how they behave to the heroes and fit into the plots of their respective novels have things in common. The ways they are presented are, however, very different. With Heep we know where we stand, or recoil, straight away: his hand is like a fish in the dark. The more David knows of him, the more odious become those fixed attributes of character associated with him from the first. David is 'attracted' to Heep 'in very repulsion' as his attention fixes on the stoppages in his nose and the sight of his mouth 'open like a post office'. His physical characteristics render all the more grotesquely unpleasant the compulsive humility which is his very essence. First impressions of others confirm our own repeatedly identical but increasingly vivid impressions. Betsy Trotwood knows him for what he is at once: 'If you're an eel, sir, conduct yourself like one; if you're a man, control your limbs, sir!', identifying physical unpleasantness with moral corruption in a traditional, even fairy-tale manner.

The presentation of Skimpole is a very different affair, although it is again contained within the frame of a first-person narrative. In all the scenes that involve Skimpole, Dickens's manipulation of Esther's narrative is consummate. Without moving out of the field of her own perception and judgement (there is nothing like Mrs. Pardiggle's 'rapacious benevolence' here) and, more surprising, without escaping from or obtruding the circumstances of her 'present' telling of the tale, Dickens has Esther record her impressions of Skimpole as she can be expected to remember receiving them at the time, with just that hint of restrospective censure – scarcely noticeable to the reader – which convinces by its restraint and, at first reading, imperceptible polite tact. Here is her first meeting:

When we went downstairs, we were presented to Mr. Skimpole, who was standing before the fire, telling Richard how fond he used to be, in his school-time, of football. He was a little bright creature, with a rather large head; but a delicate face, and a sweet voice, and there was a perfect charm in him. All he said was so free from effort and spontaneous, and was said with such a captivating gaiety, that it was fascinating to hear him talk. Being of a more slender figure than Mr. Jarndyce, and having a richer complexion, with browner hair, he looked younger. Indeed, he had more the appearance, in all respects, of a damaged young man, than a well-preserved elderly one. There was an easy negligence in his manner, and even in his dress (his hair carelessly disposed, and his neckkerchief loose and flowing, as I have seen artists paint their own portraits), which I could not separate from the idea of a romantic youth who had undergone some unique process of depreciation. It struck me as being not at all like the manner or appearance of a man who had advanced in life, by the usual road of years, cares, and experiences.

How artfully Dickens has Esther tell us the truth she found both at first meeting and now, in painting for us this introductory picture. The apparently straight descriptive 'who was standing before the fire', the *immediately* favourable conjunction of 'so free from effort' *and* 'spontaneous' (as if they were more or less the same), and the deft suspension of judgement (which itself strongly implies a judgement) of the last sentence – each of these is doing two jobs at once. The result is a sense of disturbance, of unease, in the reader. He is discovering Skimpole through a succession of barely formed judgements, and relinquishings of judgements. Esther's account, straightforwardly describing *and* unobtrusively judging, makes the reader respond with just those tensions and uncertainties, the impulse not to rush to judgement countered by the wish not to be proved a fool, that attend meetings with people in life as it is lived outside books. It is an uncertainly critical procedure used throughout these passages, but as time passes and Skimpole is observed in different situations from the vantage-point of Esther's developing awareness of what he is like, uncertainty gradually fades, and criticism fills out the perspective in which he has to be viewed: 'It seemed to me, that his off-handed professions of childishness and carelessness were a great relief to my guardian . . . and were the more readily believed in; since, to find one perfectly undesigning and candid man, among many opposites, could not fail to give him pleasure. I should be sorry to imply that Mr Skimpole divined this, and was politic.' Nevertheless she *does* imply it. 'Professions' there is approaching judgement. The verbal emphasis (in 'off-handed'), implying but not stating intention, almost confirms it. Soon we shall be prepared for his 'captivating looseness', 'airy dispensing with all principle and purpose', his '*display* of guileless candour'. Step by step 'carefree' becomes 'careless' becomes all too 'careful'. But at first it was impossible to entertain seriously the hypothesis that Skimpole was evil, evil in his carefreeness; that the man who stood in front of the fire would be the man who would

'airily' cause Jo's death by accepting Vholes's five-pound note. Yet
that is what he does. Bucket's summary nicely brings together
the venial and the totally corrupt: 'No idea of money. He takes
it though.'

Esther's point of view is made good use of here. Elsewhere, it
proves to be a clumsy way of telling the story. There are structural
reasons why she should tell her part of it, but they do not alter
the fact that we are usually happiest when we can forget her
presence and where we feel Dickens did so too. Describing Skimpole, though, she is successful, and her success depends upon
Dickens's manipulation of her as a subtle point-of-view device. It
is easy to make too much of this, especially elsewhere in her narrative, and critics have indeed made too much of it. The greatest
absurdities occur in those readings that fuse a hypothetically comprehensive point-of-view technique and a hypothetically all-
inclusive and consistent symbolism. Hence I have read an account
of *Bleak House* which attaches great importance to Esther's uncertainty, at the opening of chap. 5, as to whether the obscurity
of what she sees lies within or without: dirt on the windows or
fog outside of them. This is to impute to Dickens a post-Victorian
subtlety that has little to do with the powers of symbolic description and mimetic dramatisation that he in fact possessed. Even so,
it is worth recording his interest in using his point of view with
some consistency. Esther is careful to persuade us she really did
hear what she says she heard. She is not making it up. 'I had not
once looked up. I had not seen the visitor, and had not even
appeared to myself to hear the conversation. It surprises me to find
that I can recall it, for it seemed to make no impression on me as
it passed.' This kind of interest exists elsewhere in Dickens. In
Dombey and Son, for example, he was proud of the 'novelty' of
his treatment of Paul's illness, which should be 'only expressed in
the child's feelings – not otherwise described'. And the number
plan for *Our Mutual Friend* includes interesting notes on the
intended registration of events through Bella Wilfer's consciousness in the account of Boffin's transformation in book III, and
through Bradley Headstone's in book IV. F. W. Boege has made
much of this in an essay on 'Point of View in Dickens'.[1] Never-

[1] Also, W. J. Harvey has drawn attention to the 'dramatisation of a
limited and crippled consciousness' in the portrait of Miss Wade in *Little
Dorrit*.

theless, undue attention to what are after all clumsy Jamesian anticipations – I mean clumsy when looked at in the inappropriate context of the Jamesian approach to the structure of novels – does distort one's appreciation of Dickens. Esther's record of her changing attitude towards Skimpole is as isolated in its maintained delicacy of touch as is the presentation in the first person of the gradual change of Pip's character in *Great Expectations*. Both Bella and Bradley Headstone may gain in a kind of crude power what they lose in sensitivity of registration, but they *do* lose that. Dickensian characters are rarely sucessful as onlookers, unless they are children, unconcerned with mediating any but the most obvious moral judgements – on the Murdstones or on Magwitch, for instance.

The typically Dickensian character is ill equipped to look on, because he possesses a transforming imagination. Even the most biased onlookers, when used as devices to mediate a distorted account of events, need to possess a superficially undisturbed mind. Otherwise we cannot establish even provisional bearings from which to measure the degree of distortion. Dickens's characters are never like this. They are fit only to be looked at. What it would be like to look at the world *through* Mrs Gamp or Miss Havisham or Mrs Clennam is unthinkable. The usual explanations for this follow E. M. Forster. How silly to suppose you could look through Miss Havisham. Turn her on her side and you'll see she hasn't got anything to look through. But this explanation is unsatisfactory, depending as it does on an over-simplified division of fictional characters into two kinds, round and flat – the flat ones, unlike Steerforth's Rosa Dartle, not having even an edge.

Mr Tulkinghorn is a good example of a Dickensian character. Is he flat or round? He should be flat, because he doesn't have the capacity to surprise us. But does his inability to surprise have anything in common with Mrs Jellyby's, for instance, or Mr Turveydrop's, with Mr Vholes and his shadow or Mr Kenge and his silver trowel? Here is Tulkinghorn as we meet him in his chambers near the opening of the story, 'An Oyster of the old school, whom nobody can open':

> Like as he is to look at, so is his apartment in the dusk of the present afternoon. Rusty, out of date, withdrawing from atten-

tion, able to afford it. Heavy broad-backed old-fashioned mahogany and horsehair chairs, not easily lifted, obsolete tables with spindle-legs and dusty baize covers, presentation prints of the holders of great titles in the last generation, or the last but one, environ him. A thick and dingy Turkey-carpet muffles the floor where he sits, attended by two candles in old-fashioned silver candlesticks, that give a very insufficient light to his large room. The titles on the backs of his books have retired into the binding; everything that can have a lock has got one; no key is visible. Very few loose papers are about. He has some manuscript near him, but is not referring to it. With the round top of an inkstand, and two broken bits of sealing-wax, he is silently and slowly working out whatever train of indecision is in his mind. Now, the inkstand top is in the middle: now, the red bit of sealing-wax, now the black bit. That's not it. Mr. Tulkinghorn must gather them all up and begin again.

Here, beneath the painted ceiling, with foreshortened Allegory staring down at his intrusion as if it meant to swoop upon him, and he cutting it dead, Mr. Tulkinghorn has at once his house and office. He keeps no staff; only one middle-aged man, usually a little out at elbows, who sits in a high Pew in the hall, and is rarely overburdened with business. Mr. Tulkinghorn is not in a common way. He wants no clerks. He is a great reservoir of confidences, not to be so tapped. His clients want *him*; he is all in all. Drafts that he requires to be drawn, are drawn by special-pleaders in the Temple on mysterious instructions; fair copies that he requires to be made, are made at the stationers', expense being no consideration. The middle-aged man in the Pew, knows scarcely more of the affairs of the Peerage, than any crossing-sweeper in Holborn.

The red bit, the black bit, the inkstand top, the other inkstand top, the little sand-box. So! You to the middle, you to the right, you to the left. This train of indecision must surely be worked out now or never. – Now!

What is most striking about this long description is how little it tells us *about* Tulkinghorn, but how awfully present he is made to appear. If he is a 'great reservoir of confidences' he must immediately be seen to contain more of other people than of self,

and indeed his self is strangely independent of identifiable, or at
least specifiable, human or psychological traits. We do not even
know what he looks like – which is true of more Dickensian
characters than many people like to think (but that is probably
because of Cruikshank and Phiz). We cannot say of him what
Dickens says of Rogue Riderhood in *Our Mutual Friend*, that
'the spark of life in him is curiously separable from himself', but
we can say that that spark plays as much upon his chairs, books
and, above all, the sealing-wax he toys with, as it plays directly
on himself. We remember the dinner services and other accoutrements of Mr Dombey's christening party and the Veneering
soirées, in each case absorbing the energies, or lack of them, of the
respective hosts; and we reflect on the amount of life that is so
frequently drained from the characters to be pumped into the
things they use. But in Dickens, the more the things come to life,
the more they transmit life back to their owners. What would
Mr Tulkinghorn be without his books with titles that 'retire into
the binding', or Dombey without a 'dead dinner lying in state'?
The life of a Dickens character is very closely bound up with
his surroundings, sociable in the case of a Guppy, isolated in the
case of a Tulkinghorn – a matter of things rather than people
creating a character's identity. When he moves out of those surroundings a great deal depends on how much of the energy they
trasmit he has permanently absorbed. In Guppy's case, not much.
In Tulkinghorn's, a great deal. Smallweed finds another ambience
and becomes discontinuous – and pallid by the side of his ghastly
father.

Another thing about them is that, detached from their surroundings, they either harden into isolated 'atomic' units, or
they are in a constant process of collision with one another. Raymond Williams has made this point in his recent study of Dickens.
His characters 'do not so much relate as pass each other and
then sometimes collide. . . . They speak at or past each other,
each intent above all on defining through his words his own
identity and reality; in fixed self-description.' Dickens anticipated
Williams here in a comment on his friend Wilkie Collins's *The
Woman in White*. 'The characters', he wrote, 'are too prone to
self-analysis: they have a DISSECTIVE property in common, which
is essentially not theirs but yours; . . . my own effort would be
to strike more of what is to be got *that way* out of them by

collision with one another.' Certainly Dickens succeeded in his aim. Both characters and readers are encouraged to ignore motive, the main object of analytical modes of inquiry into character. Bucket goes out of his way to disclaim any knowledge of Tulking-horn's intentions: 'what he fully had in his mind . . . I can't quite take upon myself to say'. That 'quite' is a bathetic euphemism. The frenetic energy and inquisitiveness of the Smallweeds and Mrs Snagsby and others are also in excess of any conceivable motive. David Copperfield's testimony on Heep could apply to all Dickens's eccentrics: 'I had seen the harvest, but had never thought of the seed.'

Dickens's characters live by their creative intensity. What they are matters very little compared with the energy with which they are it. Pip can create live people out of the lettering on their tombstones, Tommy Traddles asserts a mysterious and secret self-hood by drawing skeletons on his slate between floggings. Even the weakest among them display their weakness with a panache that converts it into a kind of dramatising strength: Fascination Fledgeby and Georgiana Podsnap didn't just dry; they '*struck* each other into astonishing attitudes'. Frequently this kind of life depends on the place in which it is being lived, and some characters transplant very badly. Tulkinghorn's return to his chambers allows him to draw sustenance and dramatic life suffi-cient for any number of expeditions to Lincolnshire. But Little Dorrit, expelled from the only life she has ever known, dissolves into a dream in Venice 'quite displaced even from the last point of the old standing ground in life'.

Little Dorrit's in a singular case. Little boys and little girls had frequently been lost before in Dickens, but their sense of loss had not been demonstrated at this level of psychic activity. The energy of picaresque adventure has given way to a poetic shifting between mood and scene, the clouds above Mont Blanc and the floating pavements of Venice mirroring the sense of insubstan-tiality Little Dorrit feels in herself. This is all the more remark-able when we remember that her life at the Marshalsea, which is the 'old standing ground' referring to, presented us with an unsuccessful combination of a colourless protagonist (only elevated to that position in the third number) and a functional character we saw earlier in the form of Krook. There she represented some-thing quite different and altogether more positive than Krook had done. Even so, she was more of a mechanism through which Dickens could intervene on behalf of the forces of good than a character perpetually re-creating herself out of the energy Dickens has pumped into her. The inmates of the prison were 'largely habituated to her' and their lazy habituation rubbed off both on Little Dorrit and on our own relationship with her. Dickens tried to do something like this with Esther through the juxta-position of first- and third-person narratives in *Bleak House*, but Esther's lack of a credible inner life had rendered the experiment futile and mechanical in the earlier book.

The variety of Dickens's characters, then, is matched by the variety of his modes of presenting them and the relationships which obtain between one and another of them, and between all of them and the reader. An intense creative life may be diffused through groups of characters whose viewpoints and attitudes are continually changing; or it may be usurped by a single mon-strously unmotivated personality. Some characters are mere mech-anisms, human gloves through which Dickens can prod and poke the others into required positions and useful combinations. Most characters present themselves completely and unmistakably on first meeting. Some appear at first in a false light. Only gradually are their real outlines allowed to show through the disguises they wear. The effect of this variety of presentation, these different degrees and kinds of life and lifelikeness, is to provide a sort of mirror to the variety of ways we apprehend people in the real world. For a large part of the variousness of that world has to do with how we apprehend people, and our own relation to them, not just the diversity of character people actually display. Often it is difficult to tell the two things apart. The impression of life in a novel may well depend on the absence of fixed modes of forcing readers into acquaintance with characters, and charac-ters into acquaintance with one another.

The difference between Dickens and other Victorians – Thackeray, Mrs Gaskell, Trollope and George Eliot – becomes apparent as soon as we try to think of a character like Krook appearing in their novels. Such an event is inconceivable. It is true that characters do appear in their pages for no other reason than to get the plot moving, and consequently lack the lifelike-ness that is in one way or another bestowed upon the rest of the fictional population. One thinks of Raffles in *Middlemarch*. He is an intruder in more ways than one, a representational as well as social cuckoo in the Stone Court nest. He has to arrive, so as to expose Bulstrode and provide a reason for Lydgate's removal from the scene; just as Krook had to die, so as to bring in the Smallweeds to discover the codicil. But Krook died by Spontaneous Combustion, which was over in a moment. Raffles dies gradually, the result of accident, illness, and a form of passive assistance on Bulstrode's part which it is difficult to find a name for, but which we misleadingly over-simplify if we call it murder. George Eliot tries to bring her picture of Raffles into line with the manner in which she records action and personality in the rest of the novel – what we might for the present call fidelity to observed experience. She gives him a character that is consistent with the role he has to play and the society in which he has to move. But his role is always apparent beneath the transparency of his assumed fictional identity. His function is thinly disguised by the motives and the manners we are urged to believe are as much a part of him as those of Lydgate and Casaubon are of them.

George Eliot is unhappy with Raffles, and it is not difficult to see why. He was invented simply to fulfil an outstanding plot requirement. The action of the novel is demonstrably leading up to two important events: Bulstrode's downfall and Lydgate's surrender to his wife's ambitions. If Bulstrode is to fall and Lydgate is to leave with Rosamond for London, an event has to take place which will precipitate both actions. After all, Lydgate has been shown, in terms of George Eliot's most patient handling of her favoured procedures, imperceptibly identifying his interests with those of Bulstrode. It would therefore be a waste, a loose end, not to make use of such a carefully prepared relationship between the characters. So George Eliot does make use of it, and does kill her two birds with one stone. But the agent she uses to accomplish her design is a creature imported from the world of Victorian melodrama, who does not become acclimatised to the temperate zones of Middlemarch. In any case he is given too little time to build up a suitable character, extending credibly into a personal past that can be seen to be something more than what the Bulstrode plot requires. He is a source of intrigue (the paper in the flask) and of doubtful coincidence (Bainbridge's convenient meeting with him at Bilkley). But George Eliot will not acknowledge him as such. These events are presented in the interests of credible cause and effect. The melodrama is coated with a thin realistic veneer. Unlike Dickens, different fictional worlds are not allowed to exist together. By trying to assimilate all her creations to a single mode of fictional life, George Eliot flattens our response to the life that is in fact presented. Her characters are real, but only in respect of one dominating view of what reality is and how it is to be reproduced in fiction. This is even more true of the characters of her immediate predecessors and contemporaries.

Reality was what they all believed they were presenting. The representation of reality was what they prized above any other fictional achievement. Trollope was delighted with Hawthorne's praise of his work because it showed a 'real' world, indeed 'made a show' of it, 'as if some giant had hewn a great lump out of the earth and put it under a glass case'. This had always been Trollope's intention, to make men and women behave 'just as they do here among us . . . so that my readers might recognise human beings like to themselves. . .'. The secret was 'intimacy' or 'familiarity' with the characters. A writer makes his characters 'real' to his readers only if he 'lives with them in the full reality of established intimacy'. This is why Thackeray is to be admired more than Dickens and George Eliot; his Colonel Newcome is a triumph because the reader becomes more 'intimately acquainted' with him than with any other character in modern fiction.

Not many modern readers will agree with this view of Colonel Newcome. Indeed, the further they read through the *Autobiography*, the less they will be prepared to take seriously Trollope's ideas about what reality really is. The moment of truth comes with his chapter on 'English Novelists of the Present Day', not only in his sycophantic trust in popular appreciation which 'should go for very much, almost for everything, in criticism of the work of a novelist' (very dangerous, as we saw with Dickens, for a writer of serialised novels, though not in Trollope's own case: he had stacks of complete novels, ready for serialisation, tucked away in his desk), but also in his comments on individual novelists. These display a startling ignorance of life, which owes nothing to popular appreciation. It is all his own. Annie Thackeray's characters are 'sweet, charming, and quite true to human nature', the implication being that it is by *virtue* of their sweetness and charm that they are true to nature. Little wonder that Frederick Locker-Lampson (in *My Confidences*) felt so 'safe' with Trollope's characters. Emulating Miss Thackeray's, they live in a world where dishonest men and immodest women are punished. Again, Rhoda Broughton's novels may not be as 'sweet-savoured' as Annie Thackeray's and, 'therefore, less true to nature', but she does make her characters 'stand upright on the ground':

> And she has the gift of making them speak as men and women do speak. 'You beast!' said Nancy, sitting on the wall, to the man who was to be her husband, – thinking that she was speaking to her brother. Now Nancy, whether right or wrong, was just the girl who would, as circumstances then were, have called her brother a beast.

Trollope is identifying reality with the morally coloured version of it that he believed to be suitable for his readers. He calls novels 'sermons' elsewhere in his *Autobiography*. Whatever the earth was made of underneath that glass case, nobody got his hands dirty putting it there.

Trollope's dishonesty about how the real world is real, and the approach to fiction which it betrays, and which was widespread in the mid-Victorian period and later, had consequences which can scarcely be exaggerated. It obstructed three fruitful alternative ways of showing what was real: mottling the glass case, polishing it up, or playing about with coloured transparencies. Dickens used the mottling effect, distorting some of the 'evidence' so as to throw it into an exaggerated relation with some of the rest. Realists and naturalists were to polish it up and demonstrate that some parts of the glass gave more intereting views of what was beneath it than others. The colour transparencies I shall have to leave to my later chapters, but they involve encouraging the reader to apply to what he sees a range of concepts which may be unfamiliar to him after a hundred years or more of what was supposed to be straight description, with or without evident moral bias. By presupposing a conflation of real and ideal existences, Trollope sloughs off what might have been a useful 'pastoral'[1]

---

[1] In the sense William Empson uses the word in the first chapter of *Some Versions of Pastoral*. John Bayley refers to a similar device when he writes about 'involuntary identity'.

device at the same time as he makes life into a morality. One is reminded of V. S. Pritchett on George Eliot, noting that 'Behind her characters, awful but inescapable to the eye of conscience, loom the statues of what they ought to have been'. This same sense of the 'ought' in a person's constitution has a tendency in much Victorian fiction to come forward from behind and usurp the functions of much of a character's extra-moral life. In extreme cases the characters then assume all the rigidity and overwhelming moral expressiveness we associate with a Victorian statue.

One way of looking at the development of the novel from Trollope, through George Eliot to Arnold Bennett and Ford Madox Ford, is in terms of the use that is found for the ideal existence Trollope equates with the real. What becomes of the pastoral element, those statues? In George Eliot they have an existence which is more or less separate from the characters. No one is assimilated to the ideal role and status that is still felt to exist powerfully beyond or behind or above the action. George Eliot is aware of the perfect moral outline of a character that no character, not even Dorothea Brooke, is quite able to fill out. But the characters can be aware of what they cannot embody; they can sense the presence of their ideal potential selves, and also the duty incumbent upon them to aspire to give them substance. And this interplay between men and women as they are, and the idealised self, the sense of what they are capable of being, accounts for some of the richness of her novels, some of what is left over when many of the available kinds of reality have been excluded from the picture. With Bennett and Ford the idealised self expires; transformed into an amoral sense of alternative or foreclosed possibilities in Bennett, dispensed with in any shape or form in Ford. There is an element of determinism in this. No man lives without a shadow. Psychologically speaking, it is inclined to wander. But for Ford and his realist precursors, it is always high noon.

The secret life we failed to observe in Tulkinghorn rarely conceals itself in the other Victorians. But, alas, it is often as true in the novel as it is in the Bible, that he who loses his life shall find it, and he who finds it shall lose it. This applies to other people's characters too. Thackeray is always sniffing, and consequently snuffing them out. It is the price he pays for the unremitting exercise of his omniscience – 'for novelists have the privilege of knowing everything', as he says of Jos Sedley's dinner. Rawdon's note from Becky is equally public property. Although he 'crumpled it up and burnt it instantly in the candle', he was not fast enough – 'we had the good luck to read over Rebecca's shoulder'. 'We' pre-empt Rawdon's experience and in doing so convert it to something else, the specimen under the glass case. We no more live with Rawdon at this juncture, and at most others, than we live with Colonel Newcome or with the population of Barsetshire. By being more intimate with what is happening to him than he is, we become correspondingly less intimate with himself, always assuming that he has a self to be intimate with. Elsewhere in *Vanity Fair* the need for opacity is faintly met. Rebecca (with Lord Steyne) is 'guiltless, very likely'. 'What had happened? Was she guilty or not? She said not; but who could tell what is truth which came from those lips. . . .' Well, we are justified in replying, 'we' should be able to tell, because in most parallel cases 'we' have been the privileged source. 'We' found out about the letter, and will find out about the students in Becky's garret in Pumpernickel 'joking about the appearance of Becky's grandapa'. By what prefabricated mischance did 'we' find ourselves locked out of the bedroom? It is no trivial question, since Thackeray's chosen method of invisible observation and worldly comment calls for a representational consistency Dickens never led his readers to expect. In E. M. Forster's language, 'bouncing' is out.

Who are 'we'? One thing that can be said with certainty is that 'we' are not 'us': 'we' are not the objects of anybody else's observation, as we were in the Guppy–Jobling–Smallweed chapter of *Bleak House*. There, 'we' and 'us' were not very far apart. Observation was a part of a vicarious experience from within the situation described. In Thackeray it is very different. Because 'we' do not share in events, their uncertainty and indeed their randomness makes no impression. Instead, they come to us ready shaped and organised. ' "What is Jos eating?" do I hear you ask? "Well, come and have a look" ' is what Thackeray is saying. But who is asking? I, the reader, am presumed to be asking; and Thackeray, the writer, is prepared to gratify my request – so long as he is left to infer when the request is made. And here is the rub. 'We' are Thackeray and us. But Thackeray is all

subject – in relation to me and in relation to the characters. I am
subject in relation to the characters, when Thackeray steps out of
the way and lets me see what is happening to them – and he
usually does. But I am the audience of Thackeray's showmanship
and, as such, a sort of object. He takes me to see what is happening to the characters. Sometimes he coyly declines, lets me feel
my true position. Novelists, not readers, have the privilege of
knowing everything. So that 'very likely' is a joke at our expense.
Becky's secret life is exposed, but not to us. That is why it ceases
to exist.

What does exist is the machinery for propelling us into the situations Thackeray wants us to be in. He is quite open about it:

> Our history is destined in this chapter to go backwards and
> forwards in a very irresolute manner seemingly, and having
> conducted our story to tomorrow presently, we shall immedi-
> ately again have occasion to step back to yesterday, so that
> the whole of the tale may get a hearing . . . a little trifling
> disarrangement and disorder was excusable and becoming. We
> have only now advanced in time so far beyond Chapter
> Twenty-Two as to have got our characters. . . .

It sounds like Dowell in *The Good Soldier*,[1] but here the author,
not the character, is speaking. The primitive time-shifts are unob-
jectionable. It is the sense of living in chapters rather than in
days and in rooms that is oppressive, the guided tour through
the pages: 'This is chapter twenty-two, ladies and gentlemen,
but before we pass on to twenty-three there's a little something
back in twenty-one that I think will interest you.' The proprietor-
ial attitude towards the characters – '*our* characters' – begins to
rub off on the readers. The guide throws a provocative glance
towards the closed door with the red cord conspicuously looped
across it, and bustles us into the drawing-room. 'Nothing for us
there. Those are the family's private quarters.' Then who was
the man we saw at lunch who was *supposed* to be the real Jos
Sedley, and the lady on the sofa? The guide might insist with
Hardy, in *Two on a Tower*, that 'for the due understanding of
our present young man, his [characteristics are] most fervently
asserted, and must be as fervently believed'. There is a whiff of

---

[1] See below, pp. 124 ff.

Nigel Dennis's Hyde Mortimer about this stately book. At the conclusion the imposture is admitted, as it was hinted throughout: 'Come, children, let us shut up the box and the puppets, for our play is played out.'

What is involved is not Thackeray's ignorance of sophisticated latter-day uses of the controlled point of view, but his abuse of his own chosen controlling device, with its attendant exclusion of the reader from a position in which he is able to observe, let alone participate in, the supposed experiences of the characters. Nevertheless, it is true that the omniscient viewpoint itself, even when it plays fair by the reader, is frequently a nuisance, since it tends to deny him the right to formulate his own impressions. This is a pedestrian and commonplace caveat, but taken together with what I have written about the inconsistency in Thackeray's manipulation of the device, it does account for our sense of dissatisfaction with the way in which life is being mediated in the novels. Apart from the author, someone is always at a disadvantage. In the event of an occasional abandonment of the technique, we are at a disadvantage, because 'we' splits up into 'I' (the author) and 'you' (the readers), and 'you' are left in the dark. In the much more likely event of its functioning only too well, and drawing attention to this fact, then one or other of the characters is placed at an unfair disadvantage. Sometimes this is the character whose secret thoughts are pointed out to us so much more clearly than he can point them out to himself. 'The fact is' is the phrase usually implied on these occasions. At times it is brought out into the open, as with Dobbin's visit to the Sedley household in Chapter 12: 'The fact is, when Captain Dobbin blushed so, and looked so awkward, he remembered a circumstance of which he did not think it was necessary to inform the young ladies, viz. . . .' These 'facts', conferring unwanted privileges on the reader and simultaneously taking them away from the characters, crop up over and over again in Victorian novels. In Mrs Gaskell's *Wives and Daughters*, Mr Gibson obstructed Molly's visit to Mrs Hamley because 'he did not want to lose the companionship of his child, in fact', though unlike ourselves, now we have been informed, 'he could hardly have given his reasons for these refusals'. Mrs Kirkpatrick wore black 'In reality because . . .', and the 'real cause' of Molly's dejection over Cynthia and Roger Hamley 'was certainly this. . .'.

Wives and Daughters does not display the unfair selectivity we noticed in Thackeray's use of his omniscient technique, and because that technique is not flaunted as it is in *Vanity Fair* we are less disposed to grumble with Mrs Gaskell for not making things plain. She is careful to release the information she possesses at the most strategic points of her narrative, but she misses opportunities through unwillingness to disclose this information through a single dominant consciousness. Like Jane Austen's *Emma*, *Wives and Daughters* has at its centre a secret proposal, and as in *Emma* the novel is moving towards its close before the secret is divulged. In fact the relationship between Frank Churchill and Jane Fairfax in Jane Austen's novel is used twice in Mrs Gaskell's. Mr Preston is engaged to Cynthia, and Osborne Hamley is married to a mysterious Frenchwoman. Neither of these facts is common knowledge. We discover Osborne's secret relatively early on, but have to wait some time before we find out about Cynthia's. Of course we probably guess, since unless we assume a liaison of some kind, Mr Preston has no reason for being in the novel at all, and Cynthia no reason for behaving towards him as she does. However, in both cases the application of an engaged point of view would surely have made the situation, and the characters involved in it, very much more present to us than they are. In the matter of Osborne's marriage, our knowledge of the true state of affairs allows the comedy of Mrs Gibson's misunderstanding full play ('She had no doubt it was Cynthia who drew him thither'), but we are in need of no further encouragement to view Mrs Gibson in a comic and critical light, since everywhere else in the novel she is manoeuvred into situations where she is prevented from having justice done her as anything more than a foil to Molly. She is for ever interrupting confidences and performing trivialities in the face of other people's disasters. Her mistake about Osborne produces a local comic effect at the expense of an extension of her character that would satisfy more humane requirements on the reader's part.

Cynthia's engagement to Mr Preston is more important because its discovery, and the manner of its discovery, are pivotal to the development of the novel. The consequences of Molly's being taken into Cynthia's confidence precipitate some of the most important events towards the end: Molly's disgrace and Cynthia's freedom to reconsider her relationship with Roger Hamley. Little is made of the second of these, and the first leads nowhere. Furthermore, the seriousness of the tie that binds Cynthia to Mr Preston is difficult for us and, we should expect, Cynthia to feel. But there is a greater contrast than this to be made with Jane Austen's handling of a similar affair. The discovery of the true relationship between Frank and Jane matters so much more to Emma, and so to us. By locating the point of view in Emma's mind, and by having that mind play upon the actions of both characters separately, Jane Austen presents us with a number of what appear to be viable arrangements of the situation. This produces again that sense of alternatives and the way they can matter to the person who conceives of them. It also renders aspects of the characters who exist within that arrangement of alternatives convincingly opaque, allows us to wonder about them at the same time as we wonder about the clarity of the mind that plays upon them. The disclosure that Frank was engaged to Jane, after all that has happened, doesn't just make us laugh at Emma, as we laughed at Mrs Gibson. It makes us see the whole sequence of events in a different perspective. Frank remains culpable, but in a different way and in softened tones. Emma remains – in her past – vivaciously self-preoccupied, but now the impression she has always given of perspicacity and tact is damaged by her inability to realise what Frank thought she had realised – that he was making use of her only because he assumed she knew what was happening and was willing to play a part they both understood. Our response to Jane's character is similarly revised, and the revised version does not replace, but blends with, what we assumed before. In such a way – by virtue of the use she makes of Emma's consciousness creating hypothetical situations that we take, at least with one half of our mind, as real – Jane Austen substantiates and deepens the reality of her characters, rendering them surprising, unfathomable and lifelike. Molly's consciousness has not been allowed to work on the possible relationships existing among the young people at Hollingford. Her lack of a creative sensibility prevents those habits of speculation on the characters of others that, taken with the facts that we see, confer a real sense of life upon them. The same lack cuts off our belief in the 'shame and complicity' with which she goes about her errand to Mr Preston, and deprives Cynthia's detestation of

Mr Preston, before her disclosure to Molly, of what might have
been its Jamesian inexplicability and force.

It is amply made up for by the interest of *others* in *her*. The
scandal of her association with Mr Preston at the Book Society
creates a situation in which she becomes the object of other
people's suppositions and uncertainties. We know what really
happened, what was the real part Molly played, and so we are
not encouraged to participate in the game of creating alternatives,
as we were in Jane Austen. The people doing the supposing move
into the centre of the action as Molly moves out of it, except as a
cause of concern, a known quantity whose predicament creates
conventional suspense. We are left in the unenlightening company of the Hollingford gossips, all hope of an effective existence
for Molly removed with the tea-trays or sunk without trace in the
rich pound cake Miss Browning is discovered munching over
whist. The gossip again has no working consequence. It creates a
hypothetical situation which Molly's consciousness fails to turn to
advantage. Gossip in Middlemarch between Mrs Plymdale and
Mrs Bulstrode creates a similar situation which Lydgate and
Rosamond convert into a real one, and in the process the characters of both of them are brought into a nearer focus. But about
Molly there is no more to be known. As Laurence Lerner has
said of her, she is 'too intimately tied up with what is conventional in the book' to achieve a life which is appropriate to the
commanding position she is made to occupy.

What is and what is not conventional is a large part of the subject of this book, and since this is so I may be begging questions
by using Mr Lerner's word without defining any further what I
mean by it. I mean that the light playing upon much of the
action of *Wives and Daughters*, which should be that of Molly's
consciousness, her apprehensions of and insight (or lack of it) into
what is happening, is in effect nothing of the kind. Instead it is
shaped into a reader's guide to Hollingford and to Molly's position there. Her private interest in the events recorded through her
is subordinated to what is assumed to be the reader's convenience,
which includes his unwavering trust in her ethical and emotional
reliability. Her perceptions may be allowed to err, but her feelings never. They remain stable and predictable, and, incidentally,
always preceded by a governing subject. We always know that the
drift of such thoughts as we are offered is firmly attached to

'Molly' or 'she'; no *style indirect libre* casts them loose to the current of present occurrences and unprepared impressions of them.

We are concerned with the situation that arises when a novelist decides to use neither of the two 'naïve' methods of presenting characters in action we have looked at so far. Mrs Gaskell avoids both Dickens's eclecticism and Thackeray's omniscience. She is closer to Thackeray, but she sees the need to descend from the heights and withdraw from the keyholes. Cynicism about the characters and polite contempt for the reader disappear as we move forward from *Vanity Fair* into the high Victorian ethos of sympathetic concern for the welfare of both. In Mrs Gaskell's fiction, the need is clearly felt for a nearer identification of reader and character, but only if the character can be trusted, only if she will behave as Mrs Gaskell would like to think she would behave in the same situation – which was, as she explains in a remark about Charlotte Brontë, and as she shows in *Wives and Daughters*, very well indeed. By making her books so much better than she was, she makes characters so much less real. The real self of Molly Gibson is held in restraint, whilst the ideal self of Mrs Gaskell thrives in her place and under her name. She is the offspring of Mrs Gaskell's temptation to be good, and, as such, an undesirable medium through which to present the events of a novel.

George Eliot ran into much the same problem, though since her conception of good was less ideal and less naïve than Mrs Gaskell's, the results are more capable of answering to our experience of what life is like. Oddly enough, her method, as distinct from her manner, is at times, especially in the early novels, reminiscent of Thackeray's. She talks with Adam Bede about Mr Irwine pretty much as Thackeray must have talked with little Tow Eaves when he got him to show him Lord Steyne's house in Gaunt Square. Both novelists appear to be members of the societies they describe. Thackeray's membership, however, is of a different kind. Like George Eliot he appears to be able to materialise at will, though his dealings with Tom make fewer inroads into the fictional illusion, and therefore ensure that he is only imperfectly, as well as temporarily, assimilated to the world he describes. But it is the more extensive, *im*material presence which brings out the difference between their feeling for the characters. Thackeray's maintains a discreet distance between the characters and itself. It tiptoes behind card tables, open letters, and examines the contents of a private diary. Secrets are deliberate offences, to be investigated and made open, at the author's discretion. George Eliot doesn't behave like this. Though immaterial, she does not give the impression of being invisible. At times her presence seems to be noted by the characters, and ignored as a kind of fixture, familiar and unintimidating. Raymond Williams senses something of the sort amongst the Garths in *Middlemarch*. We see them 'as we see our own families – simply there, before anything needs to be said about them. Mary Garth is not formally described, given analysing discriminating features, until some time after she has been effectively present. It is as we might stare and reflect in some moment of adverted attention, at someone we already effectively know, simply know and are with.' Williams is looking at George Eliot seeing the Garths, but this involves the way in which the Garths can be presumed to see George Eliot. The reason they behave so naturally is that the presence of George Eliot amongst them, seeing them, is taken for granted, and since we are temperamentally identified with George Eliot as the seer, our presence is taken for granted too. The same thing happens in several of the Tulliver scenes in *The Mill on the Floss* and the Arrowpoint scenes in *Daniel Deronda*. It is a familial habit of awareness which assumes a diminishing importance as George Eliot's range extends. In Williams's view, the dominant consciousness in *Middlemarch* is quite different: 'a signifying consciousness: not of the known or the knowable but of the to-be-known; in a sense . . . the *objects* of consciousness', and this fact is to be deplored. I think it is a mistake to deplore anything which, without disturbing the sense of life as we experience it over the whole course of a novel, helps to make us aware of the multiplicity of ways it can impress us. Williams's admiration of the handling of episodes involving the Garths is a function of the critique of society operating from behind the strictly literary criticism which occupies the foreground of his book. As such it presumes upon an overwhelming provinciality of feeling on George Eliot's part (David Daiches has similar, though less carefully explained, views on the Garths) which I do not think was as decisive as Williams thinks it was. Family relationships, though important, are not the only ones it is desirable to create, and within which characters and reader alike are to be circumscribed.

In his conclusion of the unfinished *Wives and Daughters*, Frederick Greenwood expressed the view that 'as mere works of art and observation' Mrs Gaskell's later novels are 'among the first of our time':

> There is a scene in *Cousin Phillis* – where Holman, making hay with his men, ends the day with a psalm – which is not excelled as a picture in all modern fiction; and the same may be said of that chapter of this last story in which Roger smokes a pipe with the Squire after the quarrel with Osborne. There is little in either of these scenes, or in a score of others which succeed each other like gems in a cabinet, which the ordinary novel-maker could 'seize'. There is no 'material' for *him* in half-a-dozen farming men singing hymns in a field, or a discontented old gentleman smoking tobacco with his son. Still less could he avail himself of the miseries of a little girl sent to be happy in a fine house full of fine people; but it is just in such things as these that true genius appears brightest and most unapproachable.

This ability to scale down Wordsworth's ambition to make familiar things strange, by keeping them familiar at the same time as making them worth reading about, became a mounting preoccupation with late Victorian and Edwardian novelists. Trollope's 'lifelikeness' is a part of it, and so is Ernest Baker's recent description of naturalist aims as being those of dealing with 'the casual humours, the inescapable tragedies, and those tiny events the significance and decisiveness of which time alone reveals'. Many of the great 'scenes' of post-Dickensian fiction have been scenes like that in Squire Hamley's smoking-room where nothing much seems to be happening but where, in the context of all the events the novel is dealing with, everything is happening: Dorothea Casaubon in Rome, Isabel Archer by the fireside, Milly Theale in Regent's Park. Even in Dickens such scenes have a contribution to make: one thinks of Florency Dombey gazing at her father, his face obscured by the veil, and Dombey, unknown to Florence, returning her gaze. Having done so, one returns to Mrs Gaskell and notices Greenwood's choice of words to describe what she has done: 'art and *observation*'; 'excelled as a *picture*'. Like Bennett forty years later, Mrs Gaskell rarely mediates events through the intensifying consciousness of a character whose feelings compose any part of them. There is no sign of spurious concentration, of a scattering of minor incidents wrought into a drama. But that should not be the whole point. A sense of involvement can make concentration of a kind both justified and necessary. Life is sometimes felt to be a drama by the person living it. Bennett was aware of the suddenness with which this could happen, but his method precluded his doing anything more than testifying to the fact and then moving on. He did not pause to register the drama from inside. Simply, Constance or Sophia Baines are arrested for a moment – a birthday or the receipt of a Christmas card – then the action moves forward. As it does so we overcome the urge to move back to where we presume her thought would have strayed, and move forward with it. But the brief inclination to go back leaves its mark on our response to what happens from that moment on.

George Eliot's feeling for life as it is really and commonly lived comes over very clearly near the beginning of *The Mill on the Floss*. The reader is being addressed direct, and warned against being too clever about Mr Stelling's motives for offering advice to Mr Tulliver about how to put his son Tom to school:

> there is nothing more widely misleading than sagacity if it happens to get on a wrong scent; and sagacity persuaded that men usually act and speak from distinct motives, with a consciously proposed end in view, is certain to waste its energies on imaginary game. Plotting covetousness and deliberate contrivance in order to compass a selfish end, are nowhere abundant but in the world of the dramatist. [We can spoil the lives of our neighbours] by lazy acquiescence and lazy omission, by trivial falsities for which we hardly know a reason, by small frauds neutralised by small extravagancies, by maladroit flatteries, and clumsily improvised insinuations.

The comment on the world of the dramatist suggests the magnitude of the issues involved. For what George Eliot is doing here is making explicit an assumption shared by most novelists during and after her day. She is conflating metaphor and reality. Dickens got away with Krook and Tulkinghorn because each of them was two things – an assemblage of attributes amounting to a character, which did the things expected of it and was easily recognisable when it appeared; and a property which could be made to stand

for something (or things) other than itself. This gave them both
a density of existence of a very different kind from what was to
come later in more deliberately realistic novels. Where Krook
demonstrates his insubstantiality as a character, he satisfies by
projecting himself powerfully in his symbolic role, or as a device
of one kind or other that helps Dickens to manoeuvre us into the
required position vis-à-vis the fiction. Henceforth, with George
Eliot's insistence on 'realistic tragedy', these extra-representational
functions disappear. The characters are all of a piece, and their
relations with one another and the reader are existentially im-
mobile. The notion of a content lying back of the characters,
which they are used to light up at different points, in different
shapes and postures, is no longer relevant. Each piece of a character fits into another piece as the novel progresses; and as the
'picture' builds up, the shape of his relationship in time and space
with other characters is 'known'. That might involve change,
usually does, since one of the most real things about people is felt
to be the way they modify and alter their conduct as time passes
and as the area over which their experience is made to work
widens. Thus Dorothea Casaubon's relationship with her husband
is shown to be 'gradually changing with the secret motion of a
watch-hand'. Watch-hands move to predictable positions. In
George Eliot's novels, unlike Dickens's, clocks never turn out to be
time-bombs. Human beings do not spontaneously combust – as
everybody on the *Westminster Review* would have confirmed.

Events which in Dickens were dramatic and catastrophic
became 'indefinable moments', 'incalculably diffusive' in their
effect. In the 'Prelude' to *Middlemarch*, George Eliot tells us
that the struggle of the modern Saint Teresa we are to witness
would, 'to common eyes . . . seem mere inconsistency and formlessness'. Saint Teresas in general lead 'blundering lives' because
of the 'inconvenient indefiniteness' with which their natures are
made. Their passions 'tremble off and are dispersed among
hindrances, instead of centering in some long-recognizable deed' –
like receiving the stigmata, going over to the Greeks, or turning
into a statue for sixteen years. As I put it before, activity ceases
to be symbolic. 'Murder', for instance, is a symbol we use to
simplify our response to actions of a superficially similar kind.
As such the concept may have a use, as a way of finding out
more about the action it is made to represent. Everything will

depend upon the relation it is shown to bear to other concepts and actions we assemble around it, and the manner in which we go about assembling these things. But, George Eliot is saying, symbolic concepts like 'murder', 'marriage', 'seduction' have outlived their usefulness. They have hardened into things which people accept or reject irrespective of motive and circumstance. Therefore they must be de-symbolised, broken down into their constituent parts, which will prove to be different in every individual case. Instead of an 'assembling round', henceforth there will be a 'breaking apart', or a 'melting down'. This is, of course, a procedure that goes back a long way beyond George Eliot and the Victorians. But with them it becomes a matter of faith, *the* way of going about things. The double functions of the Dickensian *dramatis personae* are abandoned. Symbolic simplification gives way to sympathetic recognition of the 'real' complexities.

These were the basic presuppositions which determined the kinds of actions and the methods of dealing with them that 'modern' novelists would use. The question now was, more emphatically than ever before, how the breaking down, the melting, was to be done. In any case, at what point does symbol merge with reality? In a sense, all external actions are symbols, vivid simplifications of wishes, intentions and predispositions. At the same time, they are things people actually do. A handshake is an act, and a representation of a mental act that precedes and fuses with it. Will the handshake alone, then, 'do'? As the nineteenth century wore on, it became less and less evident to novelists that it would. Charles Reade thought he had done well with Kate Peyton in *Griffith Gaunt*: 'Her mind was in a whirl; and, were I to imitate those writers who undertake to dissect and analyze the heart of such moments, and put the exact result on paper, I should be apt to sacrifice truth to precision; I must stick to my old plan, and tell you what she did: that will surely be some index to her mind.' Not so 'surely', and 'some' is not enough, would have been George Eliot's reply. The older novelists felt that this was just the trouble with her work. Trollope thought that 'in the dissection of the mind, the outward signs seem to have been forgotten'.

To modern eyes, these outward signs appear very much more obtrusive in George Eliot's work. There are dramatic confrontations in the Red Deeps, floods at Dorlcote Mill, heroines bound for the gibbet and heroes with last-minute reprieves. Wills continue to be mysterious and the identities of handsome young men obscure. Even so, George Eliot augments the ability of the novelist to reveal 'subtle actions inaccessible by any sort of lens' and prosaicises melodrama by providing more credible links between causes and effects. Bulstrode's part may be conventionally lurid, and the manner and timing of its discovery providential. But its effect on his present consciousness almost makes us believe in it. The fluctuations of his thought (in chap. 70), his effort to 'keep his intention separate from his desire', are convincingly rendered. The movement in and out of a free indirect style – 'he could not but see the death of Raffles, and see in it his own deliverance. What was the removal of this wretched creature?' – makes the reader think *with* Bulstrode and draw apart from him in horror of a shared desire. The same could be said of Rosamond's developing dissatisfaction with Lydgate and of Dorothea's understanding of Casaubon's real nature – though in the latter case the matter is complicated by deficiencies in George Eliot's understanding of her heroine, so sensitively explored by F. R. Leavis in *The Great Tradition.* But this degree of intimacy with the secret hopes and fears of her characters (very different from the intimacy enjoined by Trollope in his comment on Colonel Newcome) was misunderstood by many of her contemporaries. Both Trollope and Reade expressed their dissatisfaction with the method by applying to it the word 'analysis', and the word continued to be used – with a gesture of fastidious disapproval as of a chemical experiment that produced nasty smells in Mudie's – by reviewers of her work from *Felix Holt* to *Daniel Deronda.*

Reviewers of *Middlemarch* held widely differing opinions about the value of the novel, and one is tempted to distinguish simply between those who took up a popular, and those who took up a professional, attitude towards it. Its serialisation by Blackwood, in spacious half-volumes, affected its readers' responses to the characters much as they must have been affected by the standard Victorian product. This emerges clearly in their speculation upon the link between the fortunes of Lydgate and Dorothea. It is obvious to us now that there *is* a link, and that it grows stronger as the action proceeds and they have more to do with each other. But for us the connection is mainly a thematic one – a matter of comparison and contrast between different forms of social idealism and egocentricity – where for the Victorians, able to speculate at leisure, between instalments, on the possible courses of action that were open, it was very much more naïve and correspondingly less 'organised'. Would Dorothea eventually marry Lydgate rather than Ladislaw after Casaubon's death and Lydgate's estrangement from his wife? This is clearly the way many reviewers, commenting on the novel as it came out at two-monthly intervals, responded. One speculates on 'an artistic relationship already in course of being established between the two characters'; another is frankly disappointed that Dorothea and Lydgate ('the real hero and heroine') do not marry at the end.

Encouraged by the manner in which *Middlemarch* was brought out, speculations like these often strayed outside the limits of accepted critical propriety, into the real world within which the characters were presumed to continue their lives after the last page was turned. W. L. Collins felt so badly about Bulstrode's 'mental agony' and his 'bitter humiliation' that he confessed to being 'inclined to take his arm, as Lydgate does, and help him to his carriage'.[1] It is hard to conceive of a more thoroughgoing naïvety than this in a reader's sense of the 'lifelikeness' of characters in fiction, yet I am sure it was and is shared by many readers. Blackwood certainly seems to have felt it; and the *Edinburgh Review* was able to sympathise with Bulstrode in spite of his having, in the opinion of that periodical, 'little real bearing on any of the three groups of characters'.

There were dissentient voices which found the reality of the characters spoilt by analysis. The *Examiner* felt that George Eliot was a 'better psychologist than a novelist', and the *Spectator* that she 'dissects her own characters till she spoils the charm of some of them . . . by subtle comment and elaborate analysis'. Leslie Stephen didn't like the loss of 'charm' in the novels after *The Mill on the Floss*. But the odd thing is how this primitive suspicion of 'analysis', which was to dog Henry James many years later, frequently went hand in hand with a 'modern' attack on what we would now call 'panoramic' method, the 'constant shifting' which Dicey found distasteful (in the *Nation*). Characters were

---

[1] In *The Victorians and their Books*, Amy Cruse quotes the view of one anonymous old lady that Bulstrode was badly let down by Raffles: 'Poor dear creature, after he had done so much for the wretch, sitting up at night and attending him and I don't believe it was the brandy that killed him.'

ruined by analysis, books by instability in the point of view. This new sophistication about the position a novelist should take up in relation to his material profoundly affected the kinds of life characters were permitted to live. Many of them emigrated, and lost weight in a new climate. We shall have to emigrate, too, for the space of a chapter, to see why conditions were as inauspicious as they seem to have been.

3
Detachment

'When you tell about life, everything changes.'
Roquentin, in Sartre's *La Nausée*

The need to stabilise the position both author and reader take up towards the events described in a novel was felt earlier in Europe, particularly in France, than it was in this country. There is nothing surprising about this. Speaking of fiction, if the English are a nation of shopkeepers, it is the French who supply the account books – and it is the characters who are brought to account. Equally unsurprising is the rapidity with which a new and scientific vocabulary emerged to ensure that every method had a name. As usually happens in these circumstances, writers and critics disagreed about what they meant by the names they had invented, and a large part of the critical debate over fiction in France from mid-century onwards took the form of a sterile bickering over whether novelist A was or was not a realist in the 'real' sense of the word, and if he were, what was to be made of novelist B, who claimed that his realism was more real. From 1856 to 1857 Edmond Duranty edited a periodical called *Réalisme* which failed to resolve the linguistic problem, and had little to say about any actual novels. After 1880, with the publication of Zola's *Le Roman expérimental*, and *Les Romanciers naturalistes* the following year, further discriminations were made between realism and naturalism. In his Preface to *Pierre et Jean*, Maupassant treated them as the same thing, but the urge to define continued to grow stronger as the actual definiteness of the definitions petered out in an accumulation of competing opinions which ceased to bear much relation to the novels themselves. Clarity was lost in a flurry of Gallic tidiness, just when the importance of what the French were supposed to be doing was impressing itself on those English men of letters who were fast becoming disenchanted with what they took to be the formlessness of the local product.

The results of this unfortunate combination of circumstances are too complex to go into in a book of this kind. Kenneth Graham has written very fully on the subject and there are many briefer and more specialised accounts. I have found M. A. Ward's review of 'Recent Fiction in England and France' in *Macmillan's Magazine* (1884) as good an example as any of the confusion into which progressive critics were thrown by the ferment of ideas on the Continent. It is as representative in its inability to distinguish between realist, naturalist and 'scientific' methods, as it is in its ambivalent attitude to the challenge which each of these methods presented. Briefly, English novelists were to counter the unhappy and degrading effects of French fiction by assaulting it with its own weapons — those of a technical expertise unknown to the early Victorians. At the same time, however, English novelists would have to 'put themselves into what they write'. This was not the professed intention of those, like George Moore, who had taken up a more uncompromising attitude; but it was believed by most of those whose opinion counted in the London reviews that the best thing that could be done in this country would be in some mysterious way to separate the technical superiority of the French from their abhorrently dispassionate point of view.

Failure to come to grips with the implications of the aesthetic superiority of the French – which usually meant Flaubert's technical superiority, his 'artistic appreciation of form and proportion' as N. H. Kennard put it in the *Nineteenth Century* (1886) – continued through the 1890s. It was not appreciated that what was taken to be the impersonality of *Madame Bovary*, and still more of the *Education sentimentale*, entailed a view of the moral purpose of fiction quite different from the one most educated English readers held. English novelists would have to use Flaubert's techniques and aspire to his formal perfection while remaining faithful to the English belief that the function of the novel was the inculcation of an acceptable morality. Realism in this country came to mean the form and proportion which contemporary English writers believed could be separated from the impersonal manner which was its controlling principle. Nowhere did any of them explain how this was to be done.

This goes some way to explain Dicey's attitude to George Eliot in the *Nation* article on *Middlemarch*. Naturally, twenty years later the charge against her is more serious. A critic of contemporary English fiction in the *Westminster Review of* 1890 traces one of the modern novelist's compositional errors to George Eliot. She is responsible for 'the habit of telling us when anything is said, *how* it is said. A writer should be able to convey the feeling, the manner, and the tone by the speech itself.' She tells us beforehand 'what is going on in the speaker's mind, analyzing the whole process, to the utter destruction of that charm of apparent unconsciousness and consequent surprise and credence which makes us feel that we are not assisting at a got-up show but living an experience'. Though there is no mention of French, and more specifically Flaubertian, realist theory, it has obviously been absorbed into the writer's way of looking at fiction and has had its effect on the critical apparatus she applies. My point is that the local techniques and devices by which Flaubert achieved the formal elegance that reviewers like these admired, were far more closely bound up with fundamental presuppositions about what a fictional world was like, and what kind of contact it was permissible for a reader to make with it, than they were able to see. They presupposed an authorial presence, of a particular kind, that put highly idiosyncratic constructions on what it means to be 'living an experience' both in and out of novels. That contribution was foreign to the traditions of representation which prevailed in English fiction before the impact of the French realists was felt.

The hinge on which the whole of Flaubert's theory of representation turns is his insistence on authorial impartiality, as expressed on many occasions during the composition of *Madame Bovary* in the 1850s, in his letters to Louise Colet at that time, and as late as a letter to George Sand in December 1875. Probably the most explicit account is contained in a letter of March 1857, the year in which *Madame Bovary* was published in book form, to Madame Leroyer de Chantepie: 'L'illusion . . . vient . . . de l'impersonalité de l'œuvre. C'est un de mes principes qu'il ne faut pas s'écrire. L'artiste doit être dans son œuvre comme Dieu dans la création, invisible et tout-puissant; qu'on le sente partout, mais qu'on ne le voie pas.' Stephen Dedalus is to have the same ambition in Joyce's *Portrait of the Artist as a Young Man*. His philosophical realism, derived from Aquinas, is equally uncompromisingly expressed by Flaubert in an earlier letter in which he expresses the view that:

La passion ne fait pas les vers; et plus vous serez personnel, plus vous serez faible. J'ai toujours péché per là, moi; c'est que j'ai fait. . . . Moins on sent une chose, plus on est apte à l'exprimer comme elle est (comme elle est toujours en elle-même, dans sa généralité et dégagée de tous ses contingents éphémères).

Although he had not achieved it, this utter impersonality of the artist was a legitimate and necessary ambition. He explained in other letters what specifically aesthetic effect was to be achieved by it. It was to be a 'méthode impitoyable'. We are unsure who is least to be pitied here: the artist, caught in the throes of a heroic struggle with reality; or the characters, shamelessly exposed in all the nakedness of their mean ambitions, petty selfishnesses and demeaning ignorance of life.

Most English writers funked both varieties of pitilessness, being too soft-hearted about themselves *and* their creations. The impersonality they approved theoretically was abhorrent to them in practice. Hence their delight at Flaubert's failure to separate Emma Bovary from himself: 'Madame Bovary, c'est moi.' What they wanted was a half-way house, avoiding what had by now become the displeasing authorial intrusions of their forebears, but stopping short of the pitiless method they championed in their criticism. It was not the case only in England. There was no national monopoly of this unnatural combination of charity and hyprocrisy. A letter from George Sand to Flaubert in January 1876 reveals little that is basically different from the expectations of later English Victorian critics.. In her opinion *Madame Bovary* would have been a better book if Flaubert had shown more clearly what opinion he had of Emma, Charles, Léon and Rodolphe – all the principal characters – and she concludes by stating categorically that 'la suprême impartialité est une chose antihumaine et un roman doit être humain avant tout'. In both France and England in the last quarter of the nineteenth century, the climate of critical opinion still favoured an explicit distribution of sympathy and disapproval by the author among his characters.

English admirers of Flaubert in the 1880s and 1890s approved his authorial impartiality, a natural consequence of his impersonal method, because the effects he managed to produce by it were the effects they thought proper to the novel: no intrusion; limitation of the scope of the fiction to the rendering of what they often called, after the French, an 'affair'; subtle revelation of character through the interplay of pictorial and scenic methods. Flaubert did not see things the same way. His aims were, in a sense, more ambitious. He believed the advantages of his method were more purely aesthetic. In spite of his respect for reality, he attached less importance to the representation of character and circumstance as he found them outside the novel than did those later English writers who claimed to have been influenced by his work. When he wrote that the most beautiful works of art, novels included, were 'sereines d'aspect et incompréhensible', he was clearly pushing the form close to the position in which John Bayley found it when he observed that 'the older idea of personalities inside a novel has been replaced by that of the personality of the novel itself'.[1] The use of an impersonal method required no justification from outside of the work, with its own laws and values. This emerges clearly in two more letters, the first to Louise Colet in January 1852:

Ce qui me semble beau, ce que je voudrais faire, c'est un livre sur rien, un livre sans attache extérieure, qui se tiendrait de lui-même par la force interne de son style, comme la terre sans être soutenue se tient en l'air, un livre qui n'aurait presque pas de sujet ou du moins où le sujet serait presque invisible, si cela se peut. Les œuvres les plus belles sont celles où il y a le moins de matière; plus l'expression se rapproche de la pensée, plus le mot colle dessus et disparaît, plus c'est beau. Je crois que l'avenir de l'Art est dans ces voies.

The second is a much later one written to George Sand in 1876. This passage follows a description of Flaubert's feelings on looking at the Acropolis:

. . . je me demande si un livre, indépendamment de ce qu'il dit, ne peut pas produire le même effet. Dans la précision des assemblages, la rareté des éléments, le poli de la surface, l'harmonie de l'ensemble, n'y a-t-il pas une vertu intrinsèque? . . . La loi des nombres gouverne donc les sentiments et

[1] See below, pp. 203 ff.

les images, et ce qui paraît être l'extérieur est tout bonnement le dedans.

The perfectly contrived novel, like the Acropolis, has an 'intrinsic virtue': it defines perfectly in terms of form an 'interior essence' which has little to do with observed reality. Indeed, in so far as the novels he wrote approximate to his ideal requirements, reality exists, if it exists, merely as the raw material out of which novels can be formed. Novels don't exist to tell us anything about reality. Reality exists to tell us something about novels.

I place the existence of reality in a conditional parenthesis to show that Flaubert was alive to the epistemological problems posed by his method. The primacy of art over life has a habit of relegating life to the realm of the hypothetical, and though it is true that in the novels we are seldom asked to doubt the facts of a situation (though the Devil doubts them in *La Tentation de Saint Antoine*), in the letters this is by no means always the case. We have already seen Flaubert admonishing George Sand that 'ce qui paraît être l'extérieure est tout bonnement le dedans', and in 1878 he asked Guy de Maupassant whether he had ever believed in the existence of things: 'Est-ce que tout n'est pas une illusion? Il n'y a de vrai que les "rapports", c'est-à-dire la façon dont nous percevons les objets.' The primacy of *rapports* over the objective existence of events that may or may not have given rise to them testifies to the presence of an epistemological concern that may go far to account for the vibrancy and immediacy of his rendering of impressions. He did not write novels about the gap between illusion and reality in any but the least philosophical senses of those words. But it is possible that his sense of there being a gap had much to do with the effort he made to ensure that the illusion, or 'impressions', in his fiction should be as acutely sensed as those outside it.

It is the quality of that immediacy and acuteness of sense that I want to define and set against the range of possibilities open to a novelist traditionally concerned with the play of character and the representation of reality. The aftermath of the Dambreuse party at the opening of part II of the *Education* is as good a place as any to begin. The gaiety and dissipation of the night are over. The orchestra has gone home. A woman dressed as a savage is stupidly imitating the monotonous rocking of a boat.

Then all is quiet and motionless. Nobody can be bothered to pretend to be anything but stupefied. Somebody gets up and opens a window:

> Le grand jour entra, avec la fraîcheur du matin. Il y eut une exclamation d'étonnement, puis un silence. Les flammes jaunes vacillaient, en faisant de temps à autre éclater leurs bobèches; des rubans, des fleurs et des perles jonchaient le parquet; des taches de punch et de sirop poissaient les consoles; les tentures étaient salies, les costumes fripés, poudreux; less nattes pendaient sur les épaules; et le maquillage, coulant avec la sueur, découvrait des faces blêmes, dont les paupières rouges clignotaient.

The effect is simple but powerful. The first two short sentences arrest the flow of the narrative. The one that follows, split up by the semi-colons, develops the description of the morning after the party with a vigour we increasingly feel is rooted in Flaubert's disgust with the scene he is describing. Notice how, after the introductory 'exclamation d'étonnement', the eye of the prose focuses on the furniture – candlesticks, discarded objects on the floor, tables, tapestries – before gradually picking out the human beings. After hints of minor accoutrements – ribbons, flowers, jewellery – attention fastens on the dresses, then the hair and shoulders, then the make-up, sweat, white faces and pupils of the eyes. By the time Flaubert has arrived at the eyes, red and blinking (presumably at what has just been described), the vigour of the prose has been allowed to run down. The last division of the last long sentence is the only one allowed dependent phrases and clauses, each of which contributes to the falling apart of the sentence, and the exhaustion of the syntax along with the exhaustion of what it helps to describe.

We are not sure who is looking here, whose eyes are gazing into those other eyes which gather into their vision the weary trail of staleness and disorder that has led us to them. What happens at the party is important to Frédéric, but he is not invariably the centre of interest. Impressions of the different phases of the party have reached us more directly, without any mental filter intervening. Though Flaubert, here as elsewhere, is interested in the possibilities of limiting his point of view, he does not feel obliged to observe any consistency in this matter: he feels free to take up the point of view of minor characters like Cisy or Deslauriers without fuss or contrivance.

In his essay on the 'Hôtel de la Mole', Erich Auerbach put the point rather differently. He was examining the scene, early in *Madame Bovary*, where Emma and Charles are dining at Tostes. The situation is not presented 'straight', but 'we are first given Emma and then the situation through her':

> It is not, however, a matter . . . of simple representation of the content of Emma's consciousness, of *what* she feels *as* she feels it. Though the light which illuminates the picture proceeds from her, she is yet herself part of the picture, she is situated within it. . . . Flaubert does nothing but bestow the power of mature expression upon the material which she affords, in its complete subjectivity. . . . So she does not simply see, but is herself seen as one seeing, and is thus judged, simply through a plain description of her subjective life, out out of her own feelings. . . . The ordering hand of the writer is present here, deliberately summing up the confusion of the psychological situation in the direction towards which it tends of itself – the direction of 'aversion to Charles Bovary'.

Such an account is not convincing. For Auerbach too, whilst apparently merely describing Flaubert's method, is forming judgements about its value and success: 'nothing but' turns out, surely, to be a great deal; 'simply through' is not simple at all. From what Auerbach says here one would suppose that language could be used transparently, as a completely neutral medium through which human behaviour can be viewed. Zola, misunderstanding Flaubert's achievement, thought it could too. In fact, of course, it cannot, because no language, no style, is neutral. Any novelist who aspires to describe reality without bias or temperamental colouring will need to write very differenty from the way Flaubert did. In the nature of things, he must be affected by what he sees. Any 'straightforward' account will have to include that affection, as a part of the situation which itself has to be seen. Whether or not this is possible is an open question. Are all the controlling predispositions of a writer ever effectively squeezed into the foreground, a disclosed content, rather than a strategic habit? I myself think not, but that is not the issue. If impersonal narrative were only impossible, we could still admire it as ideal.

But it is not only impossible, it is undesirable; and Flaubert's heroic labours to achieve it show why this is so.

The image of the successfully impersonal and impartial novelist most frequently, certainly most memorably, used by Flaubert is that of God overlooking his creation. It is, as we saw, repeated by Joyce in the person of his young artist, Stephen Dedalus. Auerbach uses it, again, of Flaubert, in his commentary on the dining passage from *Madame Bovary*: 'subjects are seen as God sees them, in their true essence'. What is the 'true essence' of that scene at Tostes? It is complete boredom, fatigue, dissatisfaction, *ennui*. What was it at Dambreuse's party? The same. For Auerbach, Flaubert 'transforms. . . the nothingness of listless and uniform days into an oppressive condition of repugnance, boredom, false hopes, paralysing disappointments, and piteous fears'. This is the result of what he calls 'objective seriousness', Flaubert's greatest contribution to the representation of reality in Western literature, 'which seeks to penetrate to the depths of the passions and entanglements of a human life, . . . without itself becoming moved'. There, in the last phrase, is the clue we are looking for: 'without itself becoming moved'. This God, who is always on the alert, always looking on, never involved with or committed to the object he contemplates, is the God of the Deists – remote, unmoved, unmoving. The eighteenth century had expressed a consuming interest in the attitudes of men and women towards such a God. It could be argued that what those interests tended to bring about – the observation of men and women in relation to one another rather than in relation to a cosmic background of animated principles and powers – was one of the most important causes of the rise of the novel in the first place. What the eighteenth century had *not* thought fit to be interested in was the attitude of such a God to men and women. In this they were wise rationalists and properly committed to the age's quest for pleasure. For such a God must be unbearably bored. That is what Flaubert is – to the extent that he achieves what he sets out to achieve. To see, and know, and yet abstain is heroic in a man, tediously unavoidable in the God Flaubert so desperately wants to be. The excitement is all in the endeavour. The inconceivable achievement would have borne barren fruit.

How barren we can guess by going back to the passage from the *Education*. How rigidly encased in the strait-jacket of Flaubert's prose are the gestures and postures he described there. The syntax and the phrasing imposed an identity on each component of the scene which is indeed merciless, merciless because final. It is an inspected scene, each item duly noted and observed in its proper relation to other items, the movement from the one to the other described in terms appropriate to the effect the whole scene of assembled particulars *must* produce, 'the direction towards which it tends of itself'. Nothing deflects that tendency, not a jaunty polysyllable nor a stray hint of good humour. Every device of style and every selected detail is a part of the 'essence' of what is presented. But what is this essence? What are the things as they truly are of Flaubert's letter – 'comme elle est toujours en elle-même, dans sa généralité et dégagée de tous ses contingents ephémères'? I am forced to a conclusion different from Flaubert's and more consonant, I should suppose, with ordinary experience. Outside Hell, as Dante described it, nothing is ever so essentially itself as Flaubert forces it to be. Somewhere someone must have smiled. The remorseless movement from the entry of daylight to the blinking of an eye could have been interrupted by at least a neutral detail, instead of accumulating at every point a more sordid trace of staleness and sweat. This would have been one of those 'contingents éphémères', true to the surface, false to the spirit of the occasion as Flaubert, from his inscrutably God-like position, sees it.

That is Flaubert's method. He aspires to a position of God-like impersonality because he wants to see things, and he wants us to see things, as they really are, not as they appear to be. Appearances are important only in so far as they confirm, by making available to the senses, the reality which lies beneath them. But from time to time, as in the letter to Maupassant, Flaubert cannot conceal his doubts about this reality. What if it is all an illusion, a matter of *rapports* rather than things, and the essences of things? There are two ways of dealing with the problem: to register the doubt in the novel itself, and so render imperfect the God above the machine; or to insist, to convince – even to create, by insistence. Flaubert chooses the second alternative. He organises his prose in such a way as to safeguard the reality of each thing he describes. Each motion of the prose corresponds with a motion of the presumed reality, so that if the reality should after all turn out to have been a shadow, its outline is graven as in steel around the silhouette, and upon the silhouette are imposed the linguistic forms of each impulsion, each thought, each uncertain appearance. Hence the furious search for the *mot juste*, the word that will not merely describe the thing, answer to the impression of the thing as we know it; but will, given its position, its sound in relation to other sounds, its proximity to or distance from other words in the sentence, stand for the thing and its relation to other things in an alternative world imposed on the uncertainly real world. Take the real world away and the linguistic tracing remains, 'un livre sans attache extérieure, qui se tiendrait de lui-même par la force interne de son style'.

A hundred years later, Flaubert's is still a beguiling dream, in America as well as in France. John Barth doesn't 'know much about Reality' and insists on an inevitable 'discrepancy between art and the Real Thing'. Susan Sontag's essays are as neo-Flaubertian as many of her subjects, though the battleground has been extended to include the cinema. In films she admires – by Resnais and Godard – the director 'makes a realistic story over into an examination of the form of emotions', and by doing so demonstrates that 'all art tends toward the formal, toward a completeness that must be formal rather than substantive'. Throughout her book, *Against Interpretation*, and most especially in its second chapter ('On Style'), Sontag is preoccupied with what she calls the 'formal' elements of a work of art, the search for that mystical formal completeness that is elevated at the expense of the substance – what we are in the habit of supposing visual and literary works of art to be about. Works of art are not *about* things in that crude sense. Far more important than what we may in our naïvety think a work of art is about, is what it *is*, even *that* it is.

Let us take as an example Resnais's *L'Année derniére à Marienbad*. Many of us supposed that this film was about a relationship between two men and a woman. We were not so stupid as to insist on using the word 'relationship' in a positive sense. It may be that the relation which exists between the woman, A . . ., and her 'lover', X . . ., is to be understood entirely in terms of its never having taken place before they met at what I will call the 'château'. Nor were we to be gulled into being seriously perplexed by the role played by the 'other man', M. . . . We were prepared to see how he functioned in the sequence of events we witnessed without simplifying that function by imposing on him a status the film itself was careful to leave indeterminate. None of this indeterminacy interfered with what we took to be the 'substance' of the film, namely 'the pathos of erotic frustration and longing' witnessed in the situation of the woman. The phrase is Sontag's. But this is not good enough: 'Not memory, but remembering is Resnais' subject: nostalgia itself becomes an object of nostalgia, the memory of an unrecapturable feeling becomes the subject of feeling.' Like *Muriel*, Resnais's next film, 'at any given moment of it, it's not about anything at all. At any given moment it is a formal composition.'

Before we protest that this explanation of the way Resnais's films work does not square with our experience of watching them, we must take note that Alain Robbe-Grillet, the scriptwriter (*ciné-romancier*) of *Marienbad*, agrees with Sontag. In an essay written shortly after the completion of the film, Robbe-Grillet said of it that' Cet homme, cette femme commencent à exister seulement lorsqu'ils apparaissent sur l'écrin pour la première fois; auparavant ils ne sont plus rien; et, une fois la projection terminée, ils ne sont plus rien de nouveau. Leur existence ne dure que ce que dure le film. Il ne peut y avoir de réalité en dehors des images que l'on voit, des paroles que l'on entend.' Later, in the same essay, he said of his novel *La Jalousie*: 'l'œuvre n'est pas un témoignage sur une réalité extérieure, mais elle est à elle-même sa propre réalité. . . . Celui-ci n'était pas une narration emmêlée d'une anecdote simple extérieure à lui, mais . . . le déroulement même d'une histoire qui n'avait d'autre réalité que celle du récit.'

L'Année dernière à Marienbad is a film about remembering. 'Not a memory, but remembering is Resnais' subject' (Sontag), and it is treated simultaneously as an act and as the object of an act – as it is experienced and as it is seen to be experienced. What is felt to be its 'formal structure' is reproduced in a succession of images which A . . . both sees and is a part of. Now one could say that *Macbeth* is a play about murdering just as *Marienbad* is a film about remembering. But that would be disingenuous. Many conflicting emotions enter into the state of mind of a man on the point of committing murder and suffering the consequences of being a man who has committed murder. The 'substance' of the act of remembering is a matter of feeling rather than of fact, of objective events. The 'substance' of the act of murdering is not a matter of feeling only, but more concretely a series of events involving other people as real, existent aids and obstructions to the end of murdering. Murdering has an end, though its consequences may be endless. Memory, remembering, may have no end because it takes place in a different sort of time. Of course, it is one of the great strengths of *Macbeth* that the protagonist is placed in a position where this sequence of time is also distorted and fragmented. But here we come to my second point of difference. *Macbeth* is not just a play about murdering. It is also a play about being murdered and responding to a murderer, about the composition of society and the removal of a threat to its wellbeing. This is the main difference, the reason why my comparison was disingenuous. At the same time I believe it was constructive. What, after all, does *Marienbad* gain from being a film about remembering as an act cut off from the actual facts that are remembered and the actual circumstances of time, place and relationship within which the remembering takes place?

I suppose Robbe-Grillet would say two things in answer to this: that by removing the external events in relation to which the memory functions, all kinds of obstructive details – obstructive because they render precise and individual a process he wants to present as general and 'formal' – are set aside; and that as a result of this what we are offered, in the film or the book, is more true, more true because more present as an act, distinct from a subject of fictional narrative. It avoids the preterite, for one thing, and all that the French associate with that tense. This is how Roland Barthes discusses its functions in the nineteenth-century fiction Robbe-Grillet and other *nouveaux romanciers* abhor:

> le passé simple est donc finalement l'expression l'un ordre, et par conséquent d'une euphorie. Grace à lui, la réalite n'est ni mystérieuse, ni absurde; elle est claire, presque familière, à chaque moment rassemblée et contenue dans la main d'un créateur; elle subit la pression ingénieuse de sa liberté. Pour tous les grands récitants du XIXe siècle, le monde est peut-être pathétique, mais il n'est pas abandonné, puisqu'il est un ensemble de rapports cohérents, puisqu'il n'y a pas de chevauchements entre les faits écrits, puisque celui qui le raconte a le pouvoir de récuser l'opacité et la solitude des existences qui le

composent, puisqu'il peut témoigner à chaque phrase d'une communication et d'une hiérarchie des actes, puisqu'enfin, pour tout dire, ces actes eux-mêmes peuvent être réduits à des signes.

It is very difficult for an English writer to enter into the spirit of this sort of thing, but it is worth the effort. There is a lot of truth in the point Barthes is making, though whether we should allow it to disturb us as much as he has allowed it to disturb him is another matter. It is true that the preterite or past-definite tense of the verb in English establishes an order of existence, a sort of safety — the safety Locker-Lampson felt in the company of Trollope's Mr Slope and Mrs Proudie — which we feel and which we, and the author, may well be inclined to deceive ourselves into supposing the characters feel, and which hardly exists in life as it is lived. Where it exists it does so only in so far as we allow our behaviour and attitudes to approximate to those of fictional characters, as Emma Bovary does in the early chapters of her novel. No wonder Flaubert is so often adverted to as the chief precursor of the *nouveau roman*. The characters in a novel by Balzac or Trollope are excused a freedom it is uncomfortable to possess. They are too clearly the objects of their authors' intentions, though not necessarily in any crude or obvious way. I am not referring to the obtrusiveness of the omniscient narrator or the patently contrived incidents we discovered in Victorian fiction. The issue is not so superficial. By being so firmly 'placed' in the past within a syntactic continuum which changes and develops under the guiding hand of the novelist, each character is bound to lack the vital freedom that comes of not having to have a point, a function, connections to make and relationships to form. This may help to account for the *nouveau romancier*'s distrust of the 'context' of fiction, of all that does not help to create an object with words that have been cleansed of their stultifyingly fictional associations and usages. None of the furniture of the new novel will be built out of prefabricated materials.

In the novels themselves, the point is most often made by the way the writing is organised, the distribution of the actions and the sequence of images. But in one of them, *La Jalousie*, Robbe-Grillet has provided an object lesson in how and how not to read a novel. On the banana plantation her husband oversees, the woman, A . . ., fills in much of her time reading novels and discussing what she has read with her lover(?), Franck. The one they are discovered reading from time to time in *La Jalousie* is set in Africa, but apart from this what happens in it bears considerable resemblance to what happens in *La Jalousie* itself. A . . . and Franck make no value judgements. They prefer to talk about the setting, the action and the characters as if they were real; and instead of attending to the 'writing' ('aucune qualité du récit') they concern themselves with trifling matters like verisimilitude, whether what happens in the novel makes sense, in the same way as happenings 'in real life' make sense:

> Ils déplorent aussi quelquefois les hasards de l'intrigue, disant que 'ce n'est pas de chance', et ils construisent alors un autre déroulement probable à partir d'une nouvelle hypothèse, 'si ça n'était pas arrivé'. D'autres bifurcations possibles se présentent, en cours de route, qui conduisent toutes à des fins différentes. Les variantes sont très nombreuses; les variantes des variantes encore plus. Ils semblent même les multiplier à plaisir, échangeant des sourires, s'excitant au jeu, sans doubte un peu grisés par cette prolifération. . . .
>
> 'Mais, per malheur, il est justement rentré plus tôt ce jour-là, ce que personne ne pouvait prévoir.'
>
> Franck balaye ainsi d'un seul les fictions qu'ils viennent d'échafauder ensemble. Rien ne sert de faire des suppositions contraires, puisque les choses sont ce qu'elles sont: on ne change rien à la réalité.

This is a typically playful and confusing example of Robbe-Grillet's method, because the speech which constitutes the second paragraph, and which appears to be spoken by Franck ('Franck balaye *ainsi* . . .'), may apply to the situation between himself and A . . . in *La Jalousie* or to the situation between the two lovers in the novel they are reading together. In either case 'he' interrupts their plans. After all, what is the difference, since in terms of the writing the situations are the same? The sole difference is that the one takes place in Africa, and the other in a place unspecified – though it is not Africa judging by A . . . 's comments on the heat, which is less excessive here than it was when she lived in Africa. Both situations are fictional. Their reality is conditioned by the fact that they are constructed out of words and appear between the covers of a single book. So the last sentence, as well as being a statement of fact (commenting on the situation that preceded it), instructs the reader how to read itself, the situation it immediately comments upon, and the linguistic context in which that situation is set. The reality of a novel is limited to what is written in it and does not extend to hypotheses, alternative possibilities, creative fabrications that irresponsible people read into the text.

At first glance there doesn't appear to be anything very startling or unreasonable about this. Isn't it usually the case that the reader of a novel is prepared to accept that, within the limits of the fictional world the writer has created, what he shows and what he says about what he shows *is* the reality? Unlike his Victorian ancestor, the modern reader does not subscribe to the naïve realist view that characters and situations precede the novels in which they appear, and move out beyond the back covers into futures about which it is his legitimate business to speculate. Nor is he likely to set great store by the guesses he makes about the way the plot will develop. What happens happens as the novelist says it does, not as the reader supposes it will, or should, or ought to have done. But of course Robbe-Grillet is claiming much more than this. He is not delivering judgements about suppositions made by the reader that the reader himself is later prepared to admit were incorrect. He is saying that the reader shouldn't have made them in the first place. Admitting they were mistaken isn't enough. The mistake lay in making suppositions at all; not *these* suppositions, but *any* suppositions. For example, on this view the point I tried to make in Chapter 2 about the importance the novelist attaches to her reader's guesses about what is the case (in *Emma* and *Wives and Daughters*)[1] is exactly the kind of thing a novelist should not encourage and a reader should not indulge. The only reality is the reality of the writing. There is nothing behind it and nothing between the parts of it. The words on the page are not there to create the illusion of a reality other than themselves. They have referents: nouns bring to our attention subjects and objects, verbs actions, prepositions and conjunctions the relations between subjects, objects and actions, etc. But these referents are important

[1] See below, pp. 50–3 ff.

only in so far as they bring our attention into line with that of the novelist. It is the link between referent, word and narrator/novelist that is the proper object of the reader's attention. With the primacy of this word/novelist relationship firmly in our minds, we can go on to observe the relationship between one word/referent and another, always looking at this in the light of the narrator/novelist's behaviour in bringing that relationship into being.

Flaubert's ideal novel about nothing, without connections with anything outside itself, held together by its internal articulations, its style, is at last a reality. What I called Flaubert's linguistic tracing no longer requires a real world to trace. The paper is opaque and the tracing *is* the reality. When he was composing *Le Voyeur*, his second novel, Robbe-Grillet was tempted to check his description of a seagull flying over the sea with an actual seagull flying over the actual sea in the world outside the book. He resisted the temptation, agreeing with Roussel and Huysmans that the reality of the mind is superior to the reality of what lies outside it. Nevertheless, Robbe-Grillet did not achieve the Flaubertian ideal until he had written his fourth novel, *Dans le labyrinthe*. His first three novels are held together by much more than a style. Character, situation and setting assume an unwarrantable significance in the reader's mind. The variations on the Oedipus plot in *Les Gommes* are dazzlingly clever, quite apart from the use to which the novelist puts them – which happens to be to erase itself as a fact from the novel in which it appears. The handling of the point of view, gradually and fitfully disclosing itself, in *La Jalousie*, is also admirable; ridding the novel of those half-creative ambiguities that it is so difficult to know how to evaluate in Ford Madox Ford's *The Good Soldier*,[1] whilst maintaining a lively interest on the reader's part in the object of its scrutiny, as well as in the formal structure of its linguistic activities. But the finest example of early Robbe-Grillet, to my mind, is *Le Voyeur*, to which I propose to turn my attention now.

Robbe-Grillet has said that there is a 'hole' at the centre of *Le Voyeur* which accounts for its structure. 'Everything is told before the "hole", then again after the "hole", and there is an effort to bring together the two edges to eliminate this

---

[1] See below, pp. 124 ff.

troublesome emptiness; but the opposite occurs, the "hole" en-
gulfs everything.' The 'hole' is the space that would be occupied
by the narrator Mathias's murder of Violette Leduc. Her body
is discovered at the bottom of a cliff the day after Mathias may
have been at the place from which she may have been pushed,
and the suspicion grows in the reader's mind that Mathias
assaulted and killed her, and then pushed her into the sea.

Before dealing with problems raised by describing the 'hole'
like this, I think it will be helpful if I summarise the rest of the
plot in conventional, pre-*nouveau roman* terms.

Mathias is a travelling salesman who has arrived by ferry-
boat at a small island – from the description of it one would
guess somewhere off the coast of Brittany, where Robbe-Grillet
was born. He carries with him an attaché case full of wrist-
watches which he intends to sell in the six and a quarter hours
he can afford to be on the island before the boat returns to the
mainland. If he is late back at the quay he will have to wait
another four days for a boat to come and take him away. This
mustn't be allowed to happen because it would mean he would
lose a great deal of time and money. With this in mind he bor-
rows a bicycle from the garage proprietor-cum-tobacconist at the
port and sets off on his tour round the island. He fails to sell any
of his watches, however, until he visits a farmhouse where his
client tells him that the youngest of her three daughters, Violette
(or is it Jacqueline?), is looking after her sheep near a cliff he
will skirt on the track that leads to the furthest point of the
island. The first part of the novel ends with Mathias at a crossroads from which he can either go on to the end of the island,
or take a side-track to the cliffs. He turns his bicycle towards the
cliffs.

The action is resumed back at the crossroads, where Mathias is
discovered talking to Madame Marek, a client he says he had
found not at home shortly before meeting her here, now, at the
crossroads. Later Madame Marek's son Julien endorses Mathias's
story, confirming the detail of his account of the visit. After the
body is found, Julien meets Mathias on the cliff-top – Mathias
has gone there to retrieve some cigarette ends and sweet wrappers
he has dropped there – and sees him throw Violette's sweater into
the sea. Whilst not directly accusing Mathias of the murder, he
reveals that he was present, a voyeur, on the cliff-top when the

'accident' took place. He describes Mathias's 'picking up *again*' the sweater in terms that more or less add up to an accusation. However, Julien does nothing about this, won't even accept the gift of a watch, and Mathias, after spending another three days on the island (he missed the boat on the first day because his bicycle broke down on his way to the port), returns unapprehended to the mainland.

I return to the description I gave of the 'hole', where I wrote that the suspicion grows in the reader's mind that Mathias killed the young girl. This must be an inappropriate way of describing what the reader's response to the novel *ought* to be because by using the word 'suspicion' the suggestion is made that an event took place that is located in a sequence of time which is different from the sequence of time constructed by the novelist as he moves from page 1, with the descriptions which appear on it, to page 2, to page 3, and so on. But the only sense in which there can be said to be a sequence of time in the novel is the one I have just mentioned. In any case, although the events described above occur in the novel more or less in that order, many of them occur more than once, or events very much like them occur before or after the places they should occupy in the narrative sequence I have extrapolated from the text. Scenes like the one Mathias sees through a lower-ground-floor window he passes on his way to the mainland port, where a man appears to be beating a woman; or like that of a young girl on the deck of the ship, of another girl who serves at the bar of the café, or of the girl at the house of 'Jean Robin', whose neck has been scratched so that the hardened blood stands out along the scratch as if it were still liquid. These scenes appear from time to time, bearing no definite causal relationship with the events that have disappeared down the 'hole' – the beating of a young woman, perhaps blood flowing from the nape of the neck as the result of a struggle. The same is true of the recurring images – a piece of string, Y marks that appear at odd intervals. Above all, figures of eight: the rusty marks left by an iron ring on the wall of the quay as it swung from side to side and bit into the stone; the shape of an imitation wood grain imprinted on the door of one of the houses Mathias visits. The significance of these we are never told – though it could have to do with a comparison that suggests itself with the figure of eight made by a rope as it is wound round a girl's wrists, or a pair of eyes watching the terrible event from a hidden vantage-point.

The reader is tempted to 'read' these events and images as if they foreshadowed or resumed the 'principal event' of the novel. The terrible violence of the murder is displaced by suggestive parallels and suppressed comparisons. The bewildering shifts and transpositions of imagery, the oblique rendering of a scene, modulating from a still to a moving picture, stopping itself when the attention of the seer has been distracted (like the sailor walking across the dock when Mathias discovers he has missed the boat) – all of these things one is tempted to explain in terms of Mathias's intention to commit the murder or his memory of having done so. But this is to surrender to outmoded habits of reading a novel. It is to take up the position of A . . . and Franck in *La Jalousie*, searching for verisimilitude as if there were a real event, a real action which existed independently of the writing. There is no such event. The expected content of a temptation to kill, a killing, a sense of guilt attending the memory of having killed, is undermined by the novelist's refusal to assemble events in such a way as to enable the reader to shuffle them into what he assumes is a coherent order. There is no linguistic key he can turn in the lock of the novel's a-temporal structure. Retrospect, actuality and anticipation occur on the same plane and therefore lose their status as indications of how the events are to be ordered in time. The only order is the order of events as they are written and as they are read, and these are the events of the novelist's imagination, not of a separate world the novelist's imagination plays on.

The fact is, though, that what I have been describing is what Robbe-Grillet intended *Le Voyeur* to be, not the novel *Le Voyeur* really is; that even readers of Éditions de Minuit do try to impose a temporal order in the events of *Le Voyeur*; and that the novel does not offer enough resistance to their doing so. Robbe-Grillet has created the events of his novel out of a preoccupation with certain objects and scenes – an attaché case, a wrist-watch, a seagull, etc. – but in the end I think we have to say that the story, the myth, imposes itself so strongly on these things that the reader finds himself trapped between them and the operations of the writer's mind that play on them. In this space he finds himself constructing a story. Events fail to stick to the linguistic

forms that express them. Mathias disengages himself sufficiently
from his creator's intentions to assume an independent existence
as a sort of Jamesian register. It follows that events we convince
ourselves are events in the real world detach themselves from
their linguistic *doppelgängers* – their roles as expressions of the
novelist's imagination – and assemble around Mathias's discrete
personality, as filings do around the poles of a magnet. The world
of the novelist and the world of Mathias split apart, and though
we see Robbe-Grillet's imagination at work making Mathias's
situation interesting, by virtue of that fact it ceases to be the
novel's own subject. Instead there is created, not a character in
the nineteenth-century sense of the word that Robbe-Grillet so
much despises, but at any rate a pressure of interest which is
exerted from somewhere other than the unobstructed centre of
the novelist's free imagination. The imagination is in servitude
to a subject. John Sturrock has written of Robbe-Gillet that his
intention is to show the power of the imagination to create what
he calls a 'consoling structure' (an interesting phrase I shall return
to in my chapter on Iris Murdoch) out of the bits and pieces of
the real world. 'But we are in no danger of confusing these mental
worlds with the real world, because they do not obey the same
laws; the relation between one image and the next is a dynamic
and affective one, the relation between one object and the next
in the everyday world is a spatial or a temporal one. The private
pattern which one of Robbe-Grillet's narrators imposes on his
stock of images cannot be one that will survive a confrontation
with the world of common reference.' But this is just what does
happen in *Le Voyeur* and, I should say, in each of Robbe-
Grillet's first three novels, because all their protagonists (Wallas
in *Les Gommes*, Mathias here, and the unnamed narrator in
La Jalousie) succeed in detaching themselves – if not as characters at any rate as what I have called pressures of interest, separate
entities we can be interested in – from the motions of the novelist's imagination. Correspondence between these motions and the
events of the novel had to wait until *Dans le labyrinthe*. It is this
novel, more than any other, which most closely conforms to
Robbe-Grillet's stipulations, in his theoretical essays, about what
the new novel should be.

In this, Robbe-Grillet's fourth novel, the identity of the speaker
is disclosed for the first time. The first word we hear is 'I'. 'I am

alone here now, safe and sheltered.' No doubt this is literally true. 'I' (the writer) am 'here' (writing) 'now' (whilst I write this) (indoors, where it is) 'safe and sheltered'. It transpires that the room is at the top of an apartment block. From the contents of the room and the view outside, a number of properties assemble in the mind of the writer. Outside it is raining, so one has to walk with one's head down. On the asphalt the wind traces parallels, curves and spiral patterns. There are marked patterns also in the dust on the varnished table-top near the writer – a circle, a square, a rectangle and other more complicated designs. A lampshade projects a circle of light on to the ceiling. There are thick red curtains drawn across the windows. Outside it is snowing. Paths have been traced by slippers across the polished floor. Another object which cannot be made out – a cross, a knife, a flower, a figurine, a dagger? – rests on the table. Outside a soldier appears, leaning against a lamp-post. The wallpaper in the room is pale grey with darker vertical stripes. The soldier carries a brown paper parcel under his arm. A box wrapped in brown paper is lying on top of a chest of drawers in the room. Above there is an engraving, a café scene which includes a *patron*, a boy and three soldiers.

This is a summary of the contents of the first fifteen pages of the novel. It shows how the writer's imagination, working on the objects around him and perhaps on the streets outside (the curtains are drawn), is freeing itself from a simple notation of what lies around it, freeing itself from making an inventory of recalcitrant objects, and converting them into a drama. The filament of the light-blub inside the room fades into the light of the lamp in the street which the soldier leans against. The café scene in the engraving, called 'The Defeat at Reichenfels', becomes the setting for a conversation between the soldier (there has been a 'cut' from the scene at the lamp-post) and the boy about a mysterious appointment the soldier must keep at one of the streets of the town to get rid of the parcel – the parcel suggested by the box wrapped in brown paper on top of the chest of drawers. The action of the rest of the novel comprises the soldier's search through the streets for the appointed place, his wounding when the enemy the town has been expecting at any moment arrives and shoots him, and his death in a room much like the one the narrator describes at the outset, and which has appeared in several places

during the soldier's search. Less than ten pages from the end the
'I' of the first pages returns. He has come to give the soldier an
injection, which is not needed because he is dead. We cannot remember the first and second injections. They have not been
described. But we can remember two woundings – one in the foot
(the back of the soldier's boot) and one in the side (the one the
soldier dies of). The novelist's efforts to kill and to revive the soldier have ended in his death. The people he met and talked to
become characters in a novel, to be identified by the roles they
have played, their actions described in the despised preterite tense
(which happens from time to time, mainly towards the end, for
example when the soldier is shot). The soldier is last seen in the
engraving on the wall, from which the eye descends to the
chest of drawers, the rain (not the snow), outside, and another
netural description of the marks on the floor of the room, 'then,
once past the front door, the succession of long corridors, the
spiral staircase, the door of the building with its stone step, and
the whole town behind me'. The novel ends as it began, with 'me'
now as an object, the trajectory of the imagination spent, the
novelist's fantasy overcome by the reality of inert matter which
reasserts its primacy over the efforts of 'I' to convert it into
drama.

The remarkable thing about *Dans le labyrinthe* is that it
holds the reader's attention in spite of the fact that, for the first
time in Robbe-Grillet's work, the protagonist (the soldier) is not
felt to be separate from the exploration of a style. What fascinates
the reader is the way the writer's imagination exerts its power
over what lies immediately within its perceptual field and then
moves out from there, combining one thing with another, and
creating a complex pattern of movements. The soldier's twists
and turns within the labyrinth of the town, and the corridors of
buildings within the town, is one with the tumescence and deli-
quescence of a style. Perhaps the soldier's movements through the
town are co-extensive with the movements of the writer's eye
along a crack in the ceiling of his room which, we are told, 'il
serait nécessaire de suivre avec application de coude [the sharp
bends in the crack or the bent elbow of the writer?] avec ses
courbes, tremblements, incertitudes, changements de direction
subits, infléchissements, reprises, légers retours en arrière, mais
il foudrait encore du temps, un peu de temps, quelques minutes,

quelques secondes, et il est déjà, maintenant, trop tard'. So, even more than Wallas, Mathias or the anonymous husband of *La Jalousie*, the soldier in this novel is absorbed into the style and imaginative impetus of the narrator, the novelist. With the exhaustion of the imaginative effort he dies, and both the novelist and the reader – who has shared the effort, the invigoration, the exhaustion of the imagination, and with that exhaustion the acknowledgement of the imagination's insufficiency (the unreality of the story and its contents) – both the novelist and the reader are returned to what is real: wallpaper, slippers, an umbrella propped against the wall.

In the end, then, character is eliminated from Robbe-Grillet's novels as well as from his polemic. It was peculiar to an age – that of the apogee of the individual, the age of Balzac and the great Victorians. By character Robbe-Grillet presumably means character in its finished, preterite sense. In its other, more nebulous but more immediate one it will presumably continue to exist. In 'Une Voie pour le Roman futur', Robbe-Grillet insists on the presence of characters who will 'donner lieu à tour les commentaires'. These 'commentaires', 'prejudices', psychological, religious, political, etc., are skin-deep and quite irrelevant to the presentation of character in fiction. 'On s'apercevra vite de leur indifférence à l'égard de ces prétendues richesses.' The insistence on them as 'riches' by the nineteenth-century novelists led to a kind of browbeating. The traditional hero was 'constamment sollicité, accaparé, détruit . . . rejeté sans cesse dans un *ailleurs* immatériel et instable, toujours plus lointain, toujours plus flou'. This '*ailleurs*' 'elsewhere', is a world which cannot be entered by the character because as a living creature he should experience as minute impingements on his consciousness what the writer insists are hardened and conventional abstractions. The future hero will be distinguished more by his presence than by his commitment to large gestures in the direction of that unconvincing '*ailleurs*'. When his presence is 'indisputable' all the perfected comments about him will seem 'inutiles, superflus, voire malhonnêtes'.

It is commonplace that Robbe-Grillet's novels have a great deal more to tell us about things than about people. If we retrace our steps through 'Une Voie pour le Roman futur' we shall find that what we were looking at there was an afterthought: 'Quant aux personnages du roman. . . .' Much of the earlier part of the essay was concerned wholly with the way in which objects might be presented in a work of fiction. Recoiling from the nausea Roquentin felt (in Sartre's *La Nausée*) when confronted with roots and pebbles, Robbe-Grillet wants to reduce the threat to the individual posed by the existence of an alien and threatening world:

> le monde n'est ni signifiant ni absurde. Il *est*, tout simplement. C'est là, en tout cas, ce qu'il a de plus remarquable. Et soudain cette évidence nous frappe avec une force contre laquelle nous ne pouvons plus rien. D'un seul coupe toute la belle construction s'écroule: ouvrant les yeux a l'improviste, nous avons éprouvé, une fois de trop, le choc de cette réalité têtue dont nous faisions semblant d'être venus à bout. Autour de nous, défiant la meute de nos adjectifs animistes ou ménagers, les choses *sont là*. Leur surface est nette et lisse, intacte, sans éclat louche ni transparence. Toute notre littérature n'a pas encore réussi à en entamer le plus petit coin, à en amollir la moindre courbe . . . il faudrait donc essayer de construire un monde plus solide, plus immédiat. Que ce soit d'abord par leur *présence* ques les objets et les gestes s'imposent, et que cette présence continue ensuite à dominer, par-dessus toute théorie explicative qui tenterait de les enfermer dans un quelconque système de référence, sentimental, sociologique, freudien, métaphysique, ou autre.

Again the emphasis falls on presence and the unimportance of meaning. But is this really how we experience the world? I think not. Robbe-Grillet is artificially excluding all the 'interests' – reminiscence, expectation, desire, possibility, etc. – which get muddled up with our sense perceptions of things and people. The way these 'interests' are used in his novels, and in *Marienbad*, robs them of their identities by falsely assimilating them to a common mode of presenting an action. We do not experience people as presences in Robbe-Grillet's sense of the word.

Robbe-Grillet's nod in the direction of character is disingenuous. He is not really interested in character; and I don't think, either, that he is very much interested in things. Except one thing: the written word. A more recent essay makes this clear. In 'Temps et description dans le récit d'aujourd'hui', Robbe-Grillet repeats his objections to the objective existence, in the nineteenth-century novel, of 'un monde que le romancier paraissait seulement re-produire, copier, transmettre'. There is no such existence and so there can be no question of reproduction. We are close to John Barth's enclosed world again, since 'Tout l'intérêt des pages descriptives – c'est-à-dire la place de l'homme dans ces pages – n'est donc plus dans la chose décrite, mais dans le mouvement même de la description'. And here we return to *Marienbad*, and to something very like Susan Sontag's comment on works of art as 'living autonomous models of consciousness':

> la durée de l'œuvre moderne n'est-elle en aucune manière un résumé, un condensé, d'une durée plus étendue et plus 'réelle' qui serait celle de l'anecdote, de l'histoire racontée... Cette histoire d'amour qu'on nous racontait comme une chose passée était en fait en train de se dérouler sous nos yeux, ici et main-tenant. Car, bien entendu, il n'y a pas plus d'*ailleurs* possible que d'*autrefois*.

The reader is deprived of any sort of confidence in what is des-cribed; the heroes are 'sans naturel comme sans identité'; the present 's'invente sans cesse, comme au fil de l'écriture'. All of this invites the reader 'à un autre mode de participation que celui dont il avait l'habitude.... Ce qu'il lui demande, ce n'est plus de recevoir tout fait un monde achevé, plein, clos sur lui-même, c'est au contraire de participier à une création.'

What has happened is that the 'density of the Word', in Barthes's phrase, freed from its responsibility in classical art to exist as part of a linguistic continuum involving relations with other words, has triumphed over the density of things and what Iris Murdoch has called 'the opacity of persons'. On the one hand we have people, characters, freed from the impositions of fiction and therefore assigned no 'place' in it; on the other a language in which a violent drive towards autonomy has deprived are of any useful imitative function. 'It is now writing which absorbs the whole identity of a literary work.' Flaubert's dream of a novel about nothing, held together by the internal binding force of its style, has come true. 'Je ne transcris pas, je construis', Robbe-Grillet writes. 'C'était déjà la vieille ambition de Flaubert: bâtir quelque chose à partir de rien, qui tienne debout tout seul sans avoir à s'appuyer sur quoi que se soit d'extérieure à l'œuvre.' And from the other side of the French argument, Sartre ends *La Nausée* in a complementarily anti-mimetic position. Roquentin, bored with Monsieur de Rollebon, decides to give up the attempt to write his life. Instead he will try to write a novel, a novel in which 'you would have to guess, behind the printed words, behind the pages, something which didn't exist, which was above existence'. Either way characters, as ends in themselves, become insignificant. As Ortega put it, 'A preoccupation with the human content of the work is in principle incompatible with aesthetic judgement'.

We must return to Flaubert and try to understand what he meant to English novelists of the late nineteenth century. It is clear that throughout the 1880s and 1890s he remained a major influence. He had died in 1880, but interest in his work was kept up by the publication of his correspondence, in France, between 1884 and 1892, though there is little evidence to show that the views on reality and representation expressed in them had any effect on his admirers. They persisted in divorcing formal from perceptual considerations, and continued to adapt 'realist' devices to representational strategies which were usually at variance with them. As the century drew to its close, however, novelists did become more and more uneasy about the French legacy. Zola, Daudet, the Goncourts lost what grudging reputation they had had. Flaubert's was a distant virtue. George Moore's progress from the calculated detachment of *Esther Waters* to the closer and less sharply focused perspectives of *The Lake* was symptomatic of the changing orientation of English fiction over the period. A more acceptable realism was being discovered, from which the moral decadence which cast a shadow over even the best of what the French produced was absent. The details of this change of heart are made available in a paper by R. A. Gettman. Clearly its most effective occasion was the discovery of the Russians and, among the Russians, of the novels of Ivan Turgenev.

From the first, Turgenev was used as a stick to beat the realists. The essays that Eugène Melchior de Vogüé wrote for the *Revue des Deux Mondes* in 1879 and 1883, and the publication of the later collection in book form, *Le Roman Russe*, in 1886, did just that. They were instrumental in bringing the emergence of the Russian school to full public notice in England and France. The view expressed was that Turgenev possesses all the virtues of the realists with none of their vices. He is thus as efficient a corrective to Victorian formal naïvety as they were. 'He never preaches', as the *London Quarterly* put it in 1884. Even so he is moral, and therefore not merely more acceptable, but more true. The *Quarterly* was consistent over the period. In 1888 it found the Russians in possession of 'the passionate realism of a faultless photographing camera, which may not choose, reject, harmonize, subdue'. The French realists are attacked on their own ground. Both French and Russians claim that they present an impression of reality unbiased by a pre-selection of details undertaken in the service of morals; but what they *see* is something quite different. The French insistence on vice betrays a failure in their apparatus of detachment: the more successful Russian variety restores virtue to its proper, commanding position.

George Moore became Turgenev's most thoughtful advocate in this country. In an essay in the *Fortnightly* in 1888 he tried to explain the difference between his response to character and that of the Victorians on the one hand and the French on the other. 'His desire is always to give utterance to a thought, to awake consciousness of that thought in the reader', and unlike the mid-Victorians – George Eliot, one would suppose, in particular – he does this by presenting an action rather than by describing the thought-processes of characters involved in it. Moore points to the scenic presentation of the Russian exiles in *Smoke*, 'dialogue where no phrase is remarkable or striking when read separately, but when taken with the context continues the picture'. It is all a matter of what he calls 'indications', casual touches that suggest the presence of an object, a thought, a nuance of feeling, without reducing it to the status of an established certainty, a fixed constituent of the scene. He refers to Irene's comments on Litvinov as a student, wearing no gloves and with ink on his hands. The point could apply as well to Flaubert's handling of Charles noticing Emma's manicure in the second chapter of *Madame Bovary*. But in Flaubert these devices are too apparent: 'they are forced down our throats as if with a silver fork'. In Turgenev they are more subtly deployed within the total method of 'instrumentation'. With Marie Nicolaevna's entrance at Polozov's, 'a physical and mental impression is given equally and so well are they contrasted that each enforces the other, and both blend and are but one picture'.

The effect is 'like life itself'. But the life is achieved without recourse to Flaubertian impersonality 'which is the vainest of illusions'. The 'pessimistic little flips at the end of every paragraph' of *Madame Bovary* make it 'the most personal of books'. In Turgenev this kind of self-deception is dropped. What he writes about is deeply and personally felt. There is a commitment to the subject of a kind that would have been foreign to Flaubert. But the 'diction' is impersonal, not in the extreme and impossible way Flaubert wanted it to be, but in the sense of not being organised so as to bestow advantages on one character or situation that it will not bestow on another. 'Impartial' can mean partial to none, or partial to all, equally. Turgenev is partial to all, interested on their behalf, even if some characters occupy a more important position in the plot than others – Turgenev usually started with 'a living person to whom the appropriate elements were later on gradually attached and added' (*Literary Reminiscences*). Each character gets the attention his position in the plot warrants, and it is an *interested* attention. The medium is therefore not transparent. No critic could mistake the gesturing hand for the silver fork. Even so, critics have objected to the method. Percy Lubbock, for instance, found that there was 'something in that constant sense of Turgenev at one's elbow, proffering the little picture' that might damage it. The urbane, sympathetic voice is in evidence throughout, not merely in *The Sportsman's Sketches* where it plays an integral part in conveying the experience of an engaging and genial eavesdropper. This is nowhere present in Flaubert. The air of relaxation, the absence of an unmitigated attention to the bounded detail, dissolves outline and drama in a meditative and casual drawl. Galsworthy must have had this in mind when he said of Turgenev that 'he thought in terms of atmosphere rather than of fact'. But 'atmosphere' is a difficult concept to define in its application to fiction. The relationship between the 'voice' of the writer and the atmosphere of the fictional world it creates is not easy to describe or to identify at specific occasions within the narrative.

Turgenev thought highly of writers like the Goncourts, Daudet and Maupassant. He recommended their books, and acted personally to help place their work in Russian reviews. He was a close friend of Flaubert in the last years of his life, was a welcome guest at the Magny dinners, translated 'La Légende de Saint Julien l'Hospitalier' and 'Hérodias' into Russian. Zola said that Turgenev had introduced him to the Russian public. Maupassant's obituary notice of him summed up all that he had meant to the realists in France: he had eschewed the old forms with their dramatic unreality. Instead he had provided slices of life, *tranches de vie*, without any hint of intrigue and manipulation.

This is what one would have expected from a writer like Maupassant. But is it a satisfactory explanation of Turgenev's literary character? Does it not miss out too much of what Moore and Ford discovered – converting him into the French novelist the English believed he so conspicuously was not? It is a question of coming closer to Galsworthy's 'atmosphere', what Ford had in mind when, in his little book on James, he recommended the 'note . . . of the enamoured watcher', so enamoured, so rapt in what he is seeing that 'the watcher disappears, becoming merely part of the surrounding atmosphere'. The self is not excluded from the narrative, felt by the reader only in the comments it makes to him direct, or in calculated intrusions into the world of the fiction. Nor is it removed altogether, working only to select what is to be treated and providing an appropriate treatment of it. It is a temperament, a sensibility; much more than Flaubert's, everywhere felt, and seldom seen – more a precipitation of the self into the very air and atmosphere of the fiction. But it is a temperament cut off from opinion, unattached to any controlling purpose and impulse to judge.

Though Flaubert and Turgenev differed in their approach to the formal arrangement of their fictions, they shared an interest in devices which had been used in more instinctive and often obstructive ways by earlier novelists, both in England and France. One such device is the 'flashback', frequently taken up by the Victorians as a clumsy short-cut to a character's past but now put to more sophisticated uses which include the summoning of the past, but place a special value on the way it is summoned and the time at which it arrives.

In the first two chapters of *Madame Bovary*, Flaubert gave an ordered and straightforward account of Charles Bovary's life before he met Emma; but it was not until he had treated the marriage and shown Emma's dissatisfaction that he projected his narrative back into the past to provide some explanation for her behaviour at the point he had reached in the story. He provides impressions of Emma's character and manners from which we can infer facts which later, by the use of flashback, are to be substantiated. In the *Education* the same method is used to deal with Madame Arnoux. It is not until part II of the novel is well advanced that we hear, in a conversation between Madame Arnoux and Frédéric, the story of her earlier relationship with her husband. By this time we have already seen Arnoux in situations which make it clear to us that the marriage is not a happy one. We infer the same from observation of Madame Arnoux's behaviour. But it is not until this point, when Frédéric is beginning to form the attachment he desires, that the crucially important details are placed before us, not the least important of which is the fact that Madame Arnoux has determined that her unhappiness must be irreparable. It is important we should discover this now because our own attitude to Frédéric's lack of impulsively effective passion must depend on a firmly based assessment of her character. We know that there are excuses for Frédéric, that he will have to fight hard against her reserve and self-mortification if he is to succeed. How far we allow such excuses to colour our judgement of him is a matter of opinion, but the criticism would have been intolerably one-sided if we had not had the facts placed at our disposal at this point, and in Madame Arnoux's own words.

Turgenev used the technique more extensively, and developed its possibilities further. In his first novel, *Rudin*, the fifth and sixth chapters are punctuated with flashbacks to Rudin's past life, but not before the hero has had time to establish his personality within Darya Mihailovna's household. Turgenev gives us a vivid impression of Rudin as he appears to Darya Mihailovna and her circle, but only after Lezhnyov has entered and become involved in a curt discussion with him do we learn about his reputation at the university and take in aspects of his character hitherto unknown to the rest of the characters and ourselves. In *A Nest of Gentlefolk* the device is more subtly handled. The first five chapters are entirely given over to establishing Marya Dimitrievna's household. They contain a minor flashback of their own – the story of Lemm's ambitions and disappointments – and serve as a prelude to the following two chapters, in which Lavretsky's arrival is described. His presence in the town has already been announced, and curiosity has subsequently been aroused about who he is and why his arrival is of such interest to everybody. So it is only after Lavretsky has been permitted to make an impression (those among whom he finds himself have already directed our attention to something out of the ordinary in his past) that we are told the story of his courtship and marriage with Petrovna and, to explain why he was so easily deceived by her, the details of his upbringing in the English manner.

Most interesting of all is the opening of *Fathers and Children*. The first six chapters of this novel have served the same purpose as the first five in *Rudin* and the first seven in *A Nest of Gentlefolk*: they set the scene within which the action of the novel is to develop. There is one difference. In both of the other cases the 'hero' had appeared at the end of the sequence, and by making an impression on the characters with whom we have already become familiar, had in turn made an impression on us, the readers. We were a second outer circle. In *Fathers and Children*, on the contrary, Bazarov, the protagonist, appears almost immediately. But the device remains essentially the same, for it is only gradually that the interest shifts from Arkady, into whose family circumstances we and the principal characters have been precipitated, to Bazarov. At the same time a shift of interest from Nikolai Petrovich, among the older generation, to his brother Pavel, is taking place. It is marked by an argument on the merits of science and poetry between Pavel and Bazarov, during which it becomes clear that Arkady slavishly follows Bazarov's anti-Romantic lead and that Pavel is a more intelligent and effective apologist for the old liberal school than Nikolai can ever be. From this point onwards Bazarov, especially in his affair with Madame Odintsov, is to become the centre of interest. But for him to be seen to be so, we must understand something more of the forces of liberal conservatism against which he has rebelled. Accordingly the next chapter (7) is wholly given over to a résumé of Pavel's own earlier affair with Princess R. It effectively demonstrates that what we have seen of him up to this point is a 'dandy' exterior protecting a man who is highly sensitive to his personal defeat and, with it, the defeat of all he stands for. The impression and the reality do not correspond. Developments in what remains of the novel show that much the same is true of Bazarov. The convincing exterior of nihilism and extreme reserve protects those as yet undeveloped possibilities of romantic idealism which are revealed in his declaration of love for Anna. Because of the way each character is used to represent quite different cultural and political attitudes to the others, this is ironic; all the more so when we remember that the climax of the book is a duel between Bazarov and Pavel which has Fenichka as its immediate, but ideological differences as its real, cause. The positioning of the flashback, at the point in the narrative after we have received our 'false' impression of Pavel, is an ironic reversal of Flaubert's method.

The uses to which Flaubert and Turgenev put the device are very different. But they do have one important thing in common. They are both concerned more with the reader than with the character, which means that readers and characters operate on different levels. The positioning of characters, and the timing of their exits and entrances, are all evidently a part of the author's strategy, and the aim of the strategy is ultimately that of catching characters out. It is not much different from what Thackeray was doing at Pumpernickel, except that what Becky and Amelia were caught out in was a good deal less credible and more dramatic. The faults and foibles of those characters were such that discovery of them, by Thackeray and the reader, hardly merits the pat on the back the author is giving himself all along, and the reader is invited to give himself at the end. But in the case of Emma Bovary and Madame Arnoux, Arkady and Bazarov, we feel we deserve it. The 'pessimistic little flips' Moore noticed at the end of Flaubert's sentences make some readers feel that, in *Madame Bovary's* case, it is a little cheap. But in *Fathers and Children*, Turgenev's impersonal diction provides a guarantee against embarrassing self-satisfaction. Embarrassment is neutralised by the pathos of it all. What a pity this is what it comes to when the reader has seen all round it and through it and beyond it. The sense of the inevitable disappointment of people, the inability of the characters to measure up to their own expectations and the author's pretended hopes for them, is very 'like life'. We, as readers, share it in our own lives. If we did not, the satisfaction we feel in catching characters out in moments of subtle self-deception would be as savage as it is in Flaubert. A muted satisfaction is what Turgenev offers, muted because we know how much it depends on the dissatisfactions of real life, when *we* are the characters who are being found out.

For the moment *they* are the characters and *we* are the readers; *they* are vulnerable, *we* are not. We can read them like a book, even if it is in small print. The naturalness with which Turgenev eases us into our position of superiority should not blind us to the fact that that is what he is doing. In no sense do we share in the lives of the characters. Our perceptual privilege prevents us from doing so. We are too clever for them, though the engaging modesty of the author's tone forbids us to make anything of it. Maybe if we were in the same situation we would behave as badly, or as weakly, as Bazarov does – that is what the tone is saying. But it is also saying, we are *not* in the same situation. And that makes all the difference.

The shortcomings of Turgenev's presentation of characters are never in respect of subtlety or understanding. They are in respect of power. Characters do not live outwards from a personal centre. The impetus of their existence is feeble. This was the gist of Maurice Baring's articles in the *Quarterly*, collected in 1910 as *Landmarks in Russian Literature*. Because it was through Turgenev that the simplicity and naturalness of the characters in Russian fiction were discovered by Europe, he received the praise 'not only due to him as an artist, but the praise for all the qualities which are inseparable from the work of any Russian'. In fact his virtues, although the same as those of Tolstoy and Dostoevsky, are 'in a less degree'. Above all, Turgenev's was a naturalness that was *noticed*. Neither Ford nor Conrad could locate the parts of the machinery, but they sensed, as every reader does, that there *was* a machinery. The characters depend on it, and to the extent that we notice them doing so, slipping back and forwards in time for our benefit, for instance, they are a degree less convincingly natural. That is what was meant by their being 'found out'. The machinery is there to make sure that we find out, and the characters do all in their power to oblige by never interfering with the machinery; with the result that they are free neither in nor of the fiction. By 1910 English writers were becoming aware of this, though they could not explain it except in Baring's terms of *degrees* of simplicity. But the difference between Turgenev and

Tolstoy is a difference in kind. To the best of my knowledge it has
taken half a century to discover in just what the difference in
kind consists.

To start with, Turgenev's characters do not have bodies. They
have physical attributes which signal their arrivals, transactions
and departures, but that is a different thing altogether. Having
a body is an experience as well as a fact. It has its effect on the
character as a subject, not merely as an object. And that effect
is very great: it converts what we understand about him in terms
of motive, opportunity, design and intention from ethical and
psychological categories into impulses, into actions. It is a large
part of what we mean when we say that a character has a sense
of himself. In this sense, Turgenev's characters have no bodies.
Their shapes and sizes are recorded for our advantage, not theirs.
Tolstoy's men and women are much more selfish, refusing to
define their physical attributes for our convenience. They are
more aware of themselves than of their readers. They have a habit
of by-passing their author's intentions, where indeed those intentions were not that they should do just that. Tolstoy will not
diminish them to the point where they can be 'found out'. 'The
assurance of his solipsism is so great that it can create a com-
parable solipsism in his characters; he does not reach them so
much by intuition and sympathy as by endowing them with the
same power of absolute and primaeval being that he has himself.'
That is how John Bayley sees it in *Tolstoy and the Novel*. It is
not a matter of 'degrees of naturalness', but of the terms according to which the novelist, the characters and the readers have to do
with one another. Must the characters accept their status as objects, set against the more or less free subjectivity of the author
and readers? During the last quarter of the nineteenth century
the argument had been about the acceptability of a variety of
methods – analysis, description, contemplation – for understanding characters. It had taken for granted the fact that all of these
methods presuppose the objectivity of the characters. It had assumed that the novelist apprehended his characters as objects –
Turgenev's attachment and addition of 'elements' to the living
person. But that is only part of the truth about how novelists
understand their characters. It is a relatively small part in Tolstoy's case, where the impression a character makes as an object
of attention is often slight compared with our sense of the energy

and self-centredness with which he goes about making it. Bayley shows very convincingly how this sense of the self belonging to a subject is dependent on his possession of a body. All Tolstoy's characters begin with a body:

> Sometimes, as occurs in real life, we begin to take the body for granted, hardly noticing it at all in our interest in what is happening inside the mind. But the body is always there, always quite separate from other bodies, and because so separated, isolated also in its mental awareness . . . this sturdy selfhood is also . . . highly selfconscious. Tolstoy's characters are physically aware of themselves . . . our enjoyment of them largely proceeds from the intensity of the satisfaction which they feel in being themselves.

In a later chapter on *Anna Karenina*, Bayley contrasts Anna's loss of this self-sufficiency – what he calls *samodovolnost* – during her affair with Vronsky, with Levin's immense appropriation of it on his return to the country after his failure with Kitty. Levin 'was himself and did not wish to be anyone else'. Anna is not even sure that she is herself. Like Little Dorrit, in very different circumstances, she has lost her grip on the forces of life, the sense of herself as a subject, with an intense conviction of unique and continuous existence.

Subjectivity can be a collective as well as an individual condition. This is what Tolstoy calls 'family understanding'. Families participate in an existence which, in rendering what goes on outside them objective (to be set against their sense of them*selves* as *self*), confirms their own mutual subjectivity. Members of a family are rarely wholly the *object* of attention of other members of the same family. Each member is part of a group which senses many of the things that go on both inside it and outside it *as* a group. The intense individuality of any one member is completed and qualified by the collective comprehension of the organism of which it is a part. Tolstoy anticipates the Rostovs and the Bolkhonskys in his general comments on families in *Youth*:

> Apart from the general faculties, which are more or less developed according to the individual, of intellect, sensibility and artistic feeling, there exists a special capacity that is more or less developed in different circles of society and especially in

families, which I call mutual *understanding*. The essence of
this capacity lies in an agreed sense of proportion and an
accepted and identical outlook on things. Two members of
the same set or the same family possessing this faculty can
always allow an expression of feeling up to a certain point beyond which they both see only empty phrases. Simultaneously
both perceive where commendation ends and irony begins,
where enthusiasm ceases and pretence takes its place – all of
which may appear quite otherwise to people possessed of a different order of apprehension. People of the same understanding see everything they can assess in an identically ludicrous,
beautiful or repellent light.

There are many families and many 'sets' in *War and Peace*, and
so this sense of a collective understanding of reality is found almost everywhere: the Rostovs' preparation for the retreat from
Moscow is probably as clear and uncomplicated an example of
'understanding' as any other. The most impressive thing is how
this way of seeing things rubs off on the reader, assimilates him
to the mode of existence of the characters. His privilege is therefore very different from the privilege he enjoyed in Turgenev.
Since the understanding between members of the family is at the
same time an understanding between Tolstoy and the reader
and between other members of the family and the reader, some
characters are deliberately made over into objects in order to
make the subjective existence of others, in whose circle the reader
finds himself moving, credible and powerful. Sonya and Vera
become 'different' so that Natasha and Nicholas can be the
'same'. As Bayley says, we accept the offer of 'insideness' at the
expense of other characters. We 'connive' at the way people like
Sonya, Vera and Berg are maltreated.

The reader's proximity to the individual or collective subject
marks off Tolstoy's method of experiencing the world from the
realists' method of looking at it, in another way. Comic behaviour
is presented less simply, perhaps less comically, because it is hardly
ever viewed entirely from the outside. Pierre's love-making with
Hélène happens to be felt by Pierre as an original mixture of
sensuality and clumsiness. Our view of it contains the absurdity
of the outside account together with the vivid confusion of Pierre's
self-projection, from inside. It is a comic incident which refuses

to be reduced to a satirical demonstration, because the comedy is clearly the product of one way of seeing it. The reductive descriptions of satirists like Milton in his picture of Satan, Swift in his picture of the Laputans (as Gulliver sees them), or Flaubert in his scene between Rodolphe and Emma at the agricultural show, are entirely absent. The author does not offer his readers a superior view of events to that of the characters who are involved in them. Our purchase on the events, and on the moral issues arising out of them, is in no way superior to that of all the characters all the time. The closeness of our way of life to theirs precludes every form of superiority but that to which so many, from the centres of so many different and well-satisfied selves, have laid their claim.

The history of the character as a subject during this century owes little, at any conscious level, to Tolstoy. Nevertheless, the 'creatural dignity' (Auerbach's phrase) his characters possess is what many of our best novelists have tried to impart to their own. There is little in what the realists did that could help them. Still, they valued Flaubert and they valued Turgenev. The complications arising out of the cross-breeding of such valuations, combined with a nagging sense of absent virtues, make up a large part of the subsequent approach to character at the turn of the century.

4
Registration

'The truth was that he had simply accepted the situation.'
Ralph Touchett in *The Portrait of a Lady*

No novels in English are more finely wrought than those of
Henry James. None so obviously and deliberately offer themselves
as exhaustive accounts of the 'affairs' they deal with. Yet the
thought that is almost always uppermost in my mind after reading
a novel by Henry James, especially one of the late novels, is that
it is incomplete; oddly, in spite of the elegance, the circumspection, the 'finish', which is not just a matter of the surface, that it
remains un-'finished'. It occurs to me also that one of the reasons
for this is that the appearance of exhaustiveness, of completeness, is too great. Paradoxically, there would be more *in* a Henry
James novel if more were taken *out*. In his compulsion to account
for everything that is going on, he leaves out of account that
large area of human experience that cannot be accounted for.
Before James all novels had had spaces in them, sometimes
enormous spaces, testifying to the blankness, the ignorance of the
novelist in face of the incomprehensibility of things. Large statements about life in general only go to show that Fielding or
George Eliot couldn't, at that point, make a small statement about
one particular life. It is a matter of approximation. The current
of the narrative dives underground and is next seen bubbling up
from a hole fifty yards downstream. From the bottom, looking up
the valley, it looks right, the vanishing stream becomes a bend or
a dip between high banks. But for James this won't do. The
stream is to be for ever above ground. Not at all times *visibly*
above ground; but at *some* time, at every point of its passage, we
are to have visible access to it. Sometimes the vantage-points are
awkwardly placed, and it takes a long time to get from the one to
the other. We always get there; but sometimes not before the
stream has reduced itself to a trickle, and our mental feet are
tired.

Whatever we think of James's novels, we have to take them into account, because the critical theory of the novel that has been most influential for more than half a century (which is to say just about the only critical theory of the novel that we have got, or *had* got until after the last war) is James's theory: the theory that governed the composition of his novels and that we can piece together from periodical essays, and the prefaces he wrote for the New York edition of his novels between 1907 and 1909. I must say that I can find no justification for the view that is commonly held that really James didn't have a theory of the novel at all and that his comments on his own novels are not to be taken as pronouncements on how all novels should be written. James's prose, especially the late prose in which the prefaces and many of the most influential essays are written, is, of course, densely equivocating. It is difficult to pin him down. But if a man is to say what James said of Dickens early and Tolstoy late (and he said, pertinently, of Dickens that he had 'need of a little philosophy' to prosecute satisfactory generalisations in his art), he must have a theory. Of course James had, and it is as finished and complete as his novels – in my view with the same lacunae that attended that completeness. He had to have a theory, because it was lack of theory, and lack of the form which was dependent on it, that had failed the Victorians whom he began his literary career writing about.

In 1875 James had found the English novel 'a ponderous, shapeless, diffuse piece of machinery, "padded" to within an inch of its life, . . . and effective, when it is effective, only by sort of brutal dead weight'. Eight years later there was no change. Effective – yes: the English 'know their way about the conscience' in a way the French do not. But satisfactory – no: they are inferior 'in audacity, in neatness, in acuteness, in intellectual vivacity, – the arrangement of material, in the art of characterizing visible things'. Why? Because they have no system. In England 'it is rather dangerous to be explicitly or consciously an artist – to have a system, a doctrine, a form'. A year later (1884) things were looking up. James was able to write his essay on 'The Art of Fiction' for *Longman's Magazine*, in which we discover that 'only a short time ago', a year ago at the most, judging from his own account in 1883, 'it might have been supposed that the English novel was not what the French call *discutable*. It had no

air of having a theory, a conviction, a consciousness of itself behind it.' With the French it was different. The French novel had
been *discutable* for some time, because of its formal sophistication; which is to say the presence in it of apparent naturalness
and hidden arrangement, the reverse of what the Victorians provided. But when James actually gets down to discussing it, discussing Flaubert in particular, what does he say? He says that it
is empty. You can discuss Flaubert, because there's nothing in
him. You can't really discuss Dickens, or Tolstoy, because there
is too much there – they are loose and baggy monsters. These
are ominous notes we have to remember when we come to the
discussions in his own novels.

Flaubert's world is empty because he was denied access to the
most private areas of experience, 'the soul' (1893). In his first
review of Flaubert, his essay on the *Tentation de Saint Antoine*
in 1874, James had written that Flaubert and the other realists
in France 'have pushed so far the education of the senses and the
cultivation of the grotesque . . . that it has left them morally
stranded and helpless'. The French are disinterested, amoral,
analytical and aware of formal beauty; the English sympathetic,
moral, unintellectual and shapeless. In the work of the Goncourts,
too, 'the attentive reader receives an indefinable impression of
perverted ingenuity and wasted power'. James was consistent in
his attack on realist practice. Unlike most of his contemporaries,
he did not exempt Flaubert from the charges he brought against
the rest of the French. In an essay on Maupassant he emphasised
that both Flaubert and Maupassant lack a sense of pity. Their
irony issues from hate. They lack 'good humour'.

> The invisible Flaubert scarcely touches; his vocabulary and
> all his methods were unadjusted and alien to it . . . he had no
> faith in the power of the moral to offer a surface. He himself
> offers such a flawless one that this hard concretion is success.

The reason for James's dislike of Flaubert begins to emerge.
Most writers in the 1880s and 1890s were too narrowly preoccupied with Flaubert's methods to get far beyond confused
admiration for his impersonality, uneasily co-existing with recoil
from his lack of sympathy. Their total assessment of Flaubert is
therefore incoherent. They fail to establish a connection between
what is admired and what is felt to be uncomfortable in his work.

But James noticed Flaubert's tendency towards an autonomy theory of language. In the 1893 essay he deprecated Flaubert's belief that 'If you pushed far enough into language you found yourself in the embrace of thought', and in 1902 he wrote of the method of *Madame Bovary* as conferring upon the 'vulgar elements of exhibition a final unsurpassable form': 'The form is in *itself* as interesting, as active, as much of the essence of the subject as the idea, and yet so close is its fit and so inseparable its life that we catch it at no moment on any errand of its own.' For Flaubert, 'expression is creation'; it 'makes reality'. Therefore 'we move in literature through a world of different values and relations . . . in which we know nothing except by style, but in which also everything is saved by it, and in which the image is thus always superior to the thing itself'.

It seemed to James that by insisting on the primacy of style Flaubert was throwing away enormous gifts. For he had hit on the device of presenting his affair through the controlled point of view of one of the characters involved. Where he went wrong was in his choice of the character. In *Madame Bovary*, Emma is altogether 'too small an affair', her 'capacity of consciousness' is too restricted. In the *Education*, the presentation of Madame Arnoux is defective for the same reason: she has 'the drawback that she is offered to us quite preponderantly through Frédéric's vision of her . . .', and Frédéric's vision is shallow, fundamentally uninteresting. A comparison with Balzac is instructive. He too was able to look at events from the point of his characters' 'pressing consciousness', though his control of the medium through which he did so was not as careful. But he chose less paltry conciousnesses and he gave them more to work on. 'Of imagination on one side all compact, he was on the other an insatiable reporter of the immediate, the material, the current combination, and perpetually moved by the historian's impulse to fix, preserve, and explain them.' In comparison, Flaubert offers 'nothing of the near, of the directly-perceived' which admits of a sufficiently interesting subjective consequence. Hence the strictures on Emma and Frédéric. In the *Education*, 'It was a mistake . . . to propose to register in so mean a consciousness as that of such a hero so large and so mixed a quantity of life'. The detail of the narrative was not justified by the mind that was produced to work on it; it did not reveal the perception of a remarkable temperament. James removes the emphasis from the details to the mind that observes them and makes use of them.

We know how James's own novels demonstrate his faith in remarkable temperaments and the interest of the way they work. So much so that contemporary critics confused his method with the 'analytical method' they had grown to deplore in George Eliot. *Blackwood's* review of *The Portrait of a Lady* shows why they disliked it:

> [James] gets more and more within the circle of [Isabel's) personality; and we have to receive both herself and her immediate surroundings, not so much as they actually are, but as they are seen through her eyes. This is always confusing; for self-knowledge at its closest has many limitations and the most impartial student will probably get more light upon it by overhearing one sharp characterization from outside than by weeks of self-examination.

This perpetual 'self-examination' was the greatest irritant to James's hostile critics, and his analytic method became the central debating-point of his work. Saintsbury's comments in the *Fortnightly* are representative of a whole tendency of early criticism. They also, conveniently, mark out the tradition of analytic writing within which James was seen to be working:

> The analyst, as he is understood by the American, French, and to some extent Russian schools . . . is in this worse off than the naturalist pure and simple, that instead of mistaking a partial for a universal method, he takes for a complete method what is not strictly a method at all. . . . The elaborate dissection of motives and characters can only result in something that stops short of being even part of a story – that is only preliminary to part of a story.

This is a case of the biter bit, for James was well aware of the dangers incurred by using the analytic method *in vacuo*, independent of a felt recording sensibility. He had criticised George Eliot for just this reason: *Romola* failed through 'excess of analysis . . . too much reflection' as early as 1873, and later Pulcheria's opinion that George Eliot's characters are 'described and analyzed to death' was dramatised as a partial but not at all totally incorrect criticism. So much depended on what was being

analysed and whether the novelist had his critical sights firmly
fixed on the character who was responsible for the analysis.

Throughout his criticism James contrasted with analysis what
he called 'immersion' – what Balzac achieved when he 'took on
all the freedom of another nature . . . by a direct process of the
senses'. 'Saturation' means the same thing. 'When saturation fails
no other presence really avails; as when, on the other hand, it
operates, no failure of method fatally interferes.' It is the novelist's job to saturate himself, immerse himself, in 'the freedom
of another nature', and only then to illuminate the consciousness
of that nature by using it as an analytical instrument. The
'nature' is not created by analysis, nor is it subjected to analysis
issuing directly from the author. It is made comprehensible to us
by that third-person analysis operating within the field of its own
possible terms of reference, subject to the limitations imposed
upon it by the range of its own experience.

It seems reasonable that if we are to raise serious doubts about
the whole strategy of James's novel-writing, we should start at
the right place and, before deciding whether or not to take James
on his own terms, understand what those terms are. What James
means by 'immersion' then becomes very important, for it is by
immersion that he intended to realise the freedom of his characters. It is not merely a matter of terminology. Thoughtless criticism of James's use of an 'analytical' method has done real
damage to our understanding of what he really did. For a start,
it suggests that he was interested in the motives underlying
behaviour as much as or more than behaviour itself. This would
have provided a comfortable explanation for his interest in George
Eliot's novels. Howells, for example, emphasised the similarity
between her writing and James's: 'No other novelist, except
George Eliot, has dealt so largely in analysis of motive . . . but
with George Eliot an ethical purpose is dominant, with Mr.
James an artistic purpose.' It is so easy to acquire a somewhat
hazy impression of the way a novel works, apply what seems to be
a suitable descriptive word to it, and then read the novel in the
light of whatever else that word suggests. Then, of course, the
further one reads, the more one is able to congratulate oneself
on the application of the word. Everything fits into place, but in
a subjective transformation of the novel into something different,
something not itself. There has to be something in the novel that

calls the word to mind at first, but it may not be anything like the controlling method of the fiction as a whole. This certainly happened to James at the end of the last century. A glance through the critical columns of the *Academy* during the period illustrates it graphically. But it was unfair. It substituted a faulty critique of the late novels for the accurate one that should have been made, but that proved hard to make when both writer and critic had been directed to the wrong debating-chamber.

James is not very much interested in motive. Usually he more or less takes it for granted. Could anything be more obvious than Kate Croy's motive for her treatment of Milly in *The Wings of the Dove*? Or the adults' treatment of Maisie in *What Maisie Knew*? Or, to put it another way, is the most pressing question in our minds when we read *The Ambassadors*, why does Strether change his mind about Chad's behaviour in Paris; or when we read *The Golden Bowl*, why does Maggie Verver conspire to have her father take Charlotte Stant back to America City? In a sense, this last question might occur to us – rather forcibly. But we shall not be inquiring about motive. I shall come back to this later. For the moment, and far beyond it, we must substitute James's own word for that of his critics. He does not analyse Kate's motives, or Maggie's. He immerses himself in their minds. His is a sort of guarded negative capability, and the critics' insistence on applying the term 'analysis' to it betrays their mistaking the nature of the process and their preoccupation with the way James qualifies it, guards it. In *What Maisie Knew*, the girl's innocence is 'saturated with knowledge'. She is 'morally at home in atmospheres it would be appalling to analyse'. The same is true elsewhere of adult protagonists. They may not be 'at home' in Lancaster Gate, in the Palazzo Leporelli, at Portland Place or at Fauns, but Milly and Maggie certainly do not analyse the atmospheres of these places, and they are consequently 'appalled' only very late in the day.

A glance back to the middle novels might help to clarify the issue. *The Portrait of a Lady* is probably the novel in which James owed most to George Eliot. Not long before it was written he had reviewed *Middlemarch* and *Daniel Deronda*, and distinctive features of the plots of both these novels find their way into his own. Furthermore, it does make sense to ask of Isabel why she turns down Ralph Touchett, Lord Warburton and Caspar Goodwood, and why she accepts Gilbert Osmond. The crises and reversals of the plot exist primarily to throw up opportunities for Isabel to display her character through the exercise of choice – choice between boldly presented alternative courses of action. But even here, in what is otherwise a relatively conventional novel, there are occasions where speculation about motives gets us nowhere. At the very end, for example. Why does Isabel go back to Osmond? Critics disagree about the reasons, or about the comparative importance of the several reasons it is possible to advance: her respect for the marriage vow; the impossibility of her situation otherwise; her duty to protect Pansy. But are reasons, these kinds of reasons, much to the point? I think we do wrong to try to establish this connection between a moral decision and a line of action consequent upon it. Isabel, and James, see it differently. One occupies a certain position, and other people occupy other positions relative to it. These positions are unstable, and they appear unstable to the minds of those who occupy and adjoin them. But the real instability and the assumed one may be different. One of the ways a person grows is in respect of his ability to separate the assumed from the real shift in relations, and to see when relations become fixed. That is what Isabel does at the end of *The Portrait*. She identifies and so accepts a real situation. To call that a motive for doing what she does seems to me an imprecise use of words. Motives precipitate decisions, not recognitions. At the most important points in the narrative, and increasingly as James develops, Jamesian protagonists make recognitions. Whether this can then be said to become a decision is doubtful. Few critics of *The Wings of the Dove* have been able to locate just *where* Milly 'decides' to deal with Densher as she does – she is 'off-stage' anyway. Maggie is 'on-stage' throughout most of part II of *The Golden Bowl*, but he would be a rash man who pointed to the passage that revealed her decision to pack Charlotte and her father off to America.

Joseph Warren Beach comes close to the real Jamesian procedures when he talks of Maggie and the Prince as 'not actors in a drama, but figures in a pattern. We do not see them doing this or that; we become aware of the fact that they have arrived at such a position in relation to one another.' This puts J. I. M. Stewart's witty description of Isabel's renunciation – 'transcendentalized good form' – into a less demeaning perspective. It is profoundly accurate. James has a habit of converting both motive and morality into formal patterns, and caring deeply about the disposition of the parts of the patterns. His characters care deeply about them too. But again, neither James nor the characters assign the elements of the pattern to categories, because their minds are too fine to be violated by ideas. James is like the small children of his Preface to *What Maisie Knew*: they had 'many more perceptions than they had terms to translate them'. Miss Wix 'is a lady with eyebrows arched like skipping-ropes and thin black stitching, like ruled lines for musical notes, on beautiful white gloves'. That is a very precise perception. No wonder James preferred Turgenev, who 'cares for the aspect of things', to George Eliot, who cares for their 'reasons'. Maisie was capable of so much. At other times James has to 'attend and amplify' with his own comments. Maisie would probably not have used the image of 'tall tumblers filled to the brim and held straight for fear of a spill'. But she and her author share a great many of the 'relational' words that are used: 'squaring' things – 'Then everyone will be squared', just as in the *Notebook* entry on *The Portrait of a Lady*, James talked of making the best of 'what groups together' – making things out, seeing one's way. It is the impression received of relations between things, and between one set of circumstances and another, that is important to him. After all, had he not written in 'The Art of Fiction' that 'Impressions are experience'?

To analyse an impression is to lose it, to turn it into something else. Vivid impressions are received by immersing oneself in the sensibility of the person receiving the impression. That is how to make the reader experience events in fiction. And that is why many readers find the experience communicated in a novel by Henry James unsatisfactory. The immersion of author and reader within the point of view of select sensibilities carries with it the obligation to share in an almost wholly passive abstraction from experience. This is part of what I meant by saying there would be more *in* the novels if more were left *out*. The unbroken train of impressions leaves no room for the indelicate and active imposition of meanings. The 'real burden' of Milly Theale's story – according to Percy Lubbock, James's most lucid and influential English apologist in the 1920s and 1930s – 'is veiled under the trembling wavering delicacy of her immediate thought', i.e. her impressions. Trembling' and 'wavering' because they are acted upon by external stimuli which they have no time to convert into ideas or meanings. It is significant that Lubbock talks of Strether's mind, in *The Ambassadors*, as being 'brushed' by new experience. Nothing substantial is put *in*; the odd bits of dirt and grit are swept *out*. The mind itself is the totally passive receptacle of impressions which bestow upon it what experience it is able to acquire. This is why the material for a short story so often fills out a whole novel. Ideas are short-cuts to truth. They give shape to meanings. James's meanings have no shape. He is too busy watching the current to see the stream.

Maisie's vocation was 'to see the world and to thrill with enjoyment to the picture'. How often in James the world is conceived as a picture, as something to be minutely scrutinised. The conjunction of 'the strain of observation and the assault of experience' is what he is always after. His prefaces are full of windows and vantage-points, his novels of eyes staring at compositions of figures arranged in a little 'scene'. The great recognition scenes are usually visual recognitions: Isabel's view of Osmond sitting and Madame Merle standing: Strether's of the boat carrying Chad and Madame de Vionnet actually sailing into a picture – the little Lambinet he has imposed on the riverside view. Again, the novels are full of painters and paintings: Miriam Rooth sitting for Nick Dormer in *The Tragic Muse*; the clutter of Bronzinos and other Mannerist portraits the heroines are persistently compared with, from *The Portrait of a Lady* to *The Wings of the Dove*. They are almost always paintings, never sculpture or ceramics; unless the plot, as in *The Golden Bowl*, demands a physical object which can be held, and dropped. The miscellaneous bric-à-brac of Lancaster Gate is swept over rapidly in the process of creating an imposing and immediate image of Mrs Lowder. At Poynton it is again a necessary property of the plot. The heroine is usually a painting, gazed at by little groups of connoisseurs and art thieves. She gazes back into their eyes in a formidable effort to see where she is hung.

Most critics have noticed the unremittingly visual emphasis of James's work. Tony Tanner, for instance, thinks that at the heart of his interests is that of deciding how we do and how we should look at the world. 'Much of James's most important drama goes on just behind the eye.' In 'Daisy Miller' we are aware of his

interest in 'eyes and minds continually active, alert, condemned
to the effort of endless response in a multi-faceted world of beguiling and deceiving brilliance'. Even when eyes are sightless,
as Maggie Verver's are at the dinner-party given to celebrate
the return of her father and stepmother to America, their effect is
'prodigious', because 'everything now so fitted for her to everything else'. Maggie has recognised the true state of affairs between
Charlotte and the Prince. She has 'taken it in', and is now
repositioning herself within the pattern of relationships the quartet
comprises, with the result that she upsets the positions occupied
by all the other members. The repositioning and the subsequent
dislocation of the existing pattern is achieved as much by looking
as by speaking. The Prince sees the shattered bowl, Maggie looks
through her window at Charlotte wandering in the garden at
Fauns, and Charlotte 'had seen she was watching her from afar'.
For Maggie, 'The sight, from the window, . . . *told* her why,
told her how, named to her . . . that other possible relation to
the whole fact which alone would bear upon her irresistibly.'
The 'arrangement' of the quartet is threatened, and 'what had
the basis of their life been . . . but that they were arranged
together'. Now Maggie has found she is 'arranged apart'. She
must remain so. 'She must be kept in position so as not to *dis-
arrange* them.' The question does arise in Maggie's own mind
at one stage 'why such promptitude of harmony should have
been important'. But it doesn't preoccupy her for long, and she
doesn't answer it. Neither does James.

Recognition must not be allowed to disrupt the formal arrangement. Only by pretending the arrangement is the same can the
evil that has entered into the heroine's field of vision be successfully ignored. Of course, this all depends on the willingness of the
other members of the arrangement to maintain the forms, on
Charlotte's not rounding on Maggie at Fauns and asking her
whether she knows, whether she has told Amerigo that she knows,
and whether Mr Verver knows that she knows and that Amerigo
has or has not been told. Luckily Charlotte prefers to be strangled
with her husband's metaphorical silken cord rather than ask a
straight question and throw everything out of position. That is her
heroism. So the arrangement remains static. The same with Milly's
discovery of her illness in *The Wings of the Dove*. The conversations between her and Kate after her visit to Sir Luke Strett

are so oblique and 'wavering' that it is difficult to judge just
where information is being released – so gently, so imperceptibly,
because the 'cup' mustn't brim over and the dispositions must
not change. If it were not for the picture of Milly on the bench
in Regent's Park, it would be some time before we ourselves
realised that she is dying. But what sort of recognition is this?
Milly has just left Sir Luke's consulting-rooms. She is alone,
elatedly; she is alone, she feels, for the first time in her life. It is
an invigorating, if undramatic, experience:

> The beauty of the bloom had gone from the small old sense
> of safety – that was distinct. She had left it behind her there
> for ever. But the beauty of the idea of a great adventure, or a
> big dim experiment or struggle in which she might, more re-
> sponsibly than ever before, take a hand, had been offered her
> instead. It was as if she had had to pluck off her breast, to
> throw away some friendly ornament, a familiar flower, a little
> old jewel, that was part of her daily dress; and to take up
> and shoulder as a substitute some queer defensive weapon,
> a musket, a spear, a battle axe – conducive possibly in a higher
> degree to a striking appearance, but demanding all the effort
> of a military posture. . . . Wonderment in truth Milly felt,
> even now attended her step: it was quite as if she saw in
> people's eyes the reflection of her appearance and pace. She
> found herself moving at times in regions visibly not haunted
> by odd-looking girls in New York, duskily draped, sable-
> plumed, all but incongruously shod and gazing about them
> with extravagance; she might, literally, have had her musket
> on her shoulder, have announced herself as freshly on the war-
> path.

The passage bristles with imagery: Milly in jewels, in an army, in
a box, assuming postures and striking appearances. The gestures
are dramatic as few of the actual gestures in 'scenes' between the
dramatis personae are allowed to be. But do they add up to anything very much? Compare them with Dorothea's gestures in
her recognition scene at the end of *Middlemarch* when she realises
that, in spite of what she thinks she has seen, she cannot simply
ignore the claims made upon her by her lover and her friends:

> All this vivid sympathetic experience returned to her now as
> a power: it asserted itself as acquired knowledge asserts itself

and will not let us see as we saw in the day of our ignorance. She said to her own irremediable grief, that it should make her more helpful, instead of driving her back from effort.

And what sort of crisis might not this be in three lives whose contact with hers laid an obligation on her as if they had been suppliants bearing the sacred branch? The objects of her rescue were not to be sought out by her fancy: they were chosen for her. She yearned towards the perfect Right, that it might make a throne within her, and rule her errant will. 'What should I do – how should I act now, this very day if I could clutch my own pain and compel it to silence and think of those three!'

It had taken long for her to come to that question, and there was light piercing into the room. She opened her curtains and looked out towards the bit of road that lay in view, with fields beyond, outside the entrance-gates. On the road there was a man with a bundle on his back and a woman carrying her baby; in the field she could see figures moving – perhaps the shepherd with his dog. Far off in the bending sky was the pearly light; and she felt the largeness of the world and the manifold workings of men to labour and endurance. She was part of that involuntary, palpitating life, and could neither look out on it from her luxurious shelter as a mere spectator, nor hide her eyes in selfish complaining.

The connections between situation, feeling and reflection are quiet different. George Eliot's vocabulary is so much more physical, so much more suggestive of the inner bodily movements that accompany deep feeling: 'power', 'driving back', 'clutch', 'involuntary, palpitating life'. These are motions of body and feeling before they are metaphors, images. By comparison, James's language is fanciful. Milly is still so preoccupied with those arrangements and appearances. Taking a hand and plucking jewels from the breast are external signs elaborating a pattern. He 'doesn't want to find things out', Wells wrote in *Boon*. 'He accepts very readily and then – elaborates.' And the elaboration is again visual – Milly strutting about and seeing her reflection in people's eyes. It has lost its attachment to a real situation, and comes back to it only as a 'charm' or a 'spell'. The picture of Milly's mind returns us to the 'scene' of the plot's arrangements without adding much substance to them. We are informed of a situation which does no more than supply the occasion for further strains to be imposed on a pattern of relationships. Eventually it enables Kate and Densher to prepare their plot. But there is no extra psychological or moral *weight*.

James's discussion of the *disponible* provides other indications of where his interests lie. In the Preface to *The Portrait of a Lady* he tells us that his 'picture' of what his novel should be about

> began . . . like Turgenev's with the vision of some person or persons, who hovered before him, soliciting him, as the active or passive figure, interesting him and appealing to him just as they were and by what they were. He saw them, in that fashion, as . . . subject to the chances, the complications of existence . . . but then had to find for them the right relations, those that would most bring them out; to imagine, to invent and select and piece together the situations most useful and favourable to the sense of the creatures themselves, the complications they would be most likely to produce and to feel.

Most commentators emphasise James's vision of the active or passive figure here, the character existing freely, and appealing to the writer just as and by what he is. I should choose to stress what James did with his character when it appealed to him, the piecing together and the creation of complications. His attention shifts from the figures to the pattern within which they are seen to exist and which they produce in combination with others created to amplify their sense of themselves. Certainly in the novels the figures tend to lose sensory definition as complications arise. Characters are not differentiated from one another in any of the obvious ways. Dialogue, for example. To my ear the conversation in the first chapter of *The Portrait of a Lady* is uniformly feminine. I cannot get used to the fact that all three characters in it are male. And I have been comparing Kate Croy's conversation with Densher in *The Wings of the Dove* with Milly's conversation with Lord Mark. Both young women, playing contrasted parts in the novel's plot, sound exactly alike. This is true also of gesture, manners, interests and tastes. Stature, tone of voice, linguistic habit are all the same. Even the imagery fails to differentiate them: both Mrs Lowder and Kate Croy are at different times compared with wild animals – a lion and a panther. Only the odd *ficelle*, like Henrietta Stackpole in *The Portrait*, sounds and behaves at all different – and she is a crude caricature.

Everything, then, depends on less tangible ways of presenting consciousness and sensibility; what was called the discovery of the 'right relations'. And this is where James's aesthetic sense so often destroys his interest in the human content. His *Notebook* entries for *The Golden Bowl* show how it came about. What worried James most about the composition of the book was the finding of a 'necessary basis' for the deployment of the pattern of relationships he had in mind. This basis turned out to be 'an intense and exceptional degree of attachment between father and daughter', which has perplexed and divided a great many of its critics. This is a most odd procedure. James has an idea of the figures he wants to develop in his book. He sees possibilities in the play of relationships among them. But to allow this pattern to emerge, one thing is missing. One piece of the jigsaw fails to fall into place. However, all is not lost. Suppose we assume that '*exceptional* degree of attachment between father and daughter'. Then everything works. All four characters face the right directions and generate 'the complications they would be most likely to produce and feel'. All the relations are 'right'. But with what qualifications and at what expense. First of all we cannot just *assume* it. It has to be there in the prose. And once it gets into the prose it has a massively descriptive effect. What *The Golden Bowl* would have been like, could have been like, if James had been able to get away with his design without this 'necessary basis' no one can say. But is it possible to imagine *The Golden Bowl* without it? Surely it dominates the plot. Everything depends on it, and it colours our attitude towards everything else that happens. We inevitably compare Maggie's feelings for her father with her feelings for the Prince, and for Charlotte. The affair between the Prince and Charlotte is inevitably set against the 'affair' between the Verver father and daughter. In other words, a basis in a novel is not a pedestal, as one would imagine looking through James's *Notebooks*. It is more like a lens. Once accepted, it determines the way we look at everything else in the book.

James doesn't see it like that. The pattern requires that such and such a relation between its constituent parts be observed, but the author attaches no interest or significance to the relation for its own sake. Stewart makes the point very neatly: 'Matter into which we ourselves want to read psychological significance [James] is accepting without psychological enquiry, simply for the sake of the action he must develop.' The emphasis has moved decisively from the characters to the patterns that can be made to emerge from their relationships, and the relationships have thus been deprived of substance. This does raise very serious questions about the nature of James's art. His immersion in the sensibilities of his characters has already produced a lack of what we might call 'scale', a feeling for the relative importance of things in any but a quantitative sense. There is a neutrality of psychological values. Then, the characters have been deprived of everything *but* sensibility: James told Edith Wharton that he had no idea that he had stripped them of what she called the 'human fringes we necessarily trail after us through life'. The result is that the principals are suspended in a void that has to be filled with what is left over – all those delicate and wavering impulses and suppositions that had been pictured for us in characters whom we had discovered over and over again 'watching each other' (again Edith Wharton's phrase). This watching, 'this rapid play of suppressed appeal and disguised response', depends on a device confessedly adopted for no other purpose. The more James works at it, the more puzzled everybody becomes about what it is, as a fact rather than as a support for other facts. And the more it fills out into a shape, acquires a sort of perverse and ghostly substance, the more comparisons and contrasts inevitably suggest themselves – comparisons and contrasts James may not have intended, and which were certainly not a part of his original scheme.

Why does John Bayley, whose approach to fiction is in general so much out of love with devices that diminish a character's capacity to exist, pick out this very novel as a masterpiece of inclusiveness and vivacity? *The Golden Bowl* is James's tribute to a 'conception of how the novelist possesses his world', and possession, there, carries no pejorative implications. The phrases Bayley uses to describe the ambience within which the Ververs, the Prince and Charlotte exist are most peculiar, almost a perverse contrast to the words I should myself prefer. He finds 'solid' what I find hollow, 'free' what for me is bound. What for him is the 'gusto of creation' is for me the attenuation of a device. As in Jane Austen, 'a loving absorption in individual personalities always precedes the working out of patterns of discernment'. This appears to me to be true only in a very special sense, which is distinctly at odds with the positive impression the words suggest.

The grounds on which Mr Bayley makes his evaluation of the novel are consonant with the views on fiction adumbrated in his essay on 'The Worlds of Love'. *The Golden Bowl* is about love, knowledge and power, and the relations which obtain between those concepts as they are experienced in the process of living. The contrast between Maggie's love of her father, and the Prince's and Charlotte's love of each other, is deliberate and at the heart of the book. Charlotte and Amerigo seem to know what they are about. They are the obvious manipulators, the active protagonists in a 'plot' to deceive the Ververs. Their line of descent can be traced back through Kate Croy and Merton Densher to Madame Merle and Gilbert Osmond. But as James developed as a novelist, his understanding of the 'plotters' increased with his appreciation of the power that might be held by the apparent victim. It becomes more and more difficult to isolate power from quite different attributes of mind and feeling. Osmond was a villain pure and simple. Densher, and even Kate, were themselves used, made over into the objects of their own design. With Charlotte and the Prince the possession of power and the deployment of design have been separated from notions of absolute corruption. Power is no longer necessarily evil. Design is no longer something one organises at arms' length, something quite separate from and uninfluential upon the person who has evolved it. Complementarily, it becomes impossible to assume that innocence, the good, is powerless. But the kind of power it possesses is obviously different from that of the 'plotters'. How, then, does it make itself felt, and how does it avoid the compromising entanglements that usually attend the exercise of power?

Crudely, Maggie and her father, the good 'victims' of *The Golden Bowl*, exercise a kind of power that comes from 'not-knowing'. This 'not-knowing' is different from ignorance, for what is so much of part II of the novel about but Maggie's growing recognition of the situation of Charlotte and the Prince? In fact, 'not-knowing' is even further removed from ignorance than knowing is. It is an active state, a refusal to know what presents itself to the mind. Why, then, is it not mere self-deception, the word Maxwell Geismar applies in his attack on this novel? Because underlying the 'decision' not to know is an acknowledgement of the human mystery that exists beneath every act of 'visibly analytic consciousness'. Basically, we don't know the 'extraordinary complications of human motive and appearance' at all. The events of the novel that we witness show this to be so. Maggie's conversation with her father at Fauns is less of a dramatic 'scene' than a 'riddle of dramatic possibility'. Drama creates motive out of less distinct activities of the mind and therefore simplifies the way human consciousness works. Hence James's lack of interest in motive. It is something abstracted from the obscure complexities of consciousness, an imposition of meaning on mystery. Maggie therefore refuses to know. She saves herself, and she saves the others, by 'deliberate ignorance' working under the guise of conventional behaviour, the observation of the forms, the maintenance of the pattern. She discovers that 'to support convention intelligently and savingly is at least as remarkable as to defy it', as Isabel did before her return to Italy from Ralph Touchett's death-bed almost a quarter of a century earlier. 'James impressively suggests the paradox that the conventional and the mysterious are closely allied, are indeed one and the same thing. It is the conventional act which challenges the imagination and produces mystery, not the daring and emancipated act.' Thus by forcing the lovers to separate and be reabsorbed into the arrangement of the marriages, Maggie compels them to be good, and because good is 'conventional' in this rather special sense of the word, she makes them interesting. The convention of not-knowing 'is allied with moral impossibility of knowing completely. The shape of the novel bears this out, for it is the shaping of an effect which is shapeless in life, the effect of queries unanswered and problems unresolved.'

This would make *The Golden Bowl* a very impressive novel. But is it really as Bayley says it is? Is the contrast he finds between the naïve knowledge of the lovers and the 'not-knowing' naïvety of the daughter (and the father, probably – but the extent of Mr Verver's 'complicity' is an even more complicated matter and literally doesn't bear thinking about) – is it really there? Apparently not. Even on Mr Bayley's evidence James does not manage to secure an effective contrast between 'the communion of Maggie and her father, and the communion of the lovers':

The contrast he attempts to indicate is the mutual silence of Maggie and her father as against the almost sensual mutual confidences of the lovers: Maggie and her father never get around to so much as mentioning 'them', which is implied as part of their instinctive and unconscious goodness. But instead of a contrast we really feel an uncomfortable resemblance, for in spite of its silence the intimacy of father and daughter seems just as exclusive, just as much closed against the others as is that of Charlotte and the Prince. Our impression of two camps is unfortunate, because the point about natural love should be that it does not constitute itself into such a camp.

It strikes me as disingenuous to call this a 'partial failure'. It is total. For it reduces the whole activity of *The Golden Bowl* to a scheme. The two 'communions' are the pivots upon which the action of the novel revolves If they are not rendered sufficiently different from each other for us to distinguish between them on any but a theoretical level, then the substance of the novel disintegrates. And of course it does. The paucity of mimetic differentiation we noticed in *The Portrait of a Lady* and *The Wings of the Dove* is here reinforced by a uniformity of positions taken up by the characters towards the world. They should be sharply distinguished, as the form of the action – and Mr Bayley's interpretation of it – suggests. But the words the characters use and the way the characters are shown to address one another prevent this from happening. In the flesh, degrees of knowledge and power lose their definition. Knowing the good and knowing you want to seduce Charlotte Stant sound very much like the same thing.

What Mr Bayley has done is to impose ideas on the flow of impressions which for James constitute experience. I do not think that for Mr Bayley they do. He believes with Mrs Assingham that he sees the lives of the characters better than they see them for themselves. It strikes him 'for very pity' that they are 'making a mess of such charming material'. Accordingly, he rescues from the flood of James's impressions the odd spar and driftwood of solid sense, material that something can be made of. Indeed his wife, Iris Murdoch, has made a great deal out of it.[1] Maggie

[1] See below, pp. 211 ff.

Verver on the connections between love and jealousy is very much like Iris Murdoch on degrees of charity. Maggie's 'contrivance of relations' which imposes an almost sacrificial burden on herself, but which might dispose of the whole complexity of the peril of others, is that of so many mythic figures in Mrs Murdoch's stories. James's 'scapegoat' is her 'unicorn' writ small. She has converted his impressions into ideas and his oblique meditations into plot. But that is to progress beyond my present argument.

5
Time and Motion

'The bill for living is that everything comes to you in time.'
Brian Moore in *An Answer from Limbo*

In book III of *The Old Wives' Tale*, Sophia Scales is taken to Auxerre by her husband Gerald and his friend Chirac to witness an execution. To Chirac, the Frenchman, 'As psychological experience . . . it will be very *intéressant*. . . . To observe one's self in such circumstances.' Gerald assumes the same attitude, but with less conviction. At dinner, before the event, Sophia looks at him with distrust: 'Gerald's pose of a calm, disinterested scientific observer of humanity gradually broke down.' Afterwards both men are somewhat the worse for wear. 'Chirac looked worn out, curiously fragile and pathetic; but Gerald was the very image of death.' Such are the trials and tribulations of dispassionate observation. The Frenchman is abashed, the Englishman completely defeated. And Gerald's reaction is a type of the reactions of English novelists to experience taken 'neat'. They couldn't face the unvarnished truth, and they couldn't understand that truth, after all, *is* varnished – that our interest in events draws over them a patina that preserves the picture and saves the painter. Even so, English realist fiction is not without its considerable achievements. One of them is *The Old Wives' Tale* itself. Another is Ford Madox Ford's *The Good Soldier*. They are very different novels, the one as expansive and continuous as the other is tight and concentrated. But they have in common the deployment of a consistent method, the attempt at a specifically novelistic manner of presenting things as they are. Ford's story is lifelike, Bennett's like life. There are both similarities and differences between the pictures of life those phrases call to mind.

Ford's opinion, as expressed in a multitude of books on the art of fiction, was that the Victorians considered the novel an impure form, and that they had no use for a theory of the novel which allotted to it as an art-form limiting, though proper and exclusive, functions. Instead they had treated it as a mixed mode, in which the novelist could pontificate, describe, dramatise, self-dramatise, and generally taken upon himself the role of mediator and judge, both in respect of relations set up within his fiction and relations between aspects of his fiction and complementary aspects of the real world. Consequently, the novel did not describe a world in relation to which the reader had a definite status. The position he occupied vis-à-vis the fiction kept on changing. He was involved and disengaged by turns. At one moment the illusion of a real world would be totally convincing. At another it would be revealed as a blatant fiction confessed to by the author in person or hinted at by tricks of style. The balance between these two kinds of writing corresponded with the balance between illusion and freedom from illusion on the part of the reader.

Ford countered this accepted view of the novel with the Continental alternative. According to this, the novel was a pure form. It had functions and methods which were quite different from those of any other literary form, having nothing to do with the sermon, the tract, the essay, the moral treatise or the writing of history. These made up its first skin, as it were, which had been sloughed off in the course of the development of the form from Madame de Lafayette and Richardson to Jane Austen and Stendhal. With Flaubert the novel had once and for all come of age. It had developed a new and glossy skin which marked it out as an altogether different species of literature. Ford traced this development in *The English Novel* in a manner which is clearly positivist, the novel having now reached a level close to perfection in the work of the French realists, James and Conrad. Further development was likely to be lateral, extending the range and subject-matter of the novel. The pure novel form achieved by the turn of the century had come into existence by a fusion of impressionistic and point-of-view techniques.

Point of view in the nineteenth-century novel had for the most part been unstable and inconsistent. This was inevitable in an impure form, made up of description and personal ancedote in unconsidered proportions:

. . . it became very early evident to us that what was the matter with the Novel, and the British Novel in particular, was that it went straight forward, whereas in your gradually making acquaintanceship with your fellows you never do go straight forward. . . . To get . . . a man into fiction you could not begin at his beginning and work his life chronologically to the end. You must first get him in with a strong impression, and then work backwards and forwards over his past.

Ford substituted for the straightforward progress in time from one description of an event to another description of a later event, a chronologically erratic grouping of impressions of different aspects of a number of events. Now the point of view remains stable at the expense of the events it apprehends, rather than the other way about. The events adapt to the modes in which they are perceived, where before, the modes could chop and change as much as the author pleased so long as the 'story line' remained straight and went on its way diagrammatically from A to B to C and so on. Another consequence was that the events became more and more *mental* events since the plot became a pattern of impressions, subjective and relatively time-free, whereas before they had been objective events which minds operated on, and were seen to operate on, from the vantage-point of the impression-free narrator. Temperamental and emotional forces themselves became events. Where the old novel was mechanical, even if the mechanism included parts of organic tissue, the new novel would be organic, even if it had an artificial valve or two inside it. The progress of the art of fiction from Flaubert to Turgenev and James was that of a reduction in the amount of visible mechanical apparatus required to make it work. Flaubert got rid of the plot but kept the events; Turgenev went some way to getting rid of the events but kept the linear time-scheme; Conrad got rid of the time-scheme, thus entirely liberating the organic, impressionist novel from its mechanical and didactic proto-form. Where earlier critics had looked for the ghost in the machine, the modern critic would have to look for the machine in the ghost; and the harder it was to find, the better the novel would be. Hence the significance of not being able to learn anything about technique from Turgenev. So much of the mechanism had been spirited away in a 'natural' sequence of impressions.

With the closer approximation to real life and the developed impressionist technique consequent upon it must go a subjectivising of the plot and a deterioration of any definite structure of events. Events will become as fluid as the minds and interests operating upon, and indeed creating them. In substituting impressions of events for the events themselves, Ford should have found that the old 'well-made' novel was beyond recall. In fact he never lost faith in the usefulness of 'well-made' novels. Somewhere there had to be found a point midway between real events – of which, unlike Flaubert, Ford nowhere seriously questioned the status – and our shifting perpections of them, and this 'somewhere' would be the point of vantage from which the novel was written. Hence point of view, time-shift and impressionist rendering of events would remain techniques. The novelist, no longer omniscient in the manner of Fielding, Scott or Thackeray, would remain in control by working his narrative techniques into a pattern as absorbing as the old plotted novel was absorbing. Impressionist point of view would be responsible for the development of whole sequences of action, and to that extent would be dominant; but the arrangement, whilst not defying impressionist principles, would be undertaken by a novelist who had reserved to himself the choice of whose point of view should open and close each sequence of scenes. The arrangement of sequences Ford called the *progression d'effet*.

The method, though not the phrase, was Flaubert's. Ford was fascinated by the way in which in *Madame Bovary* 'the most casual detail' was used to 'inevitably carry the story forward'. He noticed that the action of the *Education* is nothing but a succession of such casual details and that its plot is therefore little more than a 'constant succession of tiny unobservable surprises'. This was what all novelists should try to achieve: 'every word set on paper . . . must carry the story forward and, . . . as the story progressed, the story must be carried forward faster and faster and with more and more intensity'. In his own work Ford tried to replace this succession of details – fixed, definite and largely external – by mental agitations, plays of temperament and changes of attitude on the Jamesian and Turgenevian model. He never achieved their degree of subtlety and he often had recourse to a melodramatic or even farcical type of plotting which they had left far behind. But if Ford has a claim on posterity it is by virtue of his attempt to bring together the new preoccupation with subjective responses and impulses, and an acceptably thrusting narrative, fluctuating in its time-scheme and subject to arbitrary interruption, but able to call forth the same degree of interest and excitement that the novel composed on the old lines had done in its Victorian heyday.

He succeeded best in *The Good Soldier* (1915), a novel with a tight, dramatic form of a kind that might have been suggested by the study of French realist practice. In this case the study had been very particular. The Dedicatory Letter to his wife Stella shows that Ford was trying to emulate Maupassant's treatment of a subject in *Fort comme la mort*. This is the story of a fashionable and successful Parisian painter, Olivier Bertin, his mistress, Any de Guilleroy, and her daughter Annette. Olivier and Any are becoming aware of their decline into middle age. Olivier is falling in love with Annette. Clearly, then, the way is open for comparisons between Maupassant's novel and Ford's in respect of the subject, and these have been made by most reliable critics of *The Good Soldier*. But I wonder if this is the most useful comparison that can be made. The action of the French novel is organised around Annette's return from the country, and the effect of her presence on the liaison between the two older characters. In Ford's novel, the arrival on the scene of Nancy Rufford is a late though crucial development, and although her importance throughout is testified to by the mysterious references in part I to 'the girl' and 'the poor girl', at least as much space is occupied by Ashburnham's affairs with Maisie Maidan and Florence Dowell. Comparisons between subjects do not turn out to be quite so telling as might have been expected. Perhaps Ford had other things in mind; perhaps he was as much interested in method as in subject.

Fort comme la mort was Maupassant's fifth novel (1889), following *Pierre et Jean* and preceding *Notre cœur*. It therefore occupies a significant place within his work as a whole. None of the novels that followed it are among the best, yet *Pierre et Jean*, the year before, is one of his masterpieces. It also contains the famous preface, 'Un Roman', in which Maupassant made his clearest distinction between the *roman d'analyse* and the *roman objectif*. Unlike *Une Vie* and *Bel Ami*, *Pierre et Jean* is not completely an objective novel. E. D. Sullivan describes it as 'an extension of the objective method into the psychological domain'

Fort comme la mort is hardly an objective novel at all. Indeed there is no reason, in terms of Maupassant's own theory, why it should be, since what lies behind his preference for the objective method is his belief that the imagination is limited by the senses, and that one cannot know enough about other people's minds for the psychological method to be of much value. So: 'À lieu d'étaler la psychologie des personnages en des dissertations explicatives, il la faisait simplement apparaître par leurs actes. Les dedans étaient ainsi dévoilées par le dehors, sans aucune argumentation psychologique.' But *Fort comme la mort*, a study of an ageing artist, has a subject as closely connected with Maupassant's own life in 1888–9 as *The Good Soldier* has with Ford's in 1913–15. The psychological method was therefore permissible. But it was not effective. In the event, Maupassant proved incapable of combining objective and psychological techniques satisfactorily. Passages like those incorporating Madame de Guilleroy's reflections on her age are unnecessary and crude; they merely summarise imprecisely what has been suggested earlier through the dialogue. The action of the novel is impeded by their presence rather than placed in a different light. By manipulating Any's conscious thoughts, Maupassant is making sure we have grasped the significance of the action proper; and we can see that that is what he is doing. This makes Sullivan's assessment of the novel perfectly sound:

> Maupassant was unwilling to cut loose completely from his own objective technique and combined the objective and psychological methods, or rather, overlaid one on the other. Again and again in this novel, after having portrayed his characters through closely observed action and dialogue, he seems to remember that he is writing a psychological novel and goes back over the ground already covered and gives pages of analysis which add nothing.

To grasp the importance of this mistake, in terms of what Ford learned from it, we must be aware of another very important thing that the two novels have in common. Both deal with a process of becoming aware. Maupassant's work is about the way two middle-aged people discover that they are indeed middle-aged and that this discovery involves difficult readjustments to each other and to the circles within which they move. It is, more precisely, about Olivier Bertin's gradual discovery that he is in love with Annette de Guilleroy. As a psychological novel it tries to make the reader understand these issues from the inside; to plot, perception by perception, incident by incident, the trajectory of an intermittent, almost imperceptible, process of understanding on the part of its two main characters, and in particular of Bertin. But at each stage of the process Maupassant seems to have felt the need for summing-up of the point already reached – not, since he is a realist, from the vantage-point of an omniscient narrator, but from the point of view of the character concerned. Because this point of view is a fully conscious one, and because it duplicates insights already achieved by objective methods of dialogue and description on previous pages, it is felt to be irrelevant. The work is already done. No amount of description of conscious reflection will take it any further.

Ford's novel is also about a process of becoming aware. But in his case the awareness of his character, Dowell, is not so improved at the end of the book as is that of the reader who has followed its development. Meditations in Dowell's first-person narrative contribute a great deal more than a summing-up of what we already know, whilst functioning in a manner less pat and less academically articulated than do Bertin's conclusions in Maupassant's novel. It begins to look as if, by studying *Fort comme la mort*, Ford hit upon a method of reproducing a character's developing awareness of his situation in such a way as to allow us, the readers, to understand more about that situation than the character himself does: not *as much* or *as little* as Bertin, but *more than* Dowell. To do this he disposed of the customary method of third-person narrative.

Outside of his collaboration with Conrad at the turn of the century, Ford had never used first-person narrative before. He was to do so only once again, in *The Marsden Case*. It can therefore be assumed that he had special reasons for using it here, especially as he had taken so much time meditating how to present his story. The way he uses it in *The Good Soldier* is strange, to say the least. Usually we rely on a fictional narrator to make the story he tells clearer as it proceeds. The more he tells us, the more we understand the nature and significance of the events he is describing. If he is handled ironically, then the discrepancy between what he tells us and what we are able to infer (from the dialogue, for example) brings us by an indirect route to an understanding of what really took place. In Ford's novel this does not happen. The situation of Edward Ashburnham, involving Leonora and Florence in the first part of the book and Leonora and Nancy in the last, becomes more and more difficult to get to grips with, as the character of Dowell, who is telling us about it, becomes clearer and clearer.

This is perplexing, since Dowell is in charge of the whole affair. We are told, by him, that all the points of view of the other characters are, finally, constituents of his own. We have to rely on him almost entirely. Many critics don't like to do this, because they think he is unintelligent. I think not, and that the key to *The Good Soldier* lies in our understanding of the way Dowell's intelligence works. Taken as a whole, his narrative is not that of an imperceptive or abnormally stupid man, however much his gullibility in the face of deceptions of the grossest kind in the past might lead us to believe he ought to be. The six months during which he has been sounding the depths of the English heart have not been wasted.

Much of the confusion over Dowell's character springs from his use of a polite language which fits what we judge to have been his previous conception of himself and his friends much better than it fits him now, in his effort to communicate what he has learned and what he is till learning. He habitually uses easy expressions like 'as close as a good glove's with your hand' and 'we were thrown very much into the society of the nicer English'. That is to is to say, he is in the habit of making assumptions about the world that are inconsistent with what we discover he has learned about it. The language he uses betrays the position he occupies between two outlooks on life. The course of his narrative jolts back and forth between interpretations based on old assumptions, and others based on the undeceived outlook he is still only partly in possession of when the novel opens, and which, throughout, he fights against as much as he accepts. The most difficult problem he is left with is how to judge Edward. Conventionally, he should be the villain; but it is Leonora, the wronged wife, whom Dowell dislikes. Edward is more often 'poor' Edward, 'poor' devil, than the hated seducer of his wife. Of course, this has something to do with Dowell's basic deficiency, his feebleness and lack of passion, But more than that it is a problem because:

> I guess that I myself, in my fainter way, come into the category of the passionate, of the headstrong, and the too-truthful. For I can't conceal from myself the fact that I loved Edward Ashburnham – and that I loved him because he was just myself . . . you see, I am just as much of a sentimentalist as he was. . . .

This seems to me to be thoroughly obtuse of Dowell. Nothing he has said or done up to this point would lead one to believe that his judgement here is correct. He is not passionate and he is not headstrong. But he does love Edward Ashburnham. He is honest about what he feels but he still cannot recognise why he feels it: namely, because Edward, like himself, and like Nancy, whom he also loves, is a victim; and he automatically identifies with victims, especially when they are more attractive to others than he is. His mind dwells obsessively on this aspect of character, sometimes distilling from it images of sadistic melodrama. The self-deception he practises (even at the very end of the novel) in supposing his sense of fellow-feeling with Edward has its origin in a common strength rather than a common weakness, is evidence of the incomplete awareness he has of the situation he describes.

In a way he knows this already. He frequently confesses to ignorance of life in general as distinct from ignorance of particular aspects of it: 'I am only an ageing American with very little knowledge of life.' Dowell's reflections have not yet brought him to a proper understanding of himself. In this respect it is Ashburnham's role that is like Bertin's in *Fort comme la mort*. They both commit suicide – Ashburnham certainly, Bertin probably – as a result of what they discover about themselves in the course of their relationship with a young girl. Dowell lives on, still only half aware of what has brought him to where he is. On the other hand, we remember Maupassant's attempt to integrate passages of psychological reflection in his novel. In this respect Bertin is certainly the model for Dowell, not for Ashburnham, since all the points of view, and meditations on them and on events, are Dowell's. Both Dowell and Bertin gradually become aware of their true feelings and their reasons for them, though in Dowell's case this is an incomplete process. The difference is that by substituting Ashburnham for Bertin as a type within the narrative, and by incorporating that narrative within the first-person framework of Dowell's recollections, Ford turned the 'coming-aware' psychological passages to greater advantage. These are no longer summaries but essential parts of the plot, since it is the course of Dowell's meditations and memories which dictates the form the plot takes.

The manipulation of Dowell as speaker of a first-person narrative has another advantage: it provides additional psychological justification for the use of the time-shift which becomes, for the first time in Ford's work, a basic structural principle and not, as elsewhere, a useful technique to be applied at selected points in the novel's development. Dowell explains what it is and why he has to use it at the beginning of part IV:

> . . . when one discusses an affair – a long, sad affair – one goes back, one goes forward. One remembers points that one has forgotten, and one explains them all the more minutely since one recognizes that one has forgotten to mention them in their proper places and that one may have given, by omitting them, a false impression. I console myself with thinking that this is a real story and that, after all, real stories are probably told best in the way a person telling a story would tell them. They will then seem most real.

The way Dowell tells the story is consistent with his character. True to his amateur status, he keeps reminding us of his difficulty. The fact remains, though, that Dowell's peculiar but apparently quite natural method of organising what he has to say tells us more about *him* than he is able to tell us about Edward, Leonora, Florence and Nancy. We are almost entirely dependent on his viewpoint for our knowledge, let alone interpretation, of events involving *them*. Independent evidence is in the nature of things difficult to come by.

Where it does exist, Dowell often understands its relevance to the affair as well as we might have done ourselves if it had been presented to us in the third person. For example, it is obviously important that Leonora is a Roman Catholic. The comedy of misunderstandings at the castle at M— (part I, chap. 4) would be a much cruder thing if we had no knowledge of this, and the reason for Leonora's putting up with Edward's earlier and pettier indiscretions with women would be less intelligible. At the time, at M—, Dowell allows himself to be easily taken in by

Leonora. He takes her religious explanation of her conduct seriously, though without seeming to understand anything more about her character as a result of it; and he seems to be blind to the more obvious cause of her hysterical behaviour – namely, her realisation that Florence and her husband have been conducting an affair behind her back. His acceptance of Leonora's explanation tells us a lot about the kind of man Dowell's was then, and to some extent has remained up to the time of writing the story. For Leonora's words 'gave me the greatest relief that I have ever had in my life. They told me, I think, almost more than I had ever gathered at one moment – about myself.' What he understands about himself is his capacity to be self-deceived, not because of stupidity, but because of laziness: 'I verily believe . . . that if my suspicion that Leonora was jealous of Florence had been the reason she gave for her outburst I should have turned upon Florence with the maddest kind of rage.' Why? Because Florence would have made self-deception on his part impossible, by allowing another person to confirm suspicions he had hitherto carefully hidden from himself because he was 'too tired'. Once we grasp this characteristic of Dowell, present throughout the nine years during which he knew the Ashburnhams, it becomes less difficult to appreciate the complex, and not unintelligent, state of mind in which he tells the story. He is more of a coward than a fool, and his overriding insistence on not being bothered, on not being put to the trouble of facing the consequences of what he knows is really the case, is not eradicated by the time he writes the story. The third paragraph of the first page of the novel should have alerted us to this fact. Clearly, one thing Dowell must have learned earlier, and did not learn in the process of writing about the affair, was the spuriousness of Florence's heart condition. What he gradually becomes aware of in the course of putting down his thoughts, and in the six months before, is the extent to which his passive acceptance of a state of affairs he half knew to be dangerous has created the disastrous situation he finds himself in now. The seriousness of Dowell's behaviour and the tragedy of the situation it helps to bring about are both trivialised and misunderstood if Dowell is judged to be simply a fool. The tragedy lies in the fact that he knew well enough what he was doing, but neglected to admit to himself what the consequences might be when he and Florence

fell in with the Ashburnhams at Nauheim. The superficially convenient aspects of the friendship – his identification with Edward
as a victim of the sex war, his sympathy with Leonora as another
heart-patient nurse – override his sense of the basic danger:
Florence's promiscuity answering to Edward's. Dowell's fault is
that of seeing always and only what he wants to see. His observa-
tions on English Catholics are shrewd, because his knowledge of
them is fully consonant at this stage with his wish to avoid the
issue of Florence's adultery: Catholicism provides an explanation
for Leonora's behaviour without bringing in the other unpleasant
matter, which can therefore be disregarded. He knows enough to
want to be ignorant, and thinks he can convert the wish into a
reality by pretending hard enough that it is already granted.

This makes Dowell an interesting and complex first-person
narrator and excuses some of the uncertainty we sense in the
portrayal of Edward, who is ostensibly the main character. After
all, the plot itself, quite apart from Dowell's organisation of it, is
very complicated. It deals with Edward's affairs with at least five
women, the financial problems of the Ashburnham household
(the ups and downs of Edward's financial affairs accompany and
provide motives for much of the action of the novel), Dowell's
courtship and marriage, Florence's affair with Jimmy, and the
religious issue between Edward and Leonora. There is plenty of
material for Dowell to work on; and the fact that that is what it
is there for goes far to excuse the hints of intrigue and over-
complication left over from Ford's earlier novels. The use of the
time-shift throughout the narrative, justified by the mental habits
of the particular narrator Ford has chosen, removes the feeling of
artificiality which might otherwise have been present. The more
often Dowell returns to an awkward conjunction of incidents –
Bagshawe's arrival at Nauheim at a crucial time, for example, or
Maisie Maidan's overhearing Edward and Florence, just as
Florence, later, overhears Edward and Nancy – the less awkward,
the less of a novelist's device we feel it to be: we get used to the
fact that it happened and become absorbed in what Dowell spins
out of it, in the connections he forms between it and other incidents.

The Good Soldier is a triumph of colloquial style properly
adapted to the point-of-view method. It is also a triumph of *progression d'effet*. Ford was well aware of this, sufficiently so to

draw our attention to his subtlety in handling it. Dowell calls his story 'the saddest story' rather than 'The Ashburnham Tragedy', 'just because it is so sad and just because there was no current to draw things along to a swift and inevitable end'. We must assume that Ford is showing himself confident of his method even when proposing to adapt it to a situation which we should expect to resist it, since what is lacking, the 'current to draw things along to a swift and inevitable end' (associated with 'the elevation that accompanies tragedy' in the next sentence), is precisely what he meant by *progression d'effet*. His manipulation of the time-shift enabled him to make use of some of the strong points of both the classic drama and the novel. As in the case of the former, there is a restricted time-scale. The action revolves around two brief spaces in time: the final period at Nauheim during which Leonora struggles against Florence for possession of her husband, and Florence commits suicide; and the period at Branshaw Teleragh, during which the relationship between Edward and Nancy is broken by Leonora. There is a pendant to the latter, bringing Dowell back on to the scene and dealing with Edward's suicide. Everything else in the novel refers to one or other of these episodes; the frequent time-shifts, controlled by Dowell's changing interests, serving the same purpose as recapitulatory speeches by characters in classical tragedy. But this other material is treated novelistically, the dramatic material being incorporated in the pictorial proclivities of Dowell's temperament. Hence the compactness of the drama is accompanied by the diffuse excursions of the narrator into the past. All these excursions spring recognisably from Dowell's insistence on clarifying the meaning of what happened at Nauheim and Branshaw. The containment of the two dramatic centres of the novel within the pictorial structure of Dowell's meditation is therefore fully justified, since it is the piecing together of that structure which creates, and explains, the centres. It is the only way Dowell and ourselves (though with different conclusions) can understand their meaning. Hence the way the dramatic centres and the reflective movement backwards and forwards, from and into the past, are built up interdependently by means of the time-shift as the novel progresses, *is* the *progression d'effet*. The casual way in which Dowell says what he has to say makes the course of Edward Ashburnham's self-destruction, in spite of the imperfect rendering of his character, convincingly inevitable. The novelist's interference is not at all in evidence, and the objective record which Flaubert had achieved in the third person, and according to the conventional arrangement of the time-scheme, Ford achieved in first-person narrative, meandering according to the credible psychological impulsions of the narrator. Since the author succeeds in bringing this into line with his own requirements – those of providing readers with all the information needed to understand the affair – he remains invisible, as Flaubert did. The development of the plot of both *Madame Bovary* and *The Good Soldier* is inevitable.

In *The Good Soldier*, what must happen is shown to happen during the two brief periods at Nauheim and Branshaw which Ford singled out as the dramatic foci of the story. The significance of what has to happen only gradually discloses itself to Dowell, but it is already clear enough to enable him to realise where he can find it. He has discovered the 'affair'. All that remains is for him to exhaust it of its significance and so to know himself, as well as Edward Ashburnham, as he has never known himself before. The meaning of his life and the nature of his identity are disclosed – true, more to us than to himself – by the play of his temperament upon those two, temporally circumscribed, 'scenes'. The predominant movement of the narrative is therefore always a movement back – back from a present position which is increasingly defined by its relationship with events in the past which have made it into the present it has inevitably become. Other possibilities are foreclosed. The narrative narrows to a single point, the point at which Dowell is standing. The business of the novel is to make us see that point, and understand why it had to be there, and nowhere else.

Almost all fiction, including French realist fiction, before the First World War, was backward-looking. Dickens's first-person narrators look back from a comfortable present tense into the monstrous irregularities of the past. Flaubert opens *Madame Bovary* with a first-person narrator maing it clear that whatever happened to Charles Bovary could be contained within a narrative like this one, of his school-days. The only difference between the first few pages of the novel and the rest is that they *are* first-person. No one can say just when the first-person ends and the

third-person begins, and it doesn't matter, because they are
equally recapitulatory and 'enclosing': both contain Charles by
setting the scenes to which he belongs in a completed action
which leads to a point at which all these things can be said about
him. In both *David Copperfield* and the *Education*, 'trifles makes
the sum of life'. In Dickens they come in more interesting shapes
and, as we have seen, the shapes they come in change as we walk
around them. Even so, they are interesting because they lead to
something, something we already now about – the completion
of the narrative which adds them up. James tried to show his
characters getting the sum wrong during the addition. The result
was a fascinating series of patterns made up of expanding and
impinging errors. Ford had his narrator dicker about at the
bottom of the table, for ever running back up its columns to
check on a couple of figures he might have got wrong and so
come out with an unsatisfactory answer to himself. But, for the
most part, lives stretch out into the past which is the novel's
continuously provisional present, coming to rest at the end
where we always knew we would be – the answer to the sum, the
present that all those trifles have added up to.

   At their most rigorous, the Naturalists took this scientific
method to exhausting extremes. They preferred the physiological
sciences to mathematics, substituting medical experiments for
sums. Zola tried to apply the scientific method of Xavier Bichât
and Claude Bernard to both his own and his predecessors' novels.
In *La Cousine Bette*, Balzac was an experimentalist subjecting
his Baron Hulot to 'a series of tests'. In an early letter Zola
explained that in future the poet, by which he means the novelist,
would be able to 'discover new effects by addressing himself to
exact investigation'. Luckily, in the 1880s and 1890s few English
critics or novelists failed to flinch from those 'exact investigations',
dreading what they might find at the end of them, and unwilling
to touch pitch. Zola's stock remained low, full of prostitutes and
drunks. We have seen the English looking East for an alternative
and discovering first Turgenev, and then, very incompletely,
Tolstoy. What we have not seen is the stultifying effect this incomplete discovery had on a great many indifferent novelists at
the turn of the century and up to the war. Galsworthy is a fully
representative case. His admiration of the Russians is scattered
about *Castles in Spain* and other books of criticism, and his

pathetic impercipience is startlingly evident even in his best novels. He is, for example, a master of the neutral detail that obstinately remains neutral. The Forsytes are for ever butting sloping foreheads forward, laughing firmly and looking like lions and ''alf tame leopards'. But they never change their spots, and have patently and uselessly had them stuck on in the wings before they entered in the first place. Dartie, the gay blade, is a good example. In *The Man of Property* he is the proud possessor of an 'incorrigible commencement of whisker which, eluding the strictest attempts at shaving, seems the mark of something deeply engrained in the personality of the shaver, being especially noticeable in men who speculate'. *There* is the untelling telling detail. Seemingly irrelevant, but actually – irrelevant. Also Dartie's face 'had that look, peculiar to some men, of having been steeped in linseed oil, with its waxed moustaches and the little distinguished commencements of side whiskers, and concernedly he felt the promise of a pimple on the side of his slightly curved and fattish nose'. The generalisation is meaningless – Galsworthy is simply wrong about the physical characteristics of speculators – and the physical detail is inert. The effort at brief, pregnant summary is Tolstoyan, but its clumsiness and its finality are Galsworthy's own. The character attached to the summary is invariably stillborn. Incidentally, the Jamesian positioning of Irene, which Galsworthy draws attention to in the Preface, is no more successful. Without the details there is simply nothing at all, and the effect of Irene at Montpellier Square is as little like Milly Theale in Regents Park as the effect of Dartie's physical peculiarities (incipient pimples) is like Dolokhov's (hairy wrists). In almost every case, the debt to the Russians was in receipt of false coin: their apparent lack of method encouraged indifferent performances. In avoiding the sordid, Galsworthy and so many of his contemporaries escaped into the merely fatuous.

Novels became unlifelike not because they were melodramatic, as had been the case with the Victorians, but because of an 'air of probability' which, instead of liberating the characters, 'embalms' them. That is what Virginia Woolf felt in 1919. The quarrel was no longer with the villain in the black coat but with *l'homme moyen sensuel* dressed down to the last button 'in the fashion of the hour'. Really, life isn't like this. What it is like Virginia Woolf explained in a celebrated paragraph:

Look within and life, it seems, is very far from being 'like this'.
Examine for a moment an ordinary mind on an ordinary day.
The mind receives a myriad impressions – trivial, fantastic,
evanescent, or engraved with the sharpness of steel. From all
sides they come, an incessant shower of innumerable atoms;
and as they fall, as they shape themselves into the life of Mon-
day or Tuesday, the accent falls differently from of old; the
moment of importance came not here but there; so that, if a
writer were a free man and not a slave, if he could write what
he chose, not what he must, if he could base his work upon his
own feeling and not upon convention, there would be no plot,
no comedy, no tragedy, no love interest or catastrophe in the
accepted sense, and perhaps not a single button sewn on as the
Bond Street tailors would have it. Life is not a series of gig-
lamps symmetrically arranged; life is a luminous halo, a semi-
transparent envelope surrounding us from the beginning of
consciousness to the end. Is it not the task of the novelist to
convey this varying, this unknown and uncircumscribed spirit,
whatever abbreviation or complexity it may display, with as
little mixture of the alien and external as possible?

That is what is wrong with Wells, Galsworthy and Bennett. They
seem to be insufficiently impressionist, for Virginia Woolf's description of life reminds me of nothing more strongly than a late
Monet: his 'Houses of Parliament' could have come straight out
of *Mrs Dalloway*. And, of course, Mrs Woolf was a friend of
Roger Fry, as well as a reader of William James, whose *Principles
of Psychology* is traditionally invoked to account for the views
expressed here.

As a matter of fact, by 1910 Bennett had come round to something like the same point of view. In an article on 'Neo Impressionism and Literature' in the *New Age* that year, he permitted
himself 'to suspect that supposing some writer were to come along
and do in words what these men have done in paint, I might
conceivably be disgusted with nearly the whole of modern fiction,
and I might have to begin again.' Ford had not by this time
written *The Good Soldier*. Instead he had been trifling with
Wellsian fantasies and pastiche Jamesian social comedy. His interest in painting was mainly Pre-Raphaelite – he had written a
book on the movement and a biography of one of its admired

contemporaries, his grandfather Ford Madox Brown. But George Moore, who knew Degas in Paris, had written *Esther Waters* sixteen years earlier, and in purely visual terms I can think of no more impressionist scene in fiction than the description of the Derby in that novel. However, Moore and Ford are beside the point. Only two years before the *New Age* article, Bennett had written *The Old Wives' Tale*, and achieved for a whole life, in fact for two whole lives, what Virginia Woolf had tried to achieve for a London party, a voyage to a lighthouse, and an English garden fête. By softening and diffusing naturalist inclinations with impressionist handling of specific scenes, Bennett wrote a masterpiece. The combination of methods that runs throughout *The Old Wives' Tale* is compressed into a single, small work of art in Bennett's much earlier novel, *Anna of the Five Towns*. There Henry Mynors's pottery is described as 'a sample of the total and final achievement towards which the thousands of small, disjointed efforts that Anna had witnessed, were directed. And it seemed a miraculous, almost impossible result; so definite, precise and regular after a series of acts apparently variable, inexact and casual; so inhuman after all that intensely human labour; so vast in comparison with the minuteness of the separate endeavours.' The 'casual' brush strokes creating the regular design, the 'disjointed efforts' producing the final 'total' achievement – they might equally well produce an impressionist interior or a scene from *The Old Wives' Tale*. Novels, though, are more than separate scenes. The way scenes are linked together creates a different impression from the one we get from a single Monet painting, or even a series of Monet paintings. It is a measure of Virginia Woolf's own failure that her novels rarely get beyond the single frame.

Bennett's contribution to the *New Age* was uncharacteristically modest. He knew what he had to do. Four years later he wrote in *The Author's Craft* that the novelist 'can, by obtaining a broad notion of the whole, determine with some accuracy the position and relative importance of the particular series of phenomena to which his instinct draws him. If he does not thus envisage the immense background of his special interests, he will lose the most precious feeling for interplay and proportion.' He might almost have been replying to Virginia Woolf when he continued that 'No human phenomenon is adequately seen until the imagination has placed it back into its past and forward into its future'. Throughout the novels, this is how Bennett sees people, busily involved in their own private concerns, and acting from the centre of them, quite unaware of their representative status. In *The Old Wives' Tale*, Samuel Povey and Constance Baines are forced into producing their own labels and lettering to draw attention to the quality of their goods. Without realising it, they were 'making history'. 'They had no suspicion that they were the forces of the future insidiously at work to destroy what the forces of the past had created, but such was the case.' So much for the final achievement, of which neither Sam nor Constance is aware, because they are too involved with their 'duty to the shop' to stand apart from themselves and see the act either as a watershed in the history of commerce, or as a significant part of a life. It is just one of those 'small disjointed efforts' that make up the whole life, both personal and historic, that it is rarely the privilege of the man who lives it to see. Later, when Sophia Baines returns to Bursley after thirty years in Paris, she has one of those rare, privileged moments. Her life is 'so queer', though 'every part of it separately seemed ordinary enough'. That is what Bennett is trying to show. There are unusual things that happen in *The Old Wives' Tale*, from the death of an elephant to the siege of Paris. On the whole, though, the lives we are shown are rarely unusual at any one point in the living of them, and they are certainly not often felt to be so by the characters. It is only as a whole that they look 'queer', distinctive, different from all other lives. The characters see their lives as wholes as infrequently as we do. It is the coincidence of our view and theirs (both of us 'readers' of a whole life), at one or two points in the narrative, that lifts us out of a process of living and allows us to see the life that is being produced. The process is impressionist, the thing produced naturalist – but the combination of techniques robs naturalism of all the harshness and certainty inherent in its determinist view of life. The act of seeing what one is has to be added to the existence which is seen, before any life is fully accounted for. And that is impossible, because capable of infinite extension. It is a different view of life altogether from the dismissive and accountable view of the French.

Even so, Bennett owed something to France. After all, he wrote *The Old Wives' Tale* at Fontainebleau, not Burslem, and in

Charles Critchlow he produced a deliberate companion piece to Flaubert's Homais. Even some of the mannerisms are Flaubertian: the reference to Sophia's charlady in Paris having died of smallpox, 'thus losing a good situation', is one of those pessimistic little flips at the ends of sentences that Moore noticed throughout *Madame Bovary*. Its petty triumph is quite out of place in Bennett's novel. And again he surely knows it. When Sam Povey loses his temper and his dignity during his proposal to Mrs Baines, 'he might have appeared somewhat grotesque to the strictly impartial observer of human nature' – to Flaubert, for example. Much more suggestive than these minor instances, however, part III as a whole reads like a rather superior version of Flaubert, especially the Flaubert of the *Education*: like Flaubert because of its rapid movement and unflinching attention to the details of feeling; superior to Flaubert because such details include passages like this one from v.3, describing Sophia's feelings about Madame Foucault, a feckless courtesan who has nursed her through the terrible fever she caught after Gerald Scales left her with Chirac's bills to pay:

> Madame Foucault would not treat her as an ordinary lodger, now that the illness was past. She wanted, as it were, to complete brilliantly what she had begun, and to live in Sophia's memory as a unique figure of lavish philanthropy. This was a sentiment, a luxury that she desired to offer herself: the thought that she had played providence to a respectable married lady in distress; she frequently hinted at Sophia's misfortunes and helplessness. But she could not afford the luxury. She gazed at it as a poor woman gazes at costly stuffs through the glass of a shop-window. The truth was, she wanted the luxury for nothing.

There is plenty in Flaubert as damaging as that, but there is nothing as fair. Madame Foucault descends to her proper level, but not below it. Sophia does not have all the right on her side when she refuses to admit that 'Madame Foucault's devotion as a nurse entitled her to the satisfaction of being a philanthropist when there was no necessity for philanthropy'.

Bennett's source for *The Old Wives' Tale* was not Flaubert, however, but Maupassant. He appears to have felt about *Une Vie* what Ford was to feel about *Fort comme la mort*. It is

equally difficult to see why he should have admired Maupassant
so much. *Une Vie* is a superficial little story of a commonplace
marriage, commonplace adulteries and commonplace filial in-
gratitude. Furthermore, these are felt to be commonplace, which
means that the characters are seen to be in a demonstrably inferior position to their author. Pure women are stupid and romantic: Emma Bovary had read bad novels – even worse than Maupassant's; Jeanne Le Perthuis de Vauds makes up stories about
fairy-tale tapestries. Young men are superficial and licentious or
superficial and extravagant. Norman *curés* are worldly-wise and
jolly or ascetic and censorious. The manner in which they are
these things is unremitting, predictable and beneath contempt –
except in the case of Jeanne, who can't help the way she has been
brought up and who has a certain peasant doggedness flowing
beneath her aristocratic gentility and inexperience. Thom Gunn
wrote of Proust that:

> All are unmasked as perverts sooner or later,
> With one notable exception – the narrator.

There are no perverts in this particular book, but that does not
stop Maupassant unmasking the characters as ordinary human
beings and therefore disgusting: Julien, la contesse, la petite
maman, Rosalie, all are revealed to be no better than they should
be and probably a great deal worse. Nobody, not even the baron,
expects them to be, except the Comte de Fourville who was crazy
anyway. Only Maupassant, in the whole novel, knows what
human beings are really like, *and* can bear it. He is the notable
exception of Gunn's couplet.

Irrespective of the attitude he took up to what he saw around
him, Bennett made great changes to what he found in *Une Vie*.
What attracted him was the fact that Maupassant had traced the
course of a single life from adolescence to old age. What attracted
him still more was the effect he felt he could produce by doing
the same thing with two lives, going their own ways but never
losing contact of a kind, even if not a geographical kind, with
each other. Constance and Sophia Baines are as obviously of
Baines stock as they are all we come to see is meant by the one
being Constance and the other being Sophia. Their 'generic' and
individual qualities are always in evidence, the one co-existing
with the other even when what is done would appear to set them

at variance with each other or develop the one at the expense of the other. Sophia running Frensham's in the rue Lord Byron is both like and unlike Constance running Baines's drapery shop in the Square at Bursley. Sophia's personality is both stronger and less resilient than Constance's, and strength and resilience are both Baines qualities, and in a different way the qualities of two separate individuals called Constance and Sophia. In France, long before Constance writes to her, Sophia is aware of her sister as a force which is ever-present, always to be reckoned with; that she is to be compared with and not to be put to shame by. In Burslem, it is not just Christmas cards that keep Constance aware of Sophia's existence, although by this time this is an existence running on totally different (and unknown) plot lines to Constance's own.

The presence of two characters instead of one at the centre of the book is the most obvious difference between *Une Vie* and *The Old Wive's Tale*. The way in which Bennett sees to it that the one is always in the background of the life of the other ensures that it is not just a matter of duplication or addition. But though it is the most obvious, it is not the most important. The most important difference lies in the novelist's quite distinctive attitude to his characters, of which the doubling of the female centre is only a symptom. Bennett himself, writing of Constance when Sophia receives her first letter in thirty years, calls it 'sublime acceptance': 'Just a sublime acceptance of the situation as it was, and the assurance of undiminished love.' Nowhere, I think, is this brought out more clearly than in the description of Sophia's reaction to Gerald's death. Maupassant has a similar scene in *Une Vie*, when Jeanne mourns the ridiculous death of her husband Julien – like Gerald a philanderer, but, unlike him, a miser too.

Voilà que maintenant son âme était pénétrée par des souvenirs attendris, doux et mélancholiques, des courtes joies d'amour que lui avait autrefois données son mari. Elle tressaillait à tout moment à des réveils inattendus de sa mémoire; et elle le revoy-ait tel qu'il avait été en ces jours de fiancailles, et tel aussi qu'elle l'avait chéri en ses seules heures de passion écloses sous le grand soleil de la Corse. Tous les défauts diminuaient, toutes les duretés disparaissaient, les infidélités elles-mêmes s'atténu-uaient maintenant dans l'éloignement grandissant du tombeau

fermé. Et Jeanne, envahie par une sorte de vague gratitude
posthume pour cet homme qui l'avait tenue en ses bras, par-
donnait les souffrances passées pour ne songer qu'aux moments
heureux. Puis le temps marchant toujours et les mois tombant
sur les mois poudrèrent d'oubli, comme d'une poussière ac-
cumulée, toutes ses réminiscences et ses douleurs; et elle se
donna tout entière à son fils.

That is all Maupassant can manage, not as dismissive as we might
have expected, but just as conventional and reductive of his subject's personality. Here is the (much longer) equivalent passage
from Bennett. Sophia has arrived in Manchester, at Mr Boldero's
jeweller's shop in Deansgate, just too late to find Gerald, whom
she has not seen for over twenty years, alive:

Sophia went into the room, of which the white blind was
drawn. She appreciated Mr. Boldero's consideration in leaving
her. She was trembling. But when she saw, in the pale gloom,
the face of an aged man peeping out from under a white sheet
on a naked mattress, she started back, trembling no more –
rather transfixed into an absolute rigidity. That was no conventional, expected shock that she had received. It was a
genuine unforeseen shock, the most violent she had ever had.
In her mind she had not pictured Gerald as a very old man.
She knew that he was old; she had said to herself that he must
be very old, well over seventy. But she had not pictured him.
This face on the bed was painfully, pitiably old. . . The body
whose outlines were clear under the sheet, was very small, thin,
shrunk, pitiable as the face. And on the face was a general expression of final fatigue, of tragic and acute exhaustion; such
as made Sophia pleased that the fatigue and exhaustion had
been assuaged in rest, while all the time she kept thinking to
herself horribly: 'Oh! how tired he must have been!'
    Sophia then experienced a pure and primitive emotion, un-
coloured by any moral or religious quality. She was not sorry
that Gerald had wasted his life, nor that he was a shame to his
years and to her. The manner of his life was of no importance.
What affected her was that he had once been young, and that
he had grown old, and was now dead. That was all. Youth and
vigour had come to that. He had ill-treated her; he had aban-

doned her; he had been a devious rascal; but how trivial were such accusations against him! The whole of her huge and bitter grievance against him fell to pieces and crumbled. She saw him young and proud, and strong, as for instance when he had kissed her lying on the bed in that London hotel – she forgot the name – in 1866; and now he was old, and worn, and horrible, and dead. It was the riddle of life that was puzzling and killing her. By the corner of her eye, reflected in the mirror of the wardrobe near the bed she glimpsed a tall, forlorn woman, who had once been young and now was old; who had once exulted in abundant strength, and trodden proudly on the neck of circumstance, and now was old. He and she had once loved and burned and quarrelled in the glittering and scornful pride of youth. But time had worn them out. 'Yet a little while', she thought, 'and I shall be lying on a bed like that! And what shall I have lived for? What is the meaning of it?' The riddle of life itself was killing her, and she seemed to drown in a sea of inexpressible sorrow.

Her memory wandered hopelessly among those past years. She saw Chirac with his wistful smile. She saw him whipped over the roof of the Gare du Nord at the tail of a balloon. She saw old Niepce. She felt his lecherous arm around her. She was as old as Niepce had been then. Could she excite lust now? Ah! the irony of such a question! To be young and seductive, to be able to kindle a man's eye – that seemed to her the sole thing desirable. Once she had been so!... Niepce must certainly have been dead for years. Niepce, the obstinate and hopeful voluptuary, was nothing but a few bones in a coffin now!

She was acquainted with affliction in that hour. All that she had previously suffered sank into insignificance by the side of that suffering.

She turned to the veiled window and idly pulled the blind and looked out. Huge red and yellow cars were swimming in thunder along Deansgate; lorries jolted and rattled; the people of Manchester hurried along the pavements, apparently unconscious that all their doings were vain. Yesterday he too had been in Deansgate, hungry for life, hating the idea of death! What a figure he must have made! Her heart dissolved in pity for him. She dropped the blind.

'My life has been too terrible!', she thought. 'I wish I was dead. I have been through too much. It is monstrous, and I cannot stand it. I do not want to die, but I wish I was dead.'

What Maupassant pays lip-service to ('une sorte de vague grati-tude posthume'), Bennett makes one feel on the pulses. I don't think it is necessary to try to prove it. Most readers feel the dis-tinction of the writing here instinctively. But I should like to single out one part of the passage that contributes to its dis-tinction because it seems to me typical of Bennett and com-pletely lacking in his French models.

I am referring to the opening of the second paragraph. 'The manner of his life was of no importance. What affected her was that he had once been young, and that he had grown old, and was now dead. That was all.' The same assured and ennobling response to death has been rendered before, in Constance's reflec-tions on Samuel, and will be again, in her reflections on Sophia at the end of the novel. In this last, Constance is 'drenched', as she gazes at Sophia's body, 'not by pity for herself, but by com-passion for the immense disaster of her sister's life. She perceived fully now for the first time the greatness of that disaster.' These are grand summings-up, by one character of another at a partic-ularly solemn moment, which include those local visions of a life taking shape amid impressions of randomness and apparent aim-lessness which the character who lives it achieves from time to time. This happens in Moore as well as Bennett. When Esther returns to Woodview and Mrs Barfield at the end of *Esther Waters*, she feels that 'everything that could happen had hap-pened to her'. She looks back on her life as a whole, with all the separate events in it run into a single unbroken shape. The time she first came to Woodview 'seemed like yesterday, yet seventeen years and more had gone by – a dream, the connecting links of which were gone'. But in *The Old Wives' Tale* it happens both more frequently and with less dramatic aplomb. The characters are from time to time intensely preoccupied with lives which are different from mere aggregations of the things they have done and the things that have been done to them. When Constance sleeps for the first time in her parents' bed, as a married woman, 'She esteemed that she knew what life was'. When she finds that her son Cyril will leave her and go to live in London, she despairs that this is what her life has come to. At the very end, 'No one but Constance could realize all that Constance had been through, all that life had meant to her'.

It would be easy to infer from this that Bennett was, after all, a Naturalist; and the dividing line between this creation of a single life out of the apparently disparate events that make up a person's experience – which in turn becomes the life he 'has' – and the conventional determinism of the Naturalists, is a very thin one. After all, Bennett himself moves from Sam Povey's becoming, for Constance, 'an indivisible whole', to what appears to be the classic determinist position of part IV, chap. 2. Constance is waiting for Sophia's return, reflecting that 'in thirty years Sophia might have grown into anything, whereas Constance had remained just Constance'. But when she arrives, 'Sophia had not changed'. As Bennett said of the concierge and his wife who sold Sophia Madame Foucault's furniture in the rue Breda, 'They lived for money, and all men have what they live for'. We shall see how V. S. Naipaul[1] deals with this matter of men getting what they live for. In Bennett's case it is not as simple as it sounds. For all men live for money, and although Sophia values it, she can hardly be said to live for it. Money is tangible, 'out there'. What both Constance and Sophia want they have to create for themselves. The sentence about the concierge, when applied to the Baines sisters, means that people create their own destinies. What they really want to be, they are; and the incompleteness of their being it is the consequence of the incompleteness of their wanting. It is really a tautology, but a profound one and a difficult one to render in fiction. We are what we are, but most of the time we don't realise it. When we do, we become something else that has to include that realisation. Ultimately, we can't do this for ourselves without making ourselves out to be noble shams. So other people have to do it for us. This is why Constance's feelings about Sam and Sophia, and Sophia's about Gerald, sound so final, so much the last word. They move from particular attributes to generic descriptions. The combination of the two is in the most meaningful sense pathetic: 'he had once been young ... and he had grown old, and was now dead. That was all'; 'A brief passion, and then nearly thirty years in a boarding-house'. These

---

[1] See below, pp. 148 ff.

moments are shattering, and deeply moving, because they are so true, and so final.

Yet, within the comprehensive, bold and simple outline of these true statements, there are other outlines which take on more and more substance the more we look at them, for these endings, these presents from which we survey the past. First of all there are the occasional 'epiphanies' of the characters themselves: 'No one but Constance could realize . . . all that life had meant for her.' Then there are the events which grow to assume the status of markings, pointers to the shape life might be taking: for instance, when Gerald is found – shamming as it turns out – at the Baineses' doorstep on New Year's Eve and 'Everybody felt: what a funny ending of the old year', or when Chirac goes up in a balloon: 'A real drama existed . . . triumphing over the accidental absurdities and pettinesses of the situation.' Lastly, on the surface of little significance but full of the rough substance of life, are those very pettinesses and absurdities, the trivialities Dickens talked about in *David Copperfield*: pulling a tooth out of a cowardly employee; having difficulties with servants; going out to see a dead elephant when you should be looking after a father, a husband or a shop.

Bennett is as good at representing the stuff of life as he is at showing how his characters shape it into significant forms. He is as interested in the variety of life as he is in its completeness. Everybody knows how skilful he is at giving his readers the impression of time passing. But I wonder how many realise how subtly he does this. Most writers cannot help being explicit. When Rawdon and Becky revisit Queen's Crawley after Sir Pitt's death, we discover that Rawdon, 'the bold and reckless young blood of ten years back was subjugated, and was turned into a torpid, submissive, middle-aged, stout gentleman'. When Molly Gibson leaves for the Towers after Cynthia Kirkpatrick's wedding and sees the bridal party wave a white handerchief to her, the incident reminds her of Roger Hamley's departure two years before; she cannot, and Mrs Gaskell cannot, resist a reflection or two on 'what changes time had brought'. Maupassant is much clumsier. Less than ten pages from the end of *Une Vie* he tries to create a spurious sentimental affection for Jeanne by emphasising how in her old age she has lost the habit of early rising which used to be so much of a habit with her. We never saw this habit, so there is no reason why we should believe it now. By contrast, Bennett's handling of the characters' responses to the passing of time is masterly in its delicacy and restraint. There are explicit reminders, in Sophia's thought when she sees the Square for the first time after her long absence. But just as good is the use of casual comparison, unremarked by the author but very much present to his readers: the abandoned room at the beginning, and the use Mr Critchlow makes of it when he buys the shop; Constance and Sophia as girls pressing their noses against the showroom window to spy on Maggie's amorous adventures, and Sophia doing the same thing to try to see the roof of her room in the rue Breda – though in the last instance Bennett does remark the comparison.

In the scene of Sophia's homecoming Bennett provides another very true, but seldom described, response to the detail of life. Sophia always knew what provinciality was, but she had never really come to terms with the provinciality of the town in which she grew up. In the nature of things it couldn't be provincial to her ('in her mind it had always been differentiated from the common *province*') just as her elopement with Gerald was not an ordinary one, 'not like a real elopement', and Constance's being twenty-seven was not like anybody else's being twenty-seven: 'it would not be a real twenty-seven; nor would Sam's forty be a real forty like other people's twenty-sevens and forties'. We often exclude ourselves from our wise recognitions of grand commonplaces of life. Bennett is very good, too, at 'making it strange', placing events in an unusual perspective. When Mrs Baines and Constance are shopping in the Square, 'whom should they both see walking all alone across the empty corner by the bank, but Sophia Baines'. The novelty, scandal and unpredictability of the event make Sophia into a separate entity, outside the family, with a surname like anybody else outside the Baines parlour. Much later, something very similar happens to her. After thirty years, Charles Critchlow is still alive when Sophia returns from Paris, and the fact of his treating her like a girl throws her out of a familiar perspective and into a strange but no less true one. It is the sense of all this personal and many-sided detail that makes the accuracy of those final summations at once so bare and so true. If Sophia's 'had not been a life at all', what was it we were living with during those three hundred pages we had just read?

And yet it is so. Sophia's hadn't been a life and it had been. It all depends what 'thirty years in a boarding-house', or thirty years in a shop in Bursley, can grow to mean for someone who, like Constance, and like Bennett, is capable not of a 'strictly impartial observance of human nature', but of a 'sublime acceptance of the situation as it was'. They sound the same, but between them lies all the space that separates *The Old Wives' Tale* from its source in Maupassant's *Une Vie*.

More than half a century and many hundred miles separate *The Old Wives' Tale* from V. S. Naipaul's *A House for Mr. Biswas*. Bursley Square and Hanuman House have little in common. Constance and Sophia Baines respond to life very differently from Mohun Biswas. With one exception. Both Biswas and the Baineses want to achieve their lives. Constance's ambitions have a lower threshold than Sophia's. Biswas's have a lower one than either of them.

Biswas is in search of simplicity, a simple house, a simple family, a simple life. But simplicity is a dangerous chimera, a will-o'-the-wisp. In Naipaul's later novel, *The Mimic Men*, Ralph Singh reminds us that 'We talk of escaping to the simple life. But we do not mean what we say. It is from simplifications such as this that we wish to escape, to return to a more elemental complexity.' Because we are creatures of illusion, we suppose that 'elemental complexity' is a clever paradox. In fact it is nothing of the kind. It is Biswas's fundamental error that he shares our illusions. That is why *A House for Mr. Biswas* is a comic novel. Biswas spends his life trying to find out what it means. He doesn't know that is what he is doing. He thinks he is looking for a house – a simple, one would suppose not so difficult-to-accomplish, ambition. But the house is merely a metaphor which Biswas mistakes for a reality. Because he does so, it fails to materialise as either, until he has reached the literal end of his endeavours.

What does a life mean to the man who lives it? Each man's life is different from another's, but if the difference is to be in his own eyes a significant one, does he not have to have planned that it should be so? A man is pulled in two directions: eager to conform to the image others have of him and so to simplify himself; at the same time insistent that there is in him 'something personal and ordained', an individual destiny that complicates his existence and marks it off from the lives of everyone else he knows. We live for others and we live for ourselves, but these lives are seldom the same. What is the relationship between them and how does a man reconcile the conflicting demands they make of him? Ralph Singh discovers at the end that 'personality hangs together. It is one and indivisible.' This had not always been his view. It had seemed to him in the past that others create our personalities for us, provide us with roles to play which become our characters, our sense of ourselves. At the end of a life it can come as a shock to confront an achieved existence quite different from what, in the act of living, it had been taken to be.

For others it is not so surprising, for a sense of destiny, of ordainment, is commonly felt, though not often coherently expressed. If it is not entirely nebulous it may take one of many forms: a position to be reached; an act to be undertaken; a book to be written. Achieved, it may or may not prove to have been sufficient. It may or may not have been important in itself. For V. S. Naipaul's Mr Biswas it is a house, his own house, somewhere to live and not to visit, that he had not known since early childhood. His memories of that house have grown more and more obscure with the passage of time. When he knew it he was too young to be able to use it as a base, a growing-point into a secure and satisfying adult life. What it has left him with is an intimation of the overriding importance of a house of his own. By the end of the novel he has achieved it and fulfilled a kind of destiny. That is what *A House for Mr. Biswas* is about.

Mr Biswas is the fourth child of an Indian family in a village in Trinidad. Although the family is of a high caste, the father is a labourer, and when he dies his children are thrown upon the mercies of kindly but miserly rich relations. Biswas escapes from this situation by marrying into a less wealthy, but even more miserly, family, the Tulsis; maintaining a scanty independence at first by continuing his work as a sign painter, then managing a store owned by the family, overseeing one of its 'estates', working as a journalist and, finally, acquiring a short-lived post in the Civil Service. His hatred of his wife's relatives and their hierarchical existence at Hanuman House is later complemented by his care for his own family, especially his daughter Savi and son Anand. The novel traces Biswas's movements from one house

to another, one group of friends and enemies to another. At the
end of it he dies, in his own house.

Throughout, his life has been impinged upon and affected by
the lives of many others, all with separate lives of their own
which we have glimpses of from time to time. Some we get to
know better than others – Mrs Biswas's wife Shama and his son
Anand, for example. Others are intriguingly set at a tangent to
the main story – Seth, the strong man of the Tulsi household,
dominating Mrs Tulsi's circle from within it, but shown to be
ineffective and humiliatingly vulnerable when forced outside; or
Jagdat, who takes over Biswas's job of reading to his uncle
Ajodha for a pittance to feed his growing illegitimate family.
Afterwards we know that Mr Biswas's life will be usurped by the
survivors of his family, only one of whom (Anand) appears to
have appreciated the fact that he had wants and ambitions
separate from them and peculiarly his own. At his mother's
funeral, Biswas had felt that Shama and the children were
'alien growths, alien affections' which 'called him away from
that part of him which yet remained purely himself, that part
which had for long been submerged and was now to disappear'.
But the assumption that this one part of his life, now irrevocably
past, is more purely himself than the present and future represented by his own family, is simply one of Mr Biswas's self-
deceptions, a failure to locate himself in one network of relationships by over-valuing another, which has conveniently sunk
out of existence. He is as much his son's father as he is his mother's
son, even though the startling prominence into which his role in
the latter relationship is thrown as a result of the mother's death
leads him to underestimate the former. By opting for the one role,
Biswas is really giving in to a simplification of his own person.
What he is must include both of them and more. Nevertheless,
his sense of loss, 'of something missed in the past', is real. He
will feel it again when he ponders the growing-up of his children.
Having missed his own childhood he now muses on the fact that
he has missed theirs. By speculating on the future as a 'void'
to be filled with the 'life' he wants to create for himself, he leaves
behind a past occupying more and more of the actual span of
time at his disposal. It takes him all his life to discover that the
life he was indefinitely postponing for the future actually lies in
the past which he had thought a preparation for it.

The disappointment that a life lived like this must entail is
continuous and mortifying, a spur to ambition compounded of
forgetfulness of the past and disregard of the present. It is the
price Mr Biswas pays for his originality. His wife Shama does not
share it. Her ambition to be unexceptional is easily realised:

> For there was no doubt . . . what Shama expected from life:
> to be taken through every stage, to fulfil every function, to have
> her share of the established emotions: joy at a birth or marriage,
> distress during illness and hardship, grief at a death. Life to be
> full had to be this established pattern of sensation. Grief and
> joy, both equally awaited, were one. For Shama and her sisters
> and women like them, ambition, if the word could be used,
> was a series of negatives: not to be unmarried, not to be child-
> less, not to be an undutiful daughter, sister, wife, mother,
> widow.

Biswas knows this about his wife. We are offered the passage as
an explanation of his feelings prompted by her preparations for
a return to Hanuman House to be with the family during her
first confinement. All the more reason for us to admire the ease
with which Naipaul manages the transition between this attack
on Shama's complacency ('her share of the established emotions',
'this established pattern of sensation') and the passage that follows
it, where Biswas discovers that Shama has made preparations for
him as well:

> His clothes had been washed and darned; and he was moved,
> though not surprised, to find on the kitchen shelf little squares
> of shop paper, on which, in her Mission-school script that
> always deteriorated after the first two or three lines, Shama
> had pencilled recipes for the simplest meals, writing with a
> disregard for grammar and punctuation which he thought
> touching. How quaint, too, to find phrases he had only heard
> her speak committed to paper in this handwriting! In her
> instructions for the boiling of rice, for example, she told him
> to 'throw in just a little pinch of salt' – he could see her bunch-
> ing her long fingers – and to use 'the blue enamel pot without
> the handle'. How often, crouched before the *chulha* fire, she
> had said to him, 'Just hand me the blue pot without the
> handle.'

The commonplace also commands its share of love and the author does not withhold it. The fact that the demands a person makes on life are conventional and crude is not allowed to impoverish the substance of such a life. Eventually the order that Biswas recognises in his own life is made up of just such moments and achievements. Shama does not stop being commonplace. At the very end of the novel Biswas's death is the occasion for a reunion between her and her sisters. 'Afterwards the sisters returned to their respective homes and Shama and the children went back in their Prefect to the empty house.' We are told no more. Whether Shama's grief, sensed in the restraint of Naipaul's prose here, is the conventional grief she wanted to feel, or whether it takes notice, as ours does, of the meanings of that Prefect and that house, we cannot know. That she goes back to the house in Sikkim Street rather than the house of one of the Tulsis suggests that it does have to do with Biswas and not just an anonymous husband. At any rate, Naipaul's treatment of the developing relationship between Biswas and his wife within the marriage ensures that in neither case shall we mistake grief for something else, which the words 'conventional', 'normal' and 'established' suggest but do not in this context permit. Besides, apart from the value Shama has in herself, she inevitably becomes a part of Biswas's own destiny, a part of the past which, entering the future in a new order, conveys to Biswas the 'significance' of his life and gives it its pattern and originality.

Yet this was a marriage, and as such an important part of his future, that Biswas did not plan and for which he does not feel himself to be responsible. It happened by accident, a combination of naïve bravado on Biswas's part and a rapacious slyness on the part of the Tulsis. Biswas had passed a note to Shama when he was decorating the Tulsi shop, and Mrs Tulsi, knowing of his high caste and appreciating the usefulness of another young man to contribute to the Tulsi businesses, had manoeuvred him into a marriage for which he was unprepared. The result is that, more than ever before, Mr Biswas feels that he is trapped, that events are beyond his control and that he is therefore not responsible for his own destiny, not a person in his own right. 'How often did he try to make events appear grander, more planned and less absurd than they were!' Now that he is absorbed into the appalling protectiveness of the Tulsi household, it seems to him even less likely that it did in his wasted youth that he will never recover the proper use of himself that is symbolised for him by a house of his own. Earlier he had waited for the coming of a Love that would transport him to a world of romance. 'He deferred all his pleasure in life until that day.' His friend Alec told him not to worry: 'these things come when you least expect them'. What came was Shama and the Tulsis. But in view of the passage describing Shama's instructions on using the 'blue pot without the handle' and others affecting us in the same way, are we to suppose that Mr Biswas missed out on romance after all? He never describes his marriage in terms approximating to those of romance, and his first escape, with Shama, from the Tulsis – when he takes over the proprietorship of The Chase – is qualified by a renewed incapacity to understand it as anything but a temporary arrangement, 'a pause, a preparation', like his youth before it.

To say that he does not *understand* it to be more than this is not the same thing as to say that he does not *experience* it as something more. Naipaul's description of the increasing familiarity of the shop, the personally important details of 'slight improvements' rendering it 'their own, and therefore supportable', lead us to believe otherwise and enable us to distinguish between what is happening and Biswas's imperfect comprehension of what is happening – as a preparation for something else. His sense of the situation is a constituent of the situation, not, as he supposes, a comprehensive record of it. Only later will it slip into place as one of the determinants of an achieved order and satisfaction in a life seen to be made up of just such 'trivial' satisfactions, hidden behind apparently overwhelming disappointments. Mrs Tulsi spoke more truly than she knew when she told Mr Biswas that 'everything comes, bit by bit', just as Alec did when he said things come to you when you least expect them. At The Chase, Mr Biswas himself finds it strange that 'these disregarded years had been years of acquisition': of a kitchen safe, a hatrack, a dressing-table – but of more than these: 'It was strange . . . for him to find one day that house and shop bore so many marks of his habitation. No one might have lived there before him, and it was hard to imagine anyone after him moving about these rooms and getting to know them as he had done.' For a short time Mr Biswas really had the house he is to spend so much of his life trying to achieve. But it takes him a whole lifetime to understand it, and to allow experiences such as this to take their place in an ordered vision of the life he has had. For the moment the only vision of himself he has is that of a boy in a white vest whom he had seen in the past, leaning against a hut and staring at the bus as it went by, 'a boy leaning against an earth house that had no reason for being there, under the dark falling sky, a boy who didn't know where the road, and that bus, went'. His attention is entirely absorbed by the future, the end of the road which is a terrible blankness 'into which past tomorrow and next week and next year, he was falling'.

It is in this frame of mind that Mr Biswas moves to Green Vale, where he undergoes his most traumatic experience of futility and personal inadequacy. No obvious sequence of events triggers it off. Shama and the children are once again away at Hanuman House and he is left alone with the wooden house he is having built on the Tulsi land. A 'great calm' has settled on him because he has decided to stop looking at the situations in which he finds himself as temporary. From now on, 'Time would never be dismissed again. No action would merely lead to another; every action was a part of his life which could not be re-called; therefore thought had to be given to every action.' In this frame of mind he sits down to read *The Hunchback of Notre Dame*, and experiences a strange disturbance which takes the form of a black cloud billowing over him. He tries to forget about the people in the book he is reading and places himself alone in 'vast white plateaux, with himself safely alone, a speck in the centre'. It is an experience made up of two occurrences in other books by Naipaul. In *The Mystic Masseur*, Pundit Ganesh's first success comes when he banishes just such a cloud from over the head of a boy who lives in terror of it. In *The Mimic Men*, Ralph Singh is aware of a camera far above him, tracking him as a speck in the centre of an enormous field of vision. What all this means for Mr Biswas is panic in the knowledge of the existence of other people, followed by a transference of the panic to experience of people and things associated with them in the past. While his life had been supportable he had not been able to realise it; and now that he does realise it, as a memory it is distorted and perverted by the present fear. Caught between a wasted past – the memory of which is terrible – and a future of meaninglessness and panic, he discovers that 'all action was irrelevant and futile'. He recovers from this breakdown only after his half-completed house has been destroyed, and he is forced to go back to Hanuman House and the Tulsis. Here, ironically, he returns to a sense of the present akin to that which caused the breakdown in the first place. Without willing it, he allows himself to be drawn into the order of the house, and is determined to use his memory of what happened at Green Vale as an experience of misery against which he will measure all future unhappiness. The disconnection of the present from the past has resulted in breakdown. But the answer is still seen in the form of a 'real' future. 'The past was counterfeit, a series of cheating accidents. Real life, and its especial sweetness, awaited; he was still beginning.'

The equanimity does not last long. A visit to the doctor in Port of Spain convinces him that the freedom he has invented for himself is false. 'The past could not be ignored; it was never counterfeit; he carried it within himself. If there was a place for him it was one that had already been hollowed out by time, by everything he had lived through, however imperfect, make-shift and cheating.' His acceptance of the past prevents panic and transforms despair into the acknowledgement of age, the transference of ambition to his son. It is in this mood that he enters upon his last profession and relinquishes his most important ambition, to own a house. 'He had lost the vision of the house.'

Even so he buys a house in the end. Before he does so, he re-visits the old Tulsi house at Arawas, and enters the room in which he had lived with Shama:

Through the Demerara window he had tried to spit on Owad and flung the plateful of food on him. In this room he had been beaten by Govind, had kicked *Bell's Standard Elocutionist* and given it the dent in the cover. Here, claimed by no one, he had reflected on the unreality of his life, and had wished to make a mark on the wall as proof of his existence. Now he needed no such proof. Relationships had been created where none had existed; he stood at their centre. In that very unreality had lain freedom. Now he was encumbered and it was at Hanuman House that he tried to forget the encumbrance: the children, the scattered furniture, the dark tenement room, and Shama, as helpless as he was and now, what he had longed for, dependent on him.

It is Mr Biswas's individual experience of one of the greatest platitudes of life. We seek the freedom we already possess and live to regret that we didn't use it when we could. In the past Mr Biswas had sought freedom in marriage, a family and above all a house. These would convince him of his reality, and upon that reality he would be able to found an order and a meaning. But as fast as these things were achieved they brought with them disappointment and encumbrance. A marriage drifted into and perpetually interrupted. Children born in his absence and named without his knowledge or permission. Houses rented, owned by others, blown down, and finally acquired in ignorance of state of repair and by means of an unrepayable debt. It is again ironic that the house Mr Biswas wanted to live in, not to visit, has first to be made to look fit to be visited even if it remains unsatisfactory to be lived in. He dies in it before the debt comes up for repayment, and although he does not know it, he has achieved an ambition, an ambition which has changed beyond all recognition. Mr Biswas's drift into encumbrance and reality has created a solid past for the children. The house in Sikkim Street presents itself to them as their home. Mr Biswas's own sense of home was destroyed by his father's death, for which he has a claim to responsibility. He therefore had to create a coherence and order out of a disordered past and a future that he saw as a void at the end of a dark road leading from no obvious source. But the lives of the children 'would be ordered, their memories coherent' as the events and memories of all the other houses they had known or heard of telescoped into memories of the house in Sikkim Street. 'So later, and very slowly, in securer times of different stresses, when the memories had lost the power to hurt, with pain and joy they would fall into place and give back the past.'

The strength of Naipaul's novel lies in its success in persuading us that this is so. What happens in it is convincing both as the record of a man living his life from the cradle to the grave, and as a memory in the minds of others, creating an order out of what was experienced for the most part as a chaos, gently teasing out the pattern that lay deeply embedded within a life characterised by apparent false beginnings, lazy acquiescence in events, and disappointing achievements. As in all lives, the trivial acts as a pointer to the important, and is frequently transformed into it. Shama's sewing-machine, cow and coffee set, unobtrusively recurring as they do, testify to the increasing intimacy of her presence, to Biswas and to ourselves. Casual mention of Dodd's Kidney Pills at the newspaper office transports us twenty years back to Biswas's school-days and his friendship with Alec, who has inexplicably disappeared from the scene – as people do. Figures like Bipti, Govind and Jagdat punctuate the story from chapter to chapter and make vivid to us the passage of time and the way some people stay the same as it laps around them. Others change. Others again, like Mungroo, Maclean and W. C. Tuttle, pass in and out of life rapidly and without trace. Insignificant people like Owad assume a sudden importance. Significant ones like Seth suddenly dwindle into contemptible shadows of themselves. Hari we only learn to value after his death: his absence from the Tulsi household leaves a gap we can find no one to fill. Mrs Tulsi's death disrupts the whole complex system of relationships we had taken to be permanent. But we get used to the new fragmentation as we get used to the fact that even Mrs Tulsi, about whose 'decreptitude' there was 'a quality of everlastingness', will die. And we get used to the fact that for the Biswas children the house at Sikkim Street was just another 'permanent' arrangement, though we had seen it as a precarious gamble likely to fail at the end of any chapter.

To be persuaded of the reality of a whole family and its network of relationships spreading out to encompass a wide variety of human beings of different ages, callings and backgrounds is to respond to something most unusual in modern fiction. To be made sensitive to the shifting moods that drift among its members, the withdrawal of trust here, the sense of strangeness between inner family and outer there, is to be aware of the persistence, in a writer of so vastly different experience, of some of the best features of Victorian and Edwardian fiction. the careful attention Naipaul pays to mundane detail, made significant by the passing of time and the recurrence of habit, reminds me of no one so much as Arnold Bennett in *The Old Wives' Tale*. *A House For Mr. Biswas* is a novel on that scale, with the same command over relationships persisting in time and founded on detail. It has its own way of showing 'what life is' and its own distinctive comic tone. Nevertheless, its preoccupations and some of its structural peculiarities go back to Bennett and, beyond him, to the Russians. I have found no more successful recipient of the inheritance in contemporary English fiction.

6

Growing Pains

'I am weary of my individuality, and simply nauseated by other people's.'

D. H. Lawrence

The novelists I have been considering in the last chapter are all realists. One hesitates to use that word, because ever since its début in English (in an essay on Balzac in the *Westminster Review* in 1853), it has been employed loosely, to cover a multitude of meanings. I use it in the sense Ford used it in his novel criticism, or as Bennett used it in his reviews for the *New Age*. 'The progress of every art is an apparent progress from conventionality to realism. The basis of convention remains, but as the art develops it finds more and more subtle methods of fitting life to the convention or the convention to life.' For Bennett, Chekhov was the perfect realist: 'He seems to have achieved absolute realism. . . . His climaxes are never strained; nothing is ever idealised, sentimentalised, etherealised; no part of the truth is left out, no part is exaggerated.' In *The Good Soldier*, Ford made use of the subtlest method his study of James and the French and Russian realists had suggested to him. He fitted the lives of Dowell, Ashburnham, Florence and the rest to the conventions of an elaborate narrative, and by doing so he provided his readers with a sophisticated and unremitting study of at least one man's temperament. I have emphasised Ford's concentration on what he called an 'affair'. The events of *The Good Soldier*, vividly and exhaustively described as they are, seem to be divorced from every other aspect of life that might have been going on around them. They are also excessively dependent on the minds that witness and create them. Nothing is 'saved' from the characters, released from their demands upon it. Everything is significant. Ford would, again, have agreed with Bennett when he wrote, in *The Author's Craft*, just a year before Ford completed *The Good Soldier*, that much depended on the stance the writer took up in relation to his fiction: 'by obtaining a broad notion of the whole' a novelist can 'deter-

mine with some accuracy the position and relative importance
of the particular series of phenomena to which his instinct draws
him'. Also, 'No human phenomenon is adequately seen until
the imagination has placed it back into its past and forward into
its future'. It is my view that Ford, even in so excellent a novel
as *The Good Soldier*, never freed himself from the implications
of his own and Bennett's terminology. We do sense what happens
in his novels – and I include the Tietjens books – as a 'series of
phenomena', and so there is a tendency for his readers to look at
them as the objects of an experiment. Throughout *The Good
Soldier* I catch myself trying to get behind Dowell, to 'place' him
as accurately as I can in the context of his own descriptions, which
I realise I cannot take at their face value. This appears to me to
be a part of the legacy of what was described as French or Flaubertian realism. The novelist places his readers in a thoroughly
artificial position, a position which has as little in common with
the positions he habitually occupies in real life as the positions that
Victorian novelists like Thackeray had tried to manoeuvre him into.
The main difference is that Thackeray lets us have the information he thinks we shall want to know at the time he judges we shall
want to know it; Ford makes us wait until he feels he can get the
maximum aesthetic effect. In both cases we cannot avoid sensing
that the writer has made a bargain with his readers over the heads
of the characters. Thackeray is more explicit about it, that is all.

In *The Old Wives' Tale*, as in one or two other, smaller corners
of his fiction, Bennett seems to me to have escaped the likely
consequences of his way of looking at the world, as it is discovered
in his critical terminology. Unlike Dickens, he does not behave
'inconsistently' in his handling of narrative. His way of presenting character does not vary. As a result of this, it would be fair to
say, the people he allows us to get to know are known less vividly,
less startlingly, than they are in Dickens. But they are *known*,
always encountered, rarely appreciated or made use of. So in spite
of Virginia Woolf's jibe about the buttons and the Bond Street
tailors, Constance and Sophia, Sam Povey and Gerald Scales,
do have something in common with Natasha and Sonya, Andrei
and Dolokhov. They are people who, in some strange way, we
meet on the same terms as we meet people in the world outside
books. Manipulation of narrative, conscious control of the reader's
attention: these take second place to the naïve representation of

recognisable, credible, though not necessarily significant aspects of the characters' behaviour. Naipaul excels at the same sort of thing in *A House for Mr Biswas*. It is not a matter of theory or of conscious and consistent method. Instead, it is a matter of a certain commitment to the assumed reality of the world that is created, a submission to its solidity, its density, its plenitude. Attention to particulars, the craftsman's care for detail, come first – even where, as in Bennett, the outline of the plot has been considered some time in advance of putting pen to paper. Out of the detail, what shape the novel has will form of itself – for actions shape themselves as they do in life, surprising us by their unlooked-for connectedness, their falling into patterns and then falling out of them, their leaving traces of themselves, the ghosts of form – all of which add up to a final glimmering of the idea of what life is like, what shape, or shapes, it takes.

Bennett and Naipaul take realism beyond itself. In one respect, however, they abide by the realist rule: they do not attempt to precipitate themselves, in whatever fictional disguise, into the forefront of their own novels. No realist is prepared to be as merciless with himself as he is with other people, and even the sentimental sort shies away from the personal subject. It is permissible to make certain inferences about the relation that may exist, for example, between the characters in Naipaul's novel and Naipaul himself, but one thing that is certain is that Biswas is not Naipaul. Even where one suspects that such a relationship may exist – which is very rare, and usually indelicate to inquire into – it exists at a distance. What is looked at is looked at as a past event. This is what I grew out of, not what I am, is the burden of the tale. At this point of Romantic correspondence between time of writing and time of feeling, of experiencing the world, realism dwindles away. It rarely arrives, and if it does, it is very unusual to find the movement into the present, and the present itself, within the covers of a single book. In D. H. Lawrence's *Sons and Lovers* this happens. The fact that it happens makes it a difficult book to approach critically, and the diffculty is not at all diminished by our realisation, with hindsight, about what happened to its author after it was written.

Most of the 'past tense' of *Sons and Lovers* is not difficult to come to terms with. The first part of it is a triumph of fictional autobiography in which Lawrence accurately describes the marriage into which he was born, the community within which the marriage was lived, and his own response, as a sensitive and difficult child, to those facts of parentage and community. One can pick out the incidents one feels to be most true, most deeply understood: Mrs Morel's argument with the pot man and her qualms of conscience after it; the Morels waiting for their eldest son, William, to return from London; William and his 'superior' girl-friend, Gyp, embarrassingly out of place in the confining and suffocating atmosphere of the house in Scargill Street. My own favourite is Paul's search for advertisements for a job:

> . . . at ten o'clock, he set off. He was supposed to be a queer, quiet child. Going up the sunny streets of the little town, he felt as if all the folk he met said to themselves: 'He's going to the Co-op reading room to look in the papers for a place. He can't get a job. I suppose he's living on his mother.' Then he crept up the stone stairs behind the drapery shop at the Co-op, and peeped in the reading-room. Usually one or two men were there, either old, useless fellows, or colliers 'on the club'. So he entered, full of shrinking and suffering when they looked up, seated himself at the table, and pretended to scan the news. He knew they would think, 'What does a lad of thirteen want in a reading-room with a newspaper? and he suffered. . . .

The passage has the vivid immediacy of Sophia Baines smarting under her mother's prohibition of her becoming a teacher, of Maggie Tulliver being supplanted in her brother's affections by Lucy Deane, or of David Copperfield before the Murdstones. It is most like Dickens. Pip, in *Great Expectations*, feels precisely this combination of guilt and being the centre of attention when he goes to the magistrate's court to be indentured to Joe. This is the 'small day-life', the 'common-place' past that is looked back to as a separate thing in the later chapters. It was not felt as commonplace at the time, but now, looking back, it can be seen as customary, completed and understood.

It comprises less than half of *Sons and Lovers*. Lawrence is able to understand what is customary and familiar, but he is not slow to get his hero out of it. It exists as a condition of Paul's growing up, but there is nothing inevitable about the way he grows up and away from it. There comes a point at which he ceases to accept his upbringing as a limiting condition. This is a simplification of the way the second part of the novel works, because there is no one clearly identifiable point and it is uncertain, at the very end, how far Paul has escaped the dominating influence of his mother's love. But it is not a badly distorting simplification. Paul does grow away from custom, and as he does so the description of his experience also stops being customary. The shaped events of his past break down and spread out into shapeless present gropings and uncertainties. Lawrence is dealing with his hero beyond the point at which he chooses to accept a defined, shapely and conditioning past.

The link with the Dickens of Pip's and David's experience, with George Eliot and Arnold Bennett, is broken. It had broken at least a year before *Sons and Lovers* was published. Lawrence enjoyed Dickens, and, of course, he owed a great deal to George Eliot's having made accessible to fiction the lives of people not so very different from those among whom he had grown up. Bennett, however, he had always detested. In October 1912 he had written to A. W. McLeod: 'I hate Bennett's resignation. Tragedy ought really to be a great kick at misery. But *Anna of the Five Towns* seems like an acceptance – so does all the modern stuff since Flaubert. I hate it.' He always did. Bennett was a 'gold watch-chain', 'a pig in clover', 'an old imitator'. Mainly because of that 'resignation', 'acceptance', the acquiescence in which your family, your background, your irremediable circumstances make of you. Because you live in a draper's shop in Bursley there is absolutely no reason why you should end up, in Bursley or Paris or anywhere, with a draper's mentality. In *Women in Love*, Birkin advises Gerald, 'instead of chopping yourself down to fit the world, chop the world down to fit yourself', and in 'St Mawr', Lou Carrington's views on the younger generation are bitterly ironic: 'Because she did not see its sources of power, she concluded it was powerless. Whereas perhaps the power of accommodating oneself to any circumstances and committing oneself to no circumstances is the last triumph of mankind.' Lawrence's heroes will never accommodate themselves to circumstances, they will create them. They will not accept, they will demand – usually what is not on offer. Beyond the age of adolescence, Bennett's description of a passive and acquiescent life either *is* a lie, or ought to be. Lawrence rarely distinguishes between 'is' and 'ought', except in terms of what is appropriate to villains and heroes, the dead and the live.

The second part of *Sons and Lovers* shows Paul, and Lawrence, moving closer and closer to the personal present which the realists had cut away from their narrative. As they do so, the events described become less and less discrete, they lose any definite contour, the relationship between the one and the other ceases to be one of cause and effect in any distinct sense. The sheet anchor of Mrs Morel's love for Paul and Paul's love for his mother pulls loose only with the mother's death, and then uncertainly; but long before, Paul has tried to understand that love as a circumstance to which he will continue to commit, not accommodate, himself. His growing realisation that he is not free to do this, that he cannot help himself, in spite of what he comes to know is destructive in their reciprocal passion, occupies a large part of the closing chapters. His mother is the last tie to which he can do no other than acquiesce. From now on Lawrence, if not Paul, will freely commit himself to whatever human relationship seems most satisfying to him. What is *there*, to be acknowledged, will become what is possible, to be created. The novels become a part of the process of that creation.

For all this, though, to throw the emphasis overwhelmingly on the role the mother plays in Paul's life is to misconstrue what is going on at the deepest levels of the novel. True, Lawrence encourages us to do this. Everything that happens, happens within the ambience of Paul's relationship with his mother, and their relationship dominates both his other affairs with women. In fact, it dominates them to such an extent that we easily fall into the error of supposing that it *explains* them, and we suspect that much of the time Lawrence fell into the same error. Lawrence has constructed his novel on the principle that to create a future in which he can participate in the right kind of relationship with the world – which means, immediately, with a woman – he must first exorcise the wrong kind which was fastened on him by his mother. By reliving his adolescence in the person of Paul Morel, and at the same time understanding it as the young man and author, D. H. Lawrence, Lawrence believed he could free himself from that accommodation to circumstance he despised in Bennett. In this sense *Sons and Lovers* is an effort to neutralise the past by comprehending it. The matter is further complicated

by the circumstances in which it was written, the last draft issuing
from the beginnings of an actual, rather than a hypothetical,
commitment – to Frieda; and earlier drafts accepting some and
rejecting other materials offered by Jessie Chambers, the 'real'
Miriam of the book. But for all these added complications, the
fact remains that throughout the writing of *Sons and Lovers*, and
especially of its second part, Lawrence sets off Paul's affairs with
Miriam and Clara against the dominating, and apparently explanatory, relationship with the mother. On a long view, this
should mean that Miriam and Clara are not to be blamed for
Paul's failures with them. The tie with the mother prevents him
from making any satisfactory tie with another person. But in
novels, long views are made up of a succession of short views, and
in this particular novel *they* tell a different story.

They tell a different story because Lawrence is constitutionally
incapable of doing himself less than justice. The further Paul
and Miriam, or Paul and Clara, move away from Mrs Morel, the
longer Mrs Morel is out of our and Lawrence's sight, the less
Lawrence trusts himself and us to remember her explanatory
function. So, Lawrence's re-enactment of his relationship with
Jessie, in Paul's relationship with Miriam, takes place doubly.
The first re-enactment is of a relationship corrupted by Mrs
Morel's hold over Paul. Miriam fails with Paul, and Paul with
Miriam, because of forces that lie outside of the control of either,
and which Paul escapes only after his mother's death, when he
has left Miriam, and Clara too. So long as we and Lawrence
remember Mrs Morel's presence within all Paul's relationships
with women, this is the re-enactment we see. It makes of Paul
something approximating to a conventional fictional hero, where
conduct is explained by reference to influential facts and considerations which act upon him and which he, in turn, reacts
against. The second re-enactment is of a relationship which Mrs
Morel has nothing to do with. The failure is one between the two
lovers, and not the responsibility of any outside party. So one of
them is to blame – unless, of course, Miriam's part in the affair
can be explained in a similar, but necessarily more external,
way to Paul's in the first re-enactment. From time to time we do
hear about the way Miriam's mother has protected her from sex,
even animal sex on the farm, and encouraged her to 'exalt everything . . . to the plane of a religious trust'. But Lawrence isn't

really happy with this sort of explanation. It shifts responsibility from the involved person, and he wants to find it there, in the person who acts, rather than the place he or she acts *from*. The difficulty is in finding out which person.

In the later novels this difficulty doesn't exist, because by that time Lawrence has convinced himself that the responsibility is never his, and when he appears in the fiction, as Birkin or Mellors for example, he tells us who is wrong and why he is wrong. The fact that Birkin is inclined to be pompous and Mellors is schizophrenic makes no difference. What they say is true, when they say it, because Lawrence is saying it through them. But in *Sons and Lovers* Paul is still young, and Lawrence not much older. Paul's self-justifications and accusations are therefore more tentative, more likely to push the reader back to the long view to discover reasons why he says what he says, rather than to pull him further into the maelstrom of passion within which Paul speaks and force him to take his bearings from the hero's explanations – which are as yet too much at the mercy of the situation to be read as doctrine.

That is what makes Paul's relationship with Miriam so difficult to understand. Lawrence gets very involved in the substance of that relationship, and as he does so he finds himself stuck in the short view of it. This happens conspicuously during the 'Test on Miriam', when Paul proposes to her that they should have sexual relations. After a long paragraph explaining Mrs Morel's anger with Miriam for taking Paul away from her and 'killing the joy and warmth in him' – handily incorporated within the mother's biased view of the matter and therefore suggestive without being in any sense a final judgement – Lawrence moves back to Paul's consciousness. He has 'hardened his soul' against his mother. 'He made himself callous towards her; but it was like being callous to his own health. It undermined him quickly; yet he persisted.' The mother is packed away, and now Paul's response to her disappointment is allowed to lapse, in so far as she is not allowed to intervene on the page as a visible influence on Paul's conduct. Lawrence is very skilful here. He allows Paul's lead-up to the proposal he has to put to Miriam to be interrupted by a single reference to the mother, which is muted through its association with the rest of the family: '*they* depend on me at home'. That ambiguous reference completes the explanatory framework for

the scene and shuts out the long view. What follows is re-enactment at a very personal level, of a relationship between two
people which is entirely their own responsibility. The further the
scene goes, the more distant does the mother's explanatory
presence get. Paul confesses that he wants Miriam:

> 'Why are you ashamed of it?' he answered. 'You wouldn't be
> ashamed before your God, why are you before people?'
> 'Nay,' she answered deeply, 'I am not ashamed.'
> 'You are,' he replied bitterly; 'and it's my fault. But you
> know I can't help being – as I am – don't you?'
> 'I know you can't help it,' she replied.
> 'I love you an awful lot – then there is something short.'
> 'Where?' she answered, looking at him.
> 'Oh, in me! It is I who ought to be ashamed – like a spiritual
> cripple. And I am ashamed. It is misery. Why is it?'
> 'I don't know,' replied Miriam.
> 'And I don't know,' he repeated. 'Don't you think we have
> been too fierce in our what they call purity? Don't you think
> that to be so much afraid and averse is a sort of dirtiness?'
> She looked at him with startled dark eyes.
> 'You recoiled away from anything of the sort, and I took the
> motion from you, and recoiled also, perhaps worse.'

Paul's interpretation of what has gone wrong is uncertain and
unstable. At least that is what it looks like. But on inspection there
proves to be a principle of motion in its instability. Each time his
thoughts come to rest, they find themselves pointing to a deficiency in Miriam. Here, Paul begins by accusing Miriam, and
goes on to confess his own fault. This 'fault' persists through his
confession that he is a 'spiritual cripple', and disappears at 'And
I don't know'. Of the two questions that follow, the second is less
rhetorical than the first, is modulating into something more like
an accusation. Then the last speech *is* an accusation: not '*we*
have been too fierce' but '*you* recoiled . . . and I took the motion
from *you*'. It is the great, unresolved problem of *Sons and Lovers*:
who takes the motion from whom? To a greater or lesser extent,
all the women exist *for* Paul, Clara exclusively, Miriam and Mrs
Morel with varying degrees of resistance. This means that all
descriptions of their feeling are designed to explain Paul, who is
the dominant consciousness. So when Lawrence tells us that none

of Miriam's movements seemed quite '*the* movement' and that 'Everything was gripped stiff with intensity, and her effort, overcharged, closed in on itself', we immediately allow the observation to be appropriated by Paul. It is not a description, but an interpretation; not 'evidence', but a record of what entered Paul's mind when he saw Miriam dandling her younger brother. As a matter of fact, shorn of the loaded words Lawrence uses to justify Paul's attitude – 'surcharged with love', 'as if she were swooned in an ecstasy of love' – Miriam's behaviour with Hubert does not seem unnatural, though the child, it is true, doesn't like it and frowns.

Again, when Miriam and Paul are reading together one evening at Willey Farm, our response to Miriam is distorted by words and phrases that substitute Paul's view of her for our picture of her *out there*. As Paul is mending a puncture in his bicycle, Miriam undertakes the daunting task of running her hands down his sides. 'She always wanted to embrace him, so long as he did not want her.' Paul's response is predictable. 'She did not seem to realize *him* in all this. He might have been an object.' Is this true or isn't it? We can't tell, because in the absence of a disinterested record we have only circumstantial evidence to help us make up our minds, and that can be made to work both ways. There is one comment which is very important. Miriam goes wrong, we are told, because 'She never realized the male he was'. A little later Paul is anguished by the fact that Miriam wants something – his 'soul' – that is not him. 'If only you could want *me*, and not want what I can reel off for you!' Perhaps Miriam is too soulful, but Paul is not the less too obscurely demanding. At least Birkin (in *Women in Love*) is to know, most of the time, what he wants from Ursula. Paul is in the invidious position of trying to arrive at being Birkin whilst assuming that Miriam should already be Ursula. Now if there is one thing worse than being Birkin, it must be becoming Birkin. On one occasion during the 'Test', Paul achieves a faint trace of Birkinian articulateness when he tells Miriam that 'To be rid of our individuality, which is our will, which is our effort . . . that is very beautiful'. But on the whole his inarticulateness tells Miriam even less about how to behave than Birkin's super-articulateness tells Ursula.

The clarity of the description of Paul's affair with Miriam suffers, because there is no account of what Paul is groping his

way to discovering is a satisfactory sexual relationship until long
after the relationship between the two of them is closed. Paul
experiences this for the first time, and only temporarily, with
Clara near the canal in chap. 13. Here, 'his experience had been
impersonal', 'it was not Clara. It was something that happened
because of her, but it was not her.' Clara herself doesn't realise
this. In fact she suspects it in Paul and, through giving voice to
her suspicion, makes him feel guilty about not considering *her*,
thus introducing a 'mechanical effort' into their loving which
ultimately destroys it. Clearly, Paul is at once too ruthless and too
diffident to create a situation in which he can satisfy either
Miriam or Clara. He has much of Birkin's intolerance with
hardly any of his certainty, which is to say that Lawrence is
writing *Sons and Lovers* out of his own uncertainty, or rather out
of a developing certainty superimposed on an earlier record of
embarrassing ignorance. We are aware of a delicate and malle-
able sensitivity being beaten into shape by a mind struggling to
formulate definite beliefs. The sensitive and uncertain assertiveness of the past is from time to time overlaid by an ideologically
simplifying assertiveness of the present. Frankly, the love affairs
represented in *Sons and Lovers* are a mess, terribly embarrassing
as most adolescent love affairs must seem when looked at from
the other side of twenty-one. Lawrence is never satisfied with a
mess. Somebody has to be to blame – which is part of his adolescence that he always carried with him. Here he is saying: Miriam
is to blame, or if Paul is to blame really it's his mother. There is
some truth in this, but it isn't the whole truth. Consequently it is
a dubious basis on which to erect a doctrine about human relationships.

It is time to look at what the doctrine is, to look at it seriously
because Lawrence did emphatically believe in it and applied it
with great consistency and delicacy to the actions of his novels
after *Sons and Lovers*. It is not a metaphor or a half-cranky
private mythology, but an assertion of value held in the teeth of
prevailing presuppositions about relationships between people in
life and between characters in fiction – which were in turn responsible for most of the attitudes human beings took up to one
another in fact and fiction from Tom Jones to Constance and
Sophia Baines. These are the more respectable examples. One
could equally well advance the names of characters in any cheap

novelette or romance. On the whole we have preserved these
attitudes, or we suppose we have. Who does not admire Jane
Austen? Even Dr Leavis, who is Lawrence's most eminent and
vociferous apologist, admires Jane Austen. Lawrence detested
her. She 'typifies "personality" instead of character, the sharp
knowing in apartness instead of knowing in togetherness' ('A
Propos of Lady Chatterley's Lover'). What does Lawrence mean
by personality as distinct from character? He means what he
shows us in Mrs Witt's view of the world, or her daughter Lou
Carrington's interpretation of it, in 'St Mawr':

> Always this same morbid interest in other people and their
> doings, their privacies, their dirty linen. Always this air of alert-
> ness for personal happenings, personalities, personalities, per-
> sonalities. Always this subtle criticism and appraisal of other
> people, this analysis of other people's motives. If anatomy pre-
> supposes a corpse, then psychology pre-supposes a world of
> corpses. Personalities, which means personal criticism and analy-
> sis, pre-supposes a whole world-laboratory of human psyches
> waiting to be vivisected. If you cut a thing up, of course, it
> will smell. Hence, nothing raises such an infernal stink, at
> last, as human psychology.

By analysis Lawrence doesn't mean anything so limited as critics
of James meant in the late nineteenth-century reviews of his
work. Lawrence would include James, but his hatred of analysis
and personality extends much further to embrace Jane Austen
and a whole tradition of human behaviour of which the writing
of novels, as undertaken in the previous century, was only one
particular expression.

What Lawrence is saying is that he is not interested in differences between people. People as entities, differentiated one from
another, are of no value. They are, in fact instruments, not agents;
levers, not hands. J. I. M. Stewart said as much when he wrote
of Will and Anna in *The Rainbow* that 'although their characters are real, we feel that their characters are largely beside the
point'. Their marriage 'is torn and riven by an incompatibility
which seems to well up from deep unconscious sources, exploiting
temperamental and intellectual differences as mere instruments'.
People, in other words, are important only by virtue of the fact
that obscure forces operate through them and *can only* operate

through them. They are important for what they have in common, which is theirs only in the sense that cells belong to tissue
or carbon belongs to coal. Any suggestion of possession is false.
Human beings do not possess what is most valuable in themselves. They simply cannot avoid allowing it to take place through
them. The quiddity of a person is *im*personal, integral to personality but alien to it, inhuman, a sort of anti-body which cannot
exist without body. Lawrence's apprehension of this is extremely
reductive, equating value with the presence of a common factor
within apparently dissimilar, though co-classifiable, entities. I used
the example of the carbon in coal because it is so suggestively
accurate an example, demonstrating the equal value of coal and
diamonds by virtue of their composition out of the carbon element
which is the common factor. It is so accurate that Lawrence himself used it in his letter to Edward Garnett (June 1914) which is
the *locus classicus* of the doctrine:

> Somehow, that which is physic – non-human in humanity, is
> more interesting to me than the old-fashioned human ele-
> ment. . . . Marinetti writes: 'It is the solidity of a blade of steel
> that is interesting by itself, that is, the incomprehending and
> inhuman alliance of its molecules in resistance to, let us say, a
> bullet. The heat of a piece of wood or iron is in fact more
> passionate, for us, than the laughter or tears of a woman' – then
> I know what he means. He is stupid, as an artist, for contrast-
> ing the heat of the iron and the laugh of the woman. Because
> what is interesting in the laugh of the woman is the same as the
> binding of the molecules of steel or their action in heat: it is
> the inhuman will, call it physiology, or like Marinetti, physi-
> ology of matter, that fascinates me. I don't so much care about
> what the woman *feels* – in the ordinary usage of the word.
> That presumes an *ego* to feel with. I only care about what the
> woman *is* – what she IS – inhumanly, physiologically, materi-
> ally – according to the use of the word. . . . You mustn't look
> in my novel for the old stable *ego* of the character. There is
> another *ego*, according to whose action the individual is un-
> recognisable, and passes through, as it were, allotropic states
> which it needs a deeper sense than any we've been used to
> exercise, to discover are states of the same single radically
> unchanged element. (Like as diamond and coal are the same

pure single element of carbon. The ordinary novel would trace
the history of the diamond – but I say, 'Diamond, what!
This is carbon.' And my diamond might be coal or soot, and
my theme is carbon.)

Lawrence is fond of using these reductive, scientific images to put
over his views. He uses them again in chap. 15 of *The Rainbow*
when he reveals Ursula in one of her crucial moments of self-
discovery. She is looking at the ciliary activity of a 'plant-animal'
through her microscope at the training college:

> For what purpose were the incalculable physical and chemical
> activities nodalized in this shadowy, moving speck under her
> microscope? What was the will which nodalized them and
> created the one thing she saw? What was its intention? To
> be itself? Was its purpose just mechanical and limited to
> itself?
>   It intended to be itself. But what self? Suddenly in her mind
> the world gleamed strangely with an intense light, like the
> nucleus of the creature world under the microscope. Suddenly
> she had passed away into an intensely-gleaming light of know-
> ledge. She could not understand what it all was. She only knew
> that it was not limited mechanical energy, nor mere purpose
> of self-preservation and self-assertion. It was a consummation,
> a being infinite. Self was a oneness with the infinite. To be
> oneself was a supreme gleaming triumph of infinity.

'But what self?' That was what Paul wanted Miriam to answer
for him. He wanted her to respond to the 'real me', something
that was neither an object nor a personality. He too had tried to
explain what he meant in biological terms, 'shimmering proto-
plasm': 'Only this shimmeriness is the real living. The shape is a
dead crust. The shimmer is inside really.' Both personalities and
objects have shapes, which are stable, definable. To lose shape,
to lose definition, they must pass through 'allotropic states'.
Having done so, they will achieve the real, the radically un-
changed elemental existence which they share with human life
generally. The business of characters is to make this elemental
existence accessible to each other or one another. I press these
alternatives, 'each other' and 'one another', because Lawrence's
view of how many people, two or more than two, are necessary

to bring to birth an awareness of elemental human *being* in a single individual varies from novel to novel.

Lawrence persuades us to approach his characters at three levels. First of all they are personalities. Like Jane Austen's characters they walk round other people's estates. Like Bennett's they teach in schools. They also go on holiday. After all, Lawrence cannot get away from the fact that human beings do things, and this makes them different from one another. The best he can do is make sure they do things in the most incongruous way possible – Birkin at the school, Ursula and Gudrun exciting the bulls at the 'Water Party' in *Women in Love*. Personality is maintained by an act of will, it is the product of consciousness and superficial self-concern, the sort of self Miriam thought she had and prized so highly. Then there is dissolution, the relaxing of personality which may take one of two forms, depending on the way Lawrence is feeling at the time of writing. It is a commitment to the blood, to dark forces, which may be destructive and purely sensual. The most extensive explanation of this negative form of dissolution occurs in the chapter called 'Moony' in *Women in Love*. Birkin remembers an African fetish which embodies the breaking down of any relation between the senses and the mind, 'leaving the experience all in one sort, mystically sensual'. This is no good. Alternatively the relaxation of will, consciousness and personality may result in the individual's passing through those allotropic states which is the necessary preliminary to final discovery. To my mind Lawrence never succeeds in explaining how we are to distinguish between these alternatives in practice, that is to say in the descriptions of such states in the novels. Lastly, there is the discovery itself, existence as a 'free proud singleness', dependent on connection with another human being or other human beings rather than sustained by an exercise of will (which is proper to conscious differentiation) and possessed of that elemental rightness which human beings share with animals but which, because we have minds, takes different and less easily accessible forms in us than it does in them.

Brief explanations cannot avoid making the dogma look ridiculous. In fact I do not find it so. Consider the magnitude of the task Lawrence had set himself. Where, outside of Tolstoy and Dostoevsky (and Conrad?), do we find in the nineteenth- or early twentieth-century novel a serious attempt to explore how, at the most fundamental levels, human beings feel themselves to be bound to one another? Where do we find this consideration for what a man should try to achieve in and for his life? Both Victorians and realists had taken for granted basic presuppositions about nature and value which made the job of recording how people do in fact behave relatively easy; their first and most helpful presupposition being that behaviour was indeed their proper subject, either in its own right, or because it could be made to represent psychological forces separable from it in theory but always, in practice, dependent upon it. Furthermore, the fact that behaviour is taken as at least the immediate subject of the novel created a situation in which the way you tended to look at human beings was pre-eminently moral. Even realists with no evidental moral bias encourage their readers to adopt moral attitudes, to judge the behaviour, and through it the temperamental and emotional predispositions, of their characters. More than this, the approach to character – because of that encouragement to take up attitudes to persons, to judge them – is overwhelmingly critical. The typical pattern of a nineteenth-century novel is that of a series of illusions the protagonist either fights his way out of, or utterly capitulates to. The principal characters of Jane Austen, Thackeray, George Eliot, Flaubert, Turgenev, Meredith, Gissing and James are for ever learning not to do the next time what they did this time, and then that the next time never presents the same temptation as this time anyway, so they have to be always on guard. There are no convincingly prolonged accounts of satisfactory relationships which are anything other then *given*, and thus transparent. Every satisfactory relationship which is visibly earned by a fully explored protagonist is an artistic failure – David and Agnes, Dobbin and Amelia, Ladislaw and Dorothea – they are all either public myths or private wish-fulfilment, often both. It is not easy to show men and women responding to the basic demands they make of each other; much easier to be critical of mistaken judgements of personality and other failures of a kind readily accessible to fiction.

In the end I think one's attitude to Lawrence's refusal to take for granted so much of what the great novelists of the nineteenth century took for granted is not in itself a literary critical matter. The way he went about replacing what was taken for granted is more properly the critic's province. But the fact that Lawrence did it at all has been, I think, most unfairly held against him, and by literary and social critics of widely divergent views. Raymond Williams,[1] for example, refuses to acknowledge that Birkin's and Ursula's marriage at the end of *Women in Love* can possibly be a healthy one, because it is marriage lived outside a normative context of social life which includes memories of the families out of which it has emerged and anticipations of the family relationships into which it must issue. The past is rendered 'irrelevant' and the future 'inconceivable'. John Bayley believes that Lawrence's novels don't give much impression of 'what people actually feel their lives to be like' in comparison with *The Old Wives' Tale*, for example. 'In removing human variety and removing individuality Lawrence is left not with human "wholeness" but with mere mind and will.'

What this means, in each case, is that the critic has his own idea of what 'wholeness' is, and that it is something 'given' – to Williams in his experience of life in Monmouthshire and his subsequent abstraction of social values from it, to Bayley I do not know in what form, but clearly his view of the function and purpose of fiction depends upon a deep satisfaction with what he takes to be 'natural', received modes of experiencing the world. Bernard Bergonzi has described this as 'contemplation', a comprehensive tolerance which eschews intervention and disruptive social commitments. As Bergonzi says, Bayley's approach to fiction gives no evidence at all of the fact that literature can be subversive as well as reassuring. Williams knows this very well, and attaches great value to it. But in his view, Lawrence's subversive ideas, which take the form of an escape from community as he had shown it in *Sons and Lovers* and in many short stories, clash head-on with his own, and what he takes to be Tolstoy's in *Anna Karenina*. What Williams is asking is, why is Lawrence so pigheaded in his refusal to see that Levin and Kitty have the right relationship and that Anna's and Vronsky's is bound to be destructive? And why, then, does he show us, in *Women in Love*, variations on the destructive Anna and Vronsky theme? Lawrence's answer would be, I think, that Anna's and Vronsky's liaison is only one, destructive, variant of an extra-marital and non-familial

---

[1] Williams has written three essays on Lawrence, in *Culture and Society*, *Modern Tragedy* and *The English Novel from Dickens to Lawrence*. I am referring to the essay in *Modern Tragedy*.

relationship, to which class of possibilities the liaisons between Gerald and Gudrun, and Birkin and Ursula, also belong. The elemental existence of Birkin and Ursula, uncertain and tentative as it is, is quite different from the existence of Gerald and Gudrun, which is willed and 'personal'. Similarly, Lawrence had seen, just as Williams has, the sort of communal, familial existence Levin and Kitty are inaugurating. He started from there in his picture of the Morel household at the beginning of *Sons and Lovers* and in his account of the marriage of Tom Brangwen and Lydia Lensky in *The Rainbow*. But that customary acceptance of life and being together, valuable as he shows it can be, is closed to him. He can see how it can be fought for, in Will and Anna – and imperfectly achieved. He can also see how, more and more, it is having to be replaced by new forms of relationship between men and women which will connect them with the same elemental certainties. That is what Ursula, with Skrebensky, and with Birkin, is trying to do.

Unlike Williams and Bayley, I propose to accept that Lawrence's views about what is, fundamentally, to be required of human beings have some substance; that it is possible to feel as Ursula feels at the end of *The Rainbow* and as Birkin feels in *Women in Love* without trivialising what I understand to be most richly human. In life, they are viable, if not normative, prescriptive – as Lawrence wants them to be. The more pressingly real problems have to do with the application of these views to the way human beings are shown to act in the novels, in a literary medium. Has Lawrence created a form and a language which can be made to demonstrate the nature of the modes of existence he insists on setting such great store by?

Let us take *The Rainbow* as our text. It is Lawrence's habit in most of the novels to take one step back before taking two steps forward. *The Rainbow* is no exception. The action of the first five chapters, before 'Anna Victrix', could have taken place in *Sons and Lovers*, and much of it in the first part. Anna's amusement at Will Brangwen's singing, and the celebrations at their wedding, are consummately and affectionately handled – like William and Gyp in the earlier book; and the description of Tom Brangwen's proposal to Lydia, and of his play with Anna while Lydia is in labour, have all the rapt intensity of Mrs Morel's response to the lilies when she was locked out of the house by her husband before Paul's birth. These early chapters are probably among the most satisfactory Lawrence ever wrote: they are massive without being blurred; intense, but never hysterical. They testify to the power of mysterious energies welling up from subconscious sources, but show them merging into a common life of both customary and individual activity.

One reason why this is so is that the past tense in which these five chapters are written is heavily underlined. The incidents leading up to Anna's marriage with Will are grasped as a whole and completed sequence, a gravely considered prelude to present events. Only gradually do the heavy, almost biblically dignifying sentences release us into a present fraught with uncertainty and incompleteness. By the time they have done so, at chap. 6 or thereabouts, a sense of the great continuities of life has been conveyed within which we are to wrestle with the problem of Will and Anna, and later Ursula and Skrebensky. Without such a sense we should be all but lost in the veering passions of the next three chapters dealing with Anna's marriage to Will. These chapters seem to me to represent the heart of the novel and to exemplify most clearly the nature of Lawrence's mature fictional procedures. Much later in *The Rainbow* we are told that Will 'moved from instinct to instinct, groping, always groping on'. It is what Lawrence also seems to be doing here – much more so than in the last half of the book, describing at greater length the progress of Ursula's affair with Skrebensky. There one feels that Lawrence knows where he stands and is prepared to sacrifice the life of the characters, particularly Skrebensky, to the demands he makes of them to demonstrate his views. Here, in Anna's marriage to Will, we have something at once more confused, more difficult to read with patience – or so I have found – and more honestly exploratory. An indication of this is that although, manifestly, the account is written in the same past tense as the previous chapters describing the earlier marriage of Tom and Lydia, it doesn't feel anything like as *far* past. Characters give the impression of being caught in the act – an act which comes into existence and continues to exist only when Lawrence begins to write about it. The event and its representation in literature occur simultaneously, and they go on occurring simultaneously for the space of at least a hundred pages of prose.

The tension between feeling and understanding communicates

itself from the characters to the reader. Much of the prose is cast in the form of imperfect explanation, of an effort to understand. The imagery (of the Church, the woodcarving, the gargoyles) assists in clarifying the issues Will and Anna feel are involved. But the emphasis falls on the effort of understanding breaking out of events that are expressed as long, intense motions of the soul or brief pin-pricks of experience. Each person tries to define himself by pitting himself against the other. For Anna, 'The thought of her soul was intimately mixed up with the thought of her own self. Indeed her soul and her own self were one and the same in her'; whereas Will 'seemed simply to ignore the fact of his own self, almost to refute it'. They are both in perpetual spiritual motion, advincing from and receding into a defined personality. Will breaks out of this self-refutation: 'Before he had only existed in so far as he had relations with another being. Now he had an absolute self – as well as a relative self.' But this is liable to lapse back into a lack of self-sufficiency. Anna maintains her identity of self and soul, at varying levels of ele-mentality – which makes all the difference. 'She wanted her own sharp self, detached, detached, active but not absorbed, active for her own part, taking, giving, but never absorbed.' The repeti-tion brings out the present urgency of the 'want', its immediate, not retrospective, occurrence, and therefore its malleability, its openness to change and transformation. Will, though, 'wanted this strange absorption with her', 'this' strange absorption because it is present, able to be pointed to and confronted.

The immediacy of events in this part of *The Rainbow* deprives the narrative of many resources available to more traditional kinds of fiction, which reserve 'present' tenses for climactic moments carefully prepared for by an arranged structure of inci-dent. I will give just one example. One of the reasons we found *The Old Wives' Tale* so lifelike was that when sorrows, or so many other things, came, they came not single spies. Events rarely wait upon other events. They occur together. So, all the time Sophia is plotting how to form a liaison with Gerald Scales, Constance is slowly developing her relationship with Sam Povey. At the same time, in the early stages, Mrs Baines is still worrying about Sophia's ambition to become a teacher. Sophia, Constance and Mrs Baines are coping with a lot of other things too. Lawrence's impulse to sink himself into the half-formed intentions and responses of his characters at their deepest levels, where incidents are ignored if they do not bear down upon the dominating issue, prevents this sort of recognition of pedestrian concurrence. What has been going on all the time happens at a later point, in a retrospective frame. Hence, all the time Will and Anna have been living their marriage, Anna's brother Tom has been visiting the farm at Cossethay and striking up a friendship with Ursula. We hear of this after the main account of the marriage has closed, when Lawrence's attention has shifted to Ursula, and he has to work in the background of her launching into life. Concentration on the most important feature of an intensely felt present has meant that less important aspects of the life Lawrence is describing become even less present, and more perfunctory, than they do in the traditional novel of common life.

Lawrence called his new method in *The Rainbow* 'exhaustive'. In another letter he told Edward Garnett he no longer enjoyed creating vivid scenes, as he had done in *Sons and Lovers*. 'I don't care much more about accumulating objects in the powerful light of emotion, and making sense of them. I have to write differently.' It is certainly true that the new method had the effect of making events less and less vivid, as their outline became more and more obscure. After the remarkable struggle to make the relationship between Will and Anna comprehensible in the second part of *The Rainbow*, I feel that for the most part Lawrence simply failed to represent the reality of personal experience in his novels. With varying degrees of ineffectiveness, the writing succeeds only in converting such experience into something very like cliché. This is true even where the cliché grows out of Lawrence's ill-considered dependence on a style he himself, with great effort and intelligence, had created. Too often the hesitant, groping patterns of the syntax are nullified by the stolid assurance of a vocabulary that is no longer fresh and alive. It becomes difficult to distinguish between different levels and varieties of passion. A similarity of vocabulary creates the impression of a similarity of values, in respect of depth and meaning of an experience described. J. I. M. Stewart has remarked how, in *Women in Love*, a casual meeting with a prostitute is described in almost exactly the same way as a later encounter between Ursula and Birkin. Lawrence makes things worse by using words to which he gives the impression he attributes very precise meanings and values in an imprecise and sometimes quite contradictory way. Birkin on sensuality in Ursula's classroom and Birkin on sensuality as he casts his mind back to the African fetish are, or should be, referring to totally different things. An experience tends to be 'final' both in a derogatory and most intimately satisfactory sense. To impose upon an experience already indefinite and confused a private vocabulary or an acutely distorted composition and phrasing would be to exhaust the reader's concentration. The alternative Lawrence provides – an insistent and emphatic use of regular constructions and 'primary' imagery, of blood, fire, darkness, etc. – is none the less confusing and ultimately untrue to the experience he is describing. It is not satisfactory that a novelist who places great emphasis on the difference between willed and elemental energy cannot be relied upon to distinguish between them in the language he uses to present them. The force and thrust of the writing peter out in shapelessness and confusion. In those three chapters from *The Rainbow*, Lawrence comes nearest to embodying in fictional form his apprehension of what moves human beings. But it is confusing, easier to experience than to understand. By contrast, the latter half of the novel is easier to understand than to experience. Much of Ursula's relationship with Skrebensky is artificially explanatory. Only the unnecessarily long chapter on her career as a schoolteacher works – at a lower level of ambition than the rest. In *Women in Love* the explanatory method has taken over most of the book, with Birkin there to act as its mouthpiece. Will and Anna share the most ambitious and most truly Lawrentian sequence from the novels.

After Will and Anna, Lawrence knows what he wants. Usually at least one of his characters knows also. The novels then cease to be exploratory and worked from the inside of the human beings who provoke the action. They comprise instead one person who knows the truth and gives persistent voice to it; many people who have no inkling of it and are therefore bitterly satirised and abused; and just a few searchers after it who are guided by the Lawrentian spokesman, and are ultimately saved or thwarted by their elemental acceptance or willed refusal of that spokesman. Birkin in *Women in Love*, Lou Carrington in 'St Mawr', Captain Hepburn in 'The Captain's Doll' and Mellors in *Lady Chatterley's Lover* are or become such spokesmen. Most of the characters

are treated as Mrs Witt treats them, 'just criticising and anni-
hilating these dreary people, and enjoying it', though in Lawrence's case even the enjoyment is often missing. Lou Carrington
is the most extreme and coherent spokesman of the later doctrine,
before Mellors's insistence on tenderness. 'Just think of St Mawr!'
she says. 'I've thought so much about him. We call him an animal,
but we never know what it means. He seems a far greater mystery
to me than a clever man. He's a horse. Why can't one say in the
same way, of a man: *He's a man*? There seems no mystery in
being a man.' So 'Why can't men get their life straight, like St
Mawr, and then think?' It has become a dogma to be applied,
not a problem to be explored. The living confusion of Will and
Anna disentangles into the solving simplicities of verbal confrontations, conducted for the most part in a more combative
variant of the language inherited from those earlier instinctive
gropings.

The novels then become a cross between a sort of Shavian
dialectic with progression from one side of the argument only –
inevitably towards the position already held by the other – and
an occasional re-creation of psychic epiphanies, during which
men and women get their lives straight and become 'pure animal'.
Abusive satire and bad-tempered knockabout fill in the gaps.
The argument and opinion issue from people who have lost most
of their identity as personalities, but who rarely display the elemental self-assurance of the animals, say, in *Birds, Beasts and
Flowers*. They think, but their thoughts issue from lives whose
straightness has to be taken on trust. Lou Carrington is far less
of an animal than an opinionated wraith. At the end of 'The
Captain's Doll', Hepburn stops being a tolerably comic character
and becomes an obtuse disciplinarian whose air of command and
authority presents itself as more willed than elemental. That is the
trouble. In the absence of a viable linguistic medium, what
Lawrence wants to display as elemental self-possession almost inevitably appears on the page as its opposite in the Lawrentian
scheme of things – a personal, willed and somewhat hysterical
preoccupation with the self. After *The Rainbow*, it is difficult not
to apply to the events in the novels either the old-fashioned judgements on character and manners or dialectical counter-claims
which the hardening of enacted opinion into applied dogma cries
out for. Either way, the novel as an explanatory tool, used to cut

a way through what is 'given' in nature or in our presuppositions about nature, has changed into something else – and in each case, novelistic or tractarian, it is something less than it was in the first half of *The Rainbow*.

Most writers know what they want from the start, and much of their work takes the form of an effort to convince us that events could prove them wrong. The novels of Richard Hughes are different, in this respect as in so many others. I choose to place his work alongside Lawrence's because both of them have a way of looking at their characters that is totally distinctive and totally at variance with accepted practices. But where Lawrence's novels, even at their most dogmatic, have an air of often hectic uncertainty and exploratory openness to experience, Hughes's have an air of equanimity and calm self-satisfaction which at first glance may look suspect and naïve. Superficially, Lawrence is all inquiry. I have tried to explain the limits within which that inquiry is conducted. Similarly, Hughes appears to be all conclusion, a writer in possession of a theory about human behaviour which should render his novels schematic and restrictive. Yet in defiance of expectation, Hughes's method opens to our relaxed contemplation much of the variety of life that Lawrences's intense involvement in the problems of human relationship either gravely diminishes, or fails to acknowledge altogether.

There is no clear and consistent theme in Hughes's work. It is fair to describe the first novels as adventure stories. *A High Wind in Jamaica* tells the story of five children – the Bas-Thortons and the Fernandezes – captured by pirates on their way from Jamaica to London near the middle of the nineteenth century. *In Hazard* is Richard Hughes's *Typhoon*: the *Archimedes*, a large single-screw turbine steamer, runs unexpectedly into a hurricane. Captain Edwardes and his officers bring her, wrecked, to safety after a six-day struggle with the elements and an abortive mutiny by the Chinese crew. *The Fox in the Attic*, although a fragment of a larger whole, is a much longer book. Its main character is a young Anglo-Welsh squire, Augustine Penry-Herbert, who finds it prudent to go on a long visit to his German relatives at Lorienburg, near Munich, after he has become involved, apparently quite innocently, in the death of a young girl. The time is 1923, which means that Augustine is precipitated on to the side-lines of the Hitler–Ludendorff *putsch* and, though he does not know it, into the cross-currents of Bavarian political life as these are represented in the figures of his uncles, cousins, and their friends and acquaintances. He also falls in love with his blind cousin, Mitzi. Back in England his sister Mary is also involved in public affairs. Her husband Gilbert is trying to advance his career as an M.P. by helping to create a reconciliation between the Asquith and Lloyd George wings of the Liberal Party. Meanwhile Mary is trying to compensate her housekeeper, Nellie, for the loss of her niece, Rachel (it turns out to be this niece whose body Augustine found on the marshes at the beginning of the novel), by setting up her sister and brother-in-law, with their remaining child, Sylvanus, in a disused folly on Gilbert's estate.

There is little to be gained by looking for a common pattern of ideas in these very different narratives. In any case, it would be premature to attempt anything approaching a comprehensive judgement on Hughes's work, discovering clear thematic continuities and the influences of other novelists. In view of his descriptive power and Augustine's claim, near the end of *The Fox in the Attic*, that 'meaning is essentially visual', we might have to trace such influences as are present to painters as much as to novelists. His wife, Frances Bazley, is a painter, and his close friends have included Augustus John.

Examples of Hughes's descriptive power abound. Take this one, from chap. 2 of *A High Wind in Jamaica*. There has been an earthquake at St Anne's, where the Bas-Thorton children are staying:

> The desolation through which they drove is indescribable. Tropical scenery is anyhow tedious, prolific, and gross: the greens more or less uniform: great tubular stems supporting thick leaves: no tree has an outline because it is crushed up against something else – no *room*. In Jamaica this profusion swarms over the very mountain ranges: and even the peaks are so numerous that on the top of one you are surrounded by others, and can see nothing. There are hundreds of flowers. Then imagine all this luxuriance smashed, as with a pestle and mortar – crushed, pulped, and already growing again!

We shall search through Ballantyne, Stevenson, Conrad, in vain for such a clear, exact and effortless description of a tropical landscape. Simply as description, a visual record of what the after-math of an earthquake must be like, this is, in Walter Allen's words, 'hallucinated': '... no tree has an outline because it is crushed up against something else – no *room*'. This sort of ac-curacy is the stuff of which Hughes's descriptions are habitually made. It takes time to get used to their freshness, reality and casualness. Later Hughes has difficulty in describing 'the inside' of Laura, the youngest child on the pirate ship, but through imagery and simile he gradually works towards a clear account of the 'feel' of Laura's 'inside'. On the way there he loses him-self in a description of an octopus:

> When swimming under water, it is a very sobering thing sud-denly to look a large octopus in the face. One never forgets it: one's respect, yet one's feeling of the hopelessness of any real intellectual sympathy. One is soon reduced to mere physical admiration, like any silly painter, of the cow-like tenderness of the eye, at the beautiful and infinitesimal mobility of that large and toothless mouth, which accepts as a matter of course that very water against which you, for your life's sake, must be holding your breath. There he reposes in a fold of rock, ap-parently weightless in the clear green medium but very large, his long arms, suppler than silk, coiled in repose, or stirring in recognition of your presence. Far above, everything is bounded by the surface of the air, like a bright window of glass. Contact with a small baby can conjure an echo of that feeling in those who are not obscured by an uprush of maternity to the brain.

How does Hughes succeed in doing this sort of thing so well? The confrontation with the octopus is like a confrontation with a baby. But the comparison is not merely visual – a matter of toothless mouths, supple arms coiled in repose. What is in-trinsic to the comparison is the medium through which the octo-pus is seen and experienced. The stems and leaves of the trees in the earlier passage were seen as a blur hardly distinguishable from their background of other leaves and other trees. They were in-definite but very much living and changing *presences*, thrust close up to the perceiver in their very blurredness. We do not experi-ence things as outlines, discrete particulars with given shapes and sizes, but as organically related objects, shifting into one another as the scarcely distinguishable parts of a field of vision, which is also a field for the exercise of other senses. Much depends on the relationship between an object and the background of which it is, as a sensed experience, a part. Foreground is just as important. Here, in the description of the octopus, we have a tangible foreground through which the creature is 'looked in the face'. It is, of course, 'that very water against which you, for your life's sake, must be holding your breath'. This makes the octopus 'apparently weightless in the clear green medium'. Then we are given the sense of everything above being 'bounded' by the surface of the air. The experience of looking at the octopus is sealed off from other kinds of experience, made peculiar and original at all points but those at which looking at a baby like Laura is similar.

We have moved away from the description of landscape and animals to a description of human beings, and how their minds work, what they are like inside. But the move has not been as abrupt as may be supposed at first glance. To begin with, Laura is at that stage in her development when the baby is about to become a child, i.e. a human being. She is three years old. Hughes compares her with a tadpole whose legs have begun to grow but whose gills have not yet dropped off. In spite of token physical features she is not yet human, rather 'one of the most developed species of the lower vertebrates'. 'In short, babies have minds which cannot work in terms and categories of their own which cannot be translated into the terms and categories of the human mind.' Children themselves, like Rachel, or like Emily who is ten and a half, are human. Their minds are 'not just more ignorant and stupider than ours' (no concessions to Romantic child psychology) 'but differ in kind of thinking (are *mad* in fact): but one can, by an effort of will and imagination, think like a child, at least in a partial degree'. But it is impossible to think like a baby, just as it is impossible to think like an octopus. What we can do, on the other hand, is to render a lucid account of our own responses to either of these foreign bodies. When we say that this is what a baby is like, we mean this is how I respond to a baby and this is what the baby does when I respond to it. Hughes's success in describing the behaviour of very young children is a result of his abiding by the limitations inherent in holding such a view. The same with animals. The best example is Thomas, the ship's monkey in *In Hazard*, which wakes up mem-

bers of the crew by opening their eyelids with its thin little fingers:
'It was Thomas, with his soft fur and his big tail, hopping away
on his unnaturally elongated feet, nervously folding and unfolding his ears.'

The older children from Rachel upwards are also more ignorant and more stupid than adults. Their minds work rationally,
they are not 'nebulous' as Laura's is; but the connections between
events, and between attitudes to what they do and what is done
to them, are rudimentary. Rachel, for example, has a conscience,
but it is a very simple one. It gave her no pain 'because it never
occurred to her as conceivable that she should do anything but
follow its dictates, or fail to see them clearly'. She tries to convert the pirates; when this doesn't succeed she sends for the police.
Both courses of action are 'right'. It doesn't very much matter
which one is successful.

The most crucial instance of the way a child's mind works,
how its whole being responds to 'what happens', is Emily's response to her killing of the Dutch captain. Emily, who is half-way
between a child and a women (Laura is half-way between a baby
and a child), has hurt her leg while playing on the deck and has
been set to guard the captain while the pirates are raiding his
ship. The captain is an innocuous and timid man, unable to speak
English. 'Emily was terrified of him. There is something much
more frightening about a man who is tied up when a man who is
not tied up – I suppose it is the fear that he may get loose.' Since
she will not respond to his begging her, in Dutch, to pass him a
knife from the cabin floor so as to cut the rope from his wrists,
he tries to get it for himself. Emily begins to scream, seizes the
knife, and 'In the course of the next five seconds she had slashed
and jabbed at him in a dozen places'. The experience has come
at a delicate stage of her growth into a person. A little earlier she
had 'suddenly realised who she was', 'a discrete person', separated from her family and thus placed in a peculiar (to her) isolation. The idea of finding out that she knows this is terrifying to
her, especially since in her confusion she is not yet sure that she
is not God – a quandary Mitzi shares in *The Fox in the Attic*.
So her killing the Dutch captain at this juncture places her in an
especially vulnerable position. As a 'piece of Nature' she is
capable of letting her friend Margaret take the blame. 'But as
Emily, she was absolutely naked, tender. It was particularly cruel

that this transition should come when so fierce a blast was blowing.' Hence her oscillation between panic and anxiety and a sort of
calm solipsism, a retreat under the bed-clothes into a world in
which the real objective issue of her action doesn't exist for her.
'But the conviction that she was the wickedest person who had
ever been born, this would not die for much longer.'

At the end of the novel the pirates are arrested as a result of
their exasperation and concern for the children, and of Emily's
betrayal. The younger children, 'having as yet little sense of contradiction', hold in their minds simultaneously what they know
happened aboard the pirate ship and what the adults assume
happened. Margaret remains a mystery – reserved and uncom-
municative; I suppose because she is adult, a fact which the children have probably recognised though they have never thought
to use that word of her. This makes her mysterious to the reader
too. Emily continues to lie about the Dutch captain's death and
this helps to sign Captain Jonsen's and the other pirates' death
warrants. 'What was in her mind now? I can no longer read
Emily's deeper thoughts, or handle their cords. Henceforth we
must be content to surmise.' In spite of its unusually dramatic
form here, this is the sort of experience which helps to form a
child's being, and hence that of the adult she will become. The
operations of the adult mind and feelings take place above this
potentially dangerous substructure: first the utterly unknowable
nebulousness of a Laura; then the simple moral impulses of a
Rachel; and finally the coming-about of a sense of continuity,
persistence and separation from other people and things of an
Emily. How do they 'settle' in the adult person? Do they leave
traces of themselves and do they affect permanently the behaviour of such persons? *A High Wind in Jamaica* does not provide the answers to these questions, since the children's parents
disappear for the greater part of the novel, and the pirates are
handled in such a way as to divert attention, for the most part,
from themselves to the children. We see them characteristically in
comic situations responding to the more active behaviour of the
children or involved in practical affairs – rummaging through
the Dutch steamer or camouflaging their own schooner as the
Lizzie Green. They are successfully created characters, but 'what
people do' is different from 'behaviour'. We do not receive a description of their behaviour as we do that of the children. The

adult world in the novel is the world that is responsible for the frame in which the children are set, the eye which perceives them. Otherwise it exists as something outside the experience of the children into which the eldest are growing, or being pre-cipitated – much to their confusion. We know it to be a world in which life will be 'no longer an incessant, automatic discharge of energy', a world in which Emily 'would remember that she was *Emily*, who had killed . . . and who was *here*'. But what does this world of continuous and related actions feel like to the people who perpetrate and undergo them? What does responsibility feel like? Emily only falteringly blunders into a half-knowledge of it. We have to wait for *In Hazard* to find out what it is really like.

Like the child's sense of 'guilt' and discontinuous development in *A High Wind in Jamaica*, the adult sense of responsibility, courage and cowardice – the success and failure of measuring up to responsibility imposed – is presented in an *extreme* form in *In Hazard*. In their different ways, Captain Edwardes in con-trol of the *Archimedes* at the heart of the Caribbean hurricane and Ao Ling fighting the Kuomintang among the Communist forces in Chingkangshan and Kiangsi both demonstrate 'a natural aptitude for virtue', a way of life in which 'Everything must be done with your whole heart, and a little more than your whole strength'. Edwardes's dedication to his craft and Ao Ling's dedi-cation to the Cause find their parallels in Mitzi's final religious experience at the end of *The Fox in the Attic*. Perverted forms of it are found also among the Bavarian Royalists and Wolff, the veteran of the Baltic wars, the fox who hides in the attic in the later book. But these are indeed perverse simulacra of what Edwardes, Ao Ling and Mitzi represent. Their twisted sense of virtue springs to a greater or lesser degree from a spiritual defic-iency of which Hitler is revealed to be the most extreme example. The Roman virtue of a Captain Edwardes or an Ao Ling de-mands the capacity for a sort of emptying-out of the self. In Captain Edwardes's case this is a potential which requires the kind of event represented by the hurricane to make it actual:

Captain Edwardes was happy as a sand-boy! Had he known, at the beginning, what was coming, would he have been happy and confident like this all through? Perhaps not. Perhaps no one could have borne that foreknowledge. But passing instead from each known moment only to the unknown moment ahead, his happiness had carried him along. . . It was the hugeness of the responsibility which made his heart so light.

In Ao Ling it is perpetually present and vigilantly itself:

From the time of his conversion, at least down to the time when they fought their way out of Chingkangshan, his mind was a blank, so far as personal things were concerned – it was filled solely with the progress of the Cause. In this ecstasy of religion, small wonder that neither the storm, nor his hunger, nor even the fire from the furnace which had seemed powerless to destroy him, could move him very greatly!. . . He sat there in a posture the design of which seemed framed on the bones of his body and the set of his ears, rather than (like most European postures) on the shape of the body's surface.

Other members of the crew experience from time to time this same capacity for heroism and virtue: Mr Bennett and Mr Watchett, for example, pouring oil for hours at a stretch, totally immersed in their task and oblivious to the danger they had felt so strongly before. Others fail to measure up to the demands of the storm: Mr Rabb, the puritanical officer, undergoes a moral collapse and becomes physically incapacitated, smelling of the fear that is literally sweating out of him. Hughes communicates his sense of what adult virtue is like in his straightforward, clear description of the physical activity and motions of the minds of his characters. There is no hint of frenzy or panic in the prose; but instead a supremely steady, even description, passing over nothing that Mr Bennett does or thinks. The substance of his thought is ridiculous – a matter of delivering a lecture on 'The Whole Art of Oil Pouring' 'in balanced periods' – but it is convincingly attested to and not at all ridiciulous in *effect*. This, we are convinced, is how the mind occupies itself and develops resistance under stress. Ao Ling's mind works differently, but the deep source of his courage is the same. Just as the sense of the importance of the relation between father and son takes very different forms in different civilisations, so it is with courage and cowardice:

The powerful innate forces in us, the few prime movers common to us all, are essentially plastic and chameleon-like. The

shape and colour which they come to present at the mind's surface bear little seeming relation to the root: appear characteristic rather of the medium through which they have struggled to
the light.

The insistence that there are essential forces in human beings
which do not change their *nature*, though they may function in
what are superficially different ways from one community or
system of belief to another, is of central importance in Hughes's
work. If we have to find a single thread running through the
novels, this would be it, though I should prefer to call it a pre-
condition of his creation of character rather than a view of life
thematically sustained and dramatised. On one level Mr Rabb
and Captain Edwardes have far more in common with each other
than with a vicious and fanatical Chinese Communist who has
made himself a minor nuisance to the authorities in Canton. But
ultimately, at the level and in the respect which really count,
Edwardes and Ao Ling are alike.

In the meantime, a crisis of the kind the crew of the *Archimedes* have just passed through does not merely reveal the true
nature of a man to himself – as it does in different ways to Captain Edwardes and Mr Rabb. It also changes him and his conception of himself. Through his endurance and heroism, Dick
Watchett becomes 'a grown man', 'a hard case', and in the process of doing so experiences a sense of something leaving him
'which he regretted':

> But it has to be like that. A man cannot stretch the gamut of
> his emotions, he can only shift it. If you reach out at one end,
> to cover the emotion of danger of death, till you can cope with
> that comfortably, you can't expect to keep a delicate sensitive-
> ness at the other end too. Just as there are baritones, tenors,
> trebles: but no one can sing the whole length of the piano. It
> was as if Dick's voice had broken now. He had some fine new
> manly notes. But the old top-notes were gone.

Hughes adds to this: 'Not perhaps, for good: the shift had been
artificial. In time security might restore him to his natural range.'
The idea of a 'natural range' in human beings, which varies as
between man and man, goes along with the belief in the kind of
'biological' development indicated in the treatment of children

at different ages in *A High Wind in Jamaica*. Development in adults does not stop but continues in the sense that people gradually discover and extend the range of their capacity for experience. The kinds of discoveries and insights that produce this extension are only in small part a matter of reason and calculation (the *Archimedes* both entered and escaped the hurricane against the laws of reason and in defiance of the instruments). As a result of this, Emily's experience in the earlier book is not entirely a child's experience. She suddenly understands that she is Emily, a discrete person, in the same way as Dick Watchett wakes up a grown man, and Augustine (in *The Fox in the Attic*) suddenly realises he is in love with Mitzi. People in Hughes's novels are always changing, discovering more of their 'natural range', losing and reviving parts of themselves as they do so. Hughes's originality is bound up with his ability to convince us of processes of character development which have little to do with the exercise of conscious choice but which are by-products, as it were, of often ordinary, sometimes extraordinary, but always apparently irrelevant occurrences. The side-effects of an action can often have more subjective consequence than the achievement or otherwise of the end proposed. Dick's changing attitudes to Sukie (the girl he has fallen in love with), as he applies himself to his duties during the storm, would be a good example of this. The consequences of Augustine's drunken conversation with Jacinto, the Brazilian sculptor, at Schwabing – i.e. his belief in the aesthetic of 'Significant Form' – would be another.

It is a measure of *The Fox in the Attic*'s superiority over the earlier novels that it takes over this way of developing character and embeds it within a carefully reconstructed and detailed historical context. The fictional characters (Augustine, Nellie, Mitzi, Franz, Wolff) and the historical ones (Hitler, Goering, Roehm, Hanfstaengl) all are grasped as people living their lives in conformity with Hughes's understanding of what might be called psychic and biological process. Walter Allen calls *A High Wind in Jamaica* a 'natural history of children'. We could borrow the phrase and call *The Fox in the Attic* a natural history of adults (and children too: as always these are wonderfully and vividly realised, in the figures of Polly, Janey and the German children). As such, it presents adults in public as well as in private roles, and makes the area of their public activity much wider than that of a ship at sea. The area extends from a small Welsh town and the countryside around Munich to Welsh and Bavarian society, and ultimately to the nature of post-war England and Germany. Much is made of the inability of representatives of these societies to understand one another, so vastly different is their experience. Augustine's views on Ernst Toller are not merely anathema but incomprehensible to his uncles and cousins. To Augustine he is a great dramatist; to them a 'Jewish scribbler'. The von Kessen children cannot believe that an Englishman can be trusted to keep his word, and Augustine can't believe that they can't believe it. Conversation between Augustine and the von Kessens is a tissue of embarrassment and misunderstanding.

Why is it so difficult? What accounts for the complete breakdown of communication between the two societies, represented here as two branches of a single family? On a personal level it destroys trust between the men and turns Augustine's love for Mitzi to waste through sheer ignorance, on both sides, of the situation in which they are living. But is it possible to grasp the fundamental causes of the breakdown, causes which lie underneath the historical causes and effects on the one hand and abstract philosophical theories on the other? Hughes believes that if we look closely at the ways in which people relate themselves to their fellow-men and the societies they comprise, this is possible. His explanation, or part of it – the whole novel (and presumably its sequel) shows the working-out of it in the characters – occupies all of chap. 26 and is prolonged to the end of book 1. Hughes is talking about the 'abiding terms of the human predicament', 'the entropy of the self':

Primitive man is conscious that the true boundary of his self is no tight little stockade round one lonely perceiving 'I', detached wholly from its setting: he knows there is always some overspill of self into penumbral regions – the perceiver's *footing* in the perceived. He accepts as naturally as the birds and beasts do his union with a part of his environment, and scarcely distinguishes that from his central 'I', at all. But he knows also his self is not infinitely extensible either: on the contrary, his very identity with one part of his environment opposes him to the rest of it, the very friendliness of 'this' implies a balancing measure of hostility in – and towards – 'all that'. Yet the whole tale of *civilized* man's long and toilsome progress from the taboos of Eden to the psychiatrist's clinic could be read as a tale of his efforts, in the name of emergent Reason, to confine his concept of self wholly within Descartes' incontestable cogitating 'I'; or alternatively, recoiling rebuffed off that adamantine pinpoint, to extend 'self' outwards infinitely – to pretend to awareness of everyone as universal 'we', leaving no 'they' anywhere at all.

Selfhood is *not* wholly curtailed within the 'I': every modern language still witnesses the perpetuity of that primitive truth. For what else but affirmations of two forms of that limited overspill of 'I'-ness are the two words 'we' and 'my' (the most potent words we have: the most ancient meanings)? These are in the full sense 'personal' pronouns for they bring others right inside our own 'person'. Moreover the very meaning of 'we' predicates a 'they' in our vocabulary, 'meum' and 'alienum'.

That primitive truth about selfhood we battle against at our peril. For the absolute solipsist – the self contained wholly within the ring-fence of his own minimal innermost 'I' and for whom 'we' and 'my' are words quite without meaning – the asylum doors gape. It is the we–they and meum–alienum divisions which draw the same man's true ultimate boundary on either side of which lie quantities of opposite sign, regions of opposite emotional charge: an electric fence (as it were) of enormous potential. Yet emergent Reason had attempted to deny absolutely the validity of any such line at all! It denies it by posing the unanswerable question: Where, in the objective world, can such a line ever reasonably be drawn? But surely it is that question itself which is invalid. By definition the whole system of 'self' lies within the observer: at the most, its shadow falls across the objective observed. Personality is a *felt* concept: the only truth ever relevant about selfhood must be emotional, not intellectual truth. We must answer then that objectively the we–they dividing line 'reasonably' lies... wherever in a given context the opposing emotional charges for the moment place it: wherever it brings into balance the feelings of owning and disowning, the feelings of loving and hating trusting and fearing... 'right' and 'wrong'. For normally (at least up to now) each of these feelings seems to predicate its opposite, and my stimulus to the one seems to stimulate the other in unregenerate man. In short, it is as if it were *the locus of this emotional balance* that circumscribes and describes the whole self, almost as the balance of opposite electrical forces describes the atom. . . .

But suppose that in the name of emergent Reason the very we–they line itself within us had been deliberately so blurred and denied that the huge countervailing charges it once carried were themselves dissipated or suppressed? The normal penumbra of the self would then become a no-man's-land: the whole self-conscious being is rendered unstable – it has lost its 'footing': the perceiver is left without emotional adhesion anywhere to the perceived, like a sea-anemone which has let go its rock.

In the next chapter Hughes explains how, before 1914, the 'Liberal mystique of Laissez-faire', based on a 'rational doctrine of total *separation of persons*', had deprived Englishmen of a sense of the 'we' in their experience and trapped them in their isolated egos. The outbreak of war had restored both the 'we' and the 'they' which are necessary to individuals *and* communities – but only to be sacrificed to the holocaust. He then shows how the catastrophic betrayal of this restored sense of identity in the war left Augustine, who had just missed being called up and sent to the trenches, as we saw him in chap. 1 and as we heard of him (before the events with which the book opens happened) from his sister and the townsfolk of Flemton. The collapse of morale after the war and the reversal of his by now accepted expectation of an early death have made him withdraw from his fellows in a retreat from the outside world broken only by his ability to get on with children, especially his niece Polly.

Looking back to Augustine's sense of himself in the gun-room at Newton Llantony in the middle of part I, chap. 2, or forwards to the contrast between Hitler and Mitzi in part III, chap. 10, we can see that aspects of the views adumbrated in the abstract in the passage quoted above are embodied in all the main characters of the novel. In the gun-room Augustine, for some time now a solitary, and (one might presume) after the finding of Rachel's dead body and its consequences likely to become even more so, suddenly acquires a sense of the 'we' relation: ' "he" was no longer cooped up entirely within his own skin'; and this in turn produces the necessary 'they', a 'hostile, alien "world"' outside the 'final envelope' of the room. The rest of the novel, in so far as it concerns Augustine, traces his coming to an awareness of a shared identity and an accompanying sense of the foreignness of his German relatives. From time to time we share his sense of the strangeness and familiarity of other people – in particular Franz and Mitzi. Mitzi herself, through her blindness, experiences a shift in the relations between herself and others. She is the opposite of Hitler (an 'ego virtually without penumbra') – 'with the shock of her crisis the central "I" had become dislodged: it had dwindled to a cloudlet no bigger than a man's hand beneath the zenith of God'. That this need not be, in the strict sense, a religious experience I suggested in my comments on Ao Ling in *In Hazard*, who undergoes a similar process of self-abnegation.

Hitler, by contrast, is a 'monistic "I"'. He exists in an unnatural isolation, 'designing and creating motions enormous and without curb'. His attitude towards human beings is powerfully and briefly defined: 'All tools have handles – this sort was fitted with ears.' Wolff's situation is in a sense the opposite of Hitler's. He has identified himself with the new Germany in the struggle for the Baltic provinces. He has failed, the others have turned against him (with the exception of Franz, whom he despises), and so his altruism 'had by now so atrophied it could no longer contain this his disaster'. He skulks in the attic at Lorienburg, holding on to his romantic love for Mitzi as a last resort. When Augustine appears to have deprived him of this, he turns to the only form of final escape, 'the absolute unreality of death', and hangs himself. The blind Mitzi is found stumbling under his feet as he hangs from a beam, unaware of her 'responsibility' for what has happened, or of what indeed *has* happened.

There is something very suggestive in this ghastly tableau, the last we see of either Wolff or Mitzi. The extremity of Wolff's self-sacrifice as a partisan, exhausted in defeat, has created in him an exorbitant demand for personal compensation. But his self is not strong enough to restrain the nihilistic energies that exploit it, and in the end murder and sadistic fantasy have no choice but to give way to self-annihilation. Mitzi, on the other hand, has failed to advance beyond the outer gates of self-abnegating fanaticism. She could not destroy herself to be with God, because the line that divided God from herself didn't exist: by destroying herself she would have destroyed God in her. As the blind girl recoils from the dead fanatic, so the forces embodied in their persons almost meet, unknowingly, but finally withdraw from each other – one into complete death, the other into a limbo (the convent) which the incompleteness of this first book of a series does not allow us to comprehend, or even presume to be final.

The scene is the last of a whole sequence which throws Augustine, Mitzi and Wolff into an unintended relationship with one another. Mitzi is at the centre of the pattern, unaware of both Augustine's love and Wolff's existence in the attic. Augustine fails to understand the situation or his own involvement in it until it is too late for him to act. His position is vividly symbolised by the ballet in the snow, during which he flutters around Mitzi, invisibly guiding her from the chapel at Lorienburg back to the hall. And all the time this mimic relationship is being played out, Wolff is watching it happen, or watching another fantasy version of it happen, since, like Augustine earlier in the story, he does not know that Mitzi is blind. The link between the characters is hardly understood by them. They occupy positions they are not aware of. Tascha on her bicycle at the Odeonsplatz, Augustine on the drive to Röttningen, even little Polly and smaller Sylvanus – in their different ways made to exist in relation to a dead girl neither of them knows ever existed – all occupy a place in a pattern of events they cannot see and yet which penetrates deep into the private psyche and extends far into the world of political action.

Unlike the characters, we can see the pattern. As yet it is not complete. This is only a part of a larger novel. But the details of it are gradually falling into shape as characters occupy new positions, or cross positions previously occupied by others. As they do so it must occur to us as readers that Hughes is doing something very strange. Unlike almost any other modern English novelist, he is observing a rigid separation between how characters respond to a situation and how the reader does so. This is why many reviewers of the book when it appeared in 1961 felt that at present the hero – Augustine – seemed to be overwhelmed by events. The point-of-view technique and close involvement with characters' feelings, in all their uncertainty and mutability, have become so much a part of our expectations of serious fiction that the absence of either of them in forms which have become familiar (and hence acceptable) leaves many readers baffled. Hughes's narrative behaviour is extraordinary. Each character's experience, as it is shown to be taking place, is subjected to methods of cross-comparison and classification which ought to stop it being interesting at all. In fact it is fascinating. Once we have got used to what at first feels like wanton jerkiness – the the rapid substitution of long-shot for close-up, the conflation of past and present activities for purposes of comparison, the use of mimetically inappropriate imagery to explain what a character feels like in a new situation – we become aware of a spaciousness, a freedom from confinement in specifically 'novelistic' devices, which confounds our expectations of what can and cannot happen in prose fiction.

What strikes the reader on a first glance at *The Fox in the Attic* is the brevity of the chapters – usually no more than four pages long, and divided into small sections of four or five short paragraphs each. Before long, it becomes apparent that the division into chapters and sub-chapters is capricious. The movement of the narrative from one group of paragraphs to the next is often very much more abrupt than the movement from chapter to chapter. We soon learn to take unsignalled changes of scene or tone or point of view in our stride. Those surprising pieces of information that (deliberately) baffle us, knock us off balance, in E. M. Forster (Gerald's notorious death in a football match in *The Longest Journey*) and Muriel Spark (the death by lightning of the secretary's companions in *Not to Disturb*), are only mildly unsettling. The book works in part on the principle of habitual unexpectedness. It is a visible refutation of Barthes's view that the past-definite tense condemns both novelist and reader to conventional ways of responding to the world. Quite the reverse. The occurrences of Hughes's novels are always felt as happening *now*, even where techniques of foreshadowing and recapitulation contrive to prevent the excitement of present action from slipping over into imprisonment in mere sensation. One of the achievements that I believe is greatly to Hughes's credit is his relaxed, unhysterical descriptions of present events. His dislocated sentence and paragraph structure has a great deal to do with this achievement.

The opening of book II, 'The White Crow', provides an unspectacular and typical example of the device. As a matter of fact the division of this chapter into three parts is less capricious than usual. The second part is a flashback to the end of the war, sandwiched between two descriptions (the last very brief) of Augustine's uncle Otto von Kessen at work in his office at Lorien-burg. But the first part of the chapter, providing the reader with his first glimpse of the German side of Augustine's family, will do as well as any to exemplify this aspect of Hughes's narrative technique:

In his little office in Lorienburg, the castle Mary had visited in her girlhood before the war, sat the magnificent Otto von Kessen she had so lately dreamed of. He was rubbing his chin, which felt pleasingly rough to touch after the papers he had been fingering all afternoon.

'Thursday November the Eight' said the calendar on the wall. The cold had come early to Bavaria this autumn, with ten degrees of frost outside. But this office was in the thickness of the castle's most ancient part: it was a tiny twilight room with a sealed double window, and it was like an oven. There were beads of sweat on Baron Otto's forehead, and the hot air over the huge blue porcelain stove quivered visibly: it kept a loose strip of wallpaper on the wall in constant agitation like a pennon.

This monumental stove was too big: with its stack of wood it more than half-filled the room and the space left only just housed the safe and the little kneehole desk Otto was sitting at. On the desk stood a huge ancient typewriter of British make, built like an ironclad and with two complete banks of keys (being pre-shiftlock), and that incubus also took up far too much space; the files and ledgers piled high beside it leaned, like Pisa. In such a cubbyhole there was no possible place to put the big wire wastepaper basket other than under the desk, yet that left a man nowhere to stretch his artificial leg in comfort and now the socket was chafing: a nerve in the mutilated hip had begun to throb neuralgically against the metal of the heavy revolver in Otto's pocket.

Otto tried hard to concentrate on the sheets of accounts in front of him (he acted as factotum for his half-brother Walther these crippled days). These were the last and craziest weeks of the Great Inflation when a retired colonel's whole year's

pension wouldn't cobble him one pair of shoes: Walther's
cheques however vast were still honoured, but only because
he was able to keep his bank account nowadays in terms of the
corn he grew and a cheque drawn for trillions of marks would
be debited as so many bushels according to the price that
actual hour. This galloping calculus of the currency, this hourly
acceleration in the rise of all prices and the fall of all real
values, made endless difficulties for Otto; and now the shoot-
ing pains in the leg which wasn't there were getting worse. . . .

'November the Eighth' said the calendar: almost five years
to the day since the old world ended.

The subordinate clauses of the first paragraph, about Mary's visit to
the castle and her recent memory of it, established a somewhat surprising link with book 1 where, several chapters back, we saw Mary
reflecting on her experiences at Lorienburg. Hughes has chosen not
to set his new scene by an abrupt and dramatic sleight of hand. The
old scenery of Wales and Dorset drifts leisurely into the wings
as the new scenery of the Bavarian countryside is wheeled as
leisurely into position. On the other hand, new information which
we are quite unprepared for is introduced as if we were already
in full possession of the facts. Hughes doesn't say that Otto had
an artificial leg, and so he wasn't comfortable at his desk, with
the wastepaper basket taking up too much room underneath it.
He brings in the artificial leg ostensibly to tell us something about
the desk, and the size of the room in which it is placed. In fact
the description of the stove, the desk, the typewriter and the
wastepaper basket is carefully organised so as to allow our eye to
travel across these things as if we were present in the room. We
notice the artificial leg only because the objects that have seized
our attention have automatically caused us to wonder how the
occupant of the room can be comfortable when the arrangements
in it are so cramping. At the same time the novelist preserves his
privilege of explaining what cannot be directly pereceived: the
office is in the thickness of the castle's most ancient part; there
is a heavy revolver (*the* heavy revolver, which makes a great deal
of difference) in Otto's pocket. Then Hughes deflects our attention to the calendar. Who reads the date first: Otto, or Hughes –
and so ourselves? The inset passage which follows, about the
German soldiers returning in shame to Munich from the war,

could be remembered by Otto or it could be reported objectively by Hughes. Otto heard the sound of marching feet. He was in the crowd that saw the soldiers returning. But Hughes's description refuses to confine itself in the frame of Otto's vision, or memory, of events. The two visions, Hughes's and Otto's, co-exist. It is rather like Flaubert's description of the Dambreuse party in *L'Education sentimentale*. But there is a difference. In the passage quoted above, the insignificant observation of the strip of wallpaper blowing 'like a pennon'; and in the following section, the fact that one of the women who spat at the soldiers wore a railwayman's peaked cap: these concessions to ordinariness and unfittingness are precisely what lay outside the reach of Flaubert's theory and his temperament. The one is jolly, where it should be a little oppressive; the other is incongruous, where it should be telling. Both are unashamedly insignificant. They are the tokens of a kind of truth, if only – and I hope I have given that word 'only' its true weight in my comments on fiction so far – the truth of appearances. It is by saving so much of the appearances, and making them vividly present, that Hughes gives his fictional world a conviction, a freedom from purpose, that, in the end, Flaubert's lacks.

'The White Crow' ends with the Munich *putsch*, a startlingly vivid presentation of events that it is difficult to believe is only ten pages long. All the more so when we see that Hughes is doing full justice to the *putsch* on two levels – as a chaotic jumble of present actions, and as a historical event presaging other events of much greater consequence. The *putsch* as a fact of history is conveyed in three ways. First, by the unavoidable associations of the names of the principal actors – Hitler, Kahr, Ludendorff, Goering. Then by the 'setting' of events in a historical context by both the author and the characters. The description opens with a contrast between the cold weather of November 1923 and the warm weather of the same month in 1918, when Kurt Eisner came to power in much the same way that the Nazis are attempting five years later. And throughout the four chapters that deal directly with the *putsch*, Ludendorff ('the fabulous, the Army's idol') is viewed as a historical figure rather than a private individual. He sees himself in this light, confident he will not be shot at by the troops on the Odeonsplatz because of his historic identity. At the same time as he stands upright for the troops, who

are firing into the marchers, his mind broods almost mystically
on the fact that both 1-9-1-4 and 1-9-2-3, the two dates of triumph
for Germany's enemies, add up to 1-5, ten and five; and that
the tenth and fifth letters of the alphabet are J and E, signifying Germany's greatest enemies, the Jews and the Jesuits. Later,
when he is taken to the police station, the sergeant professes not
to know how to spell 'Ludendorff', even though he claims he
lost an eye in the Ludendorff offensive of 1918. Finally, a historical context has been created for the *putsch* by Dr Reinhold,
who has returned from the *Bierkeller* in Munich to attend a party
given by Dr Ulrich, a friend of the von Kessens at Röttningen.
His description of what happened there (before we see for ourselves, and through Franz's friend Lothar's eyes, the events that
followed) places Goering, Hitler and the rest in a dramatically
historic perspective, almost as though it were a description of one
of those stilted German-realist historical pictures of the 1930s.

Superimposed on the historical event, recollected and made
rhetorical and heroic, is the patchwork of actions and non-actions
out of which the historical event has been created. The illusion
of reality is remarkably powerful, and in many respects compar-
able to some of the historical scenes in *War and Peace* – the
Rostovs' flight from Moscow, Pierre on his mission to assassinate
Napoleon. It is produced in large part by Hughes's technique of
rapid engagement and disengagement, a brisk movement from
event to event, or from the inside to the outside of the same
event, which does not allow the reader to settle in any one controlling position for longer than a few seconds of reading time.
A death is not prepared for by placing the reader suspiciously
close to the intended victim. Max-Erwin von Scheubner-Richter
lies on the ground with his lungs bursting from his chest before
we have ever heard his name. He is noticed because Mitzi's
émigrée Russian pen-friend, Tascha, happens to have got into
the Odeonsplatz by chance just when the soldiers open fire. As
she glances down at Max-Erwin it flashes through her mind:
'She's met him at parties: he'd had so much charm. . . .' Between
Goering dragging himself behind one of the stone lions in front
of the Residenz palace and Hitler limping to the yellow car that
is waiting for him on the Max-Josefs-Platz, the historically insignificant, indeed historically non-existent, Tascha is riding wildly
down the street on her bicycle, hoping to get plenty of splashes

of blood on the wheels. She fails to get any of Hitler's. Lothar
has seen him getting into the yellow car. 'So Tascha had to be
content with quite anonymous blood: it was mostly Willi's,
as it happened.' Willi is a friend of Lothar and Franz. To
us he is not anonymous, though it is true we don't know
much about him. Only later do we discover, far from all the
muddle and excitement, that he is not dead, only wounded in
the leg. Through all the confusion a little dog in a plaid waistcoat,
'looking important', has been trotting aimlessly through the
streets. At the end of it all we find he has rejoined his master,
'an elderly, frock-coated, elegant citizens with so neat a spade
beard it deserved a prize (he slept with it in a net)'. These abrupt
transitions from Hitler and Ludendorff to the yellow car, Tascha
on her bicycle, the dog in the plaid waistcoat, are the mechanisms
by which we are convinced of the reality of the situation. From
where we are standing, on a clear view of events, Hitler and the
little dog are of equal importance. They both occupy defined
positions within a field of vision. The present picture is excitingly
chaotic. The historical perspective, set back from the present,
controls the chaos and explains the significance of what is happening, or did happen. The two ways of looking meet in a historic
present which has all the clarity of epic narrative; and it is as a
combination of epic and romance narrative that Hughes, on his
own suggestion, hopes that his novel will succeed.

As Wolff looks down on Mitzi from his attic, we are reminded
of Chaucer's 'Knight's Tale', of Palamon in his Athenian tower
catching sight of Emily in the garden below. Mitzi's yellow hair
was also 'broyed in a tresse/ Behinde hir back, a yerde long I
gesse', and like Palamon (Hughes tells us) the moment he saw it
Wolff too had 'bleynte, and cryde "A!"/ As if he stongen were
unto the herte'. Wolff is the last person to summon these lines
to mind. Hughes has put them there to expand the possibilities of
the situation. Like so much of the imagery – including the almost
epic similes which stud the narrative with references to politics,
the Bible, classical mythology, and including also the descriptive
set pieces – the lines from Chaucer have the effect not of concentration, of bearing down ever more heavily on one pressing
point of consciousness, but of an airy expansion, a sense of the
continuity of the action with the vast continuum of human life
which stretches out beyond the interlocking action of this one

book. Unlike Lawrence's, Hughes's preoccupation with forces lying beneath the level of differentiated character does not involve his readers either in the toils of passion or the thin air of an abstracted argument. Instead, there is something Chaucerian in the effect of the novel as a whole: as in the *Troilus*, all is referred to a dominating metaphysical schema, and then back again to the teeming and patterned multiplicity of the world at large.

7
Plots

'In life everything is different. Everything is in the providence of God.'

Charmian, in Muriel Spark's *Memento Mori*

'A false doctor is not a kind of doctor, but a false god is a kind of god.'

Nigel, in Iris Murdoch's *Bruno's Dream*

. . . the greatest English literature is not about the Human Condition. We might say that it is about 'Nature', a term which has no equivalent in the Franco-American critical vocabulary which is current today. . . . It implies, above all, an absence of purpose, of insistence, and of individual insight; the portrayal of 'Nature' suggests an almost involuntary fidelity to what is constant in human types and human affairs; to the repetition of birth and death, joy and sorrow; to the humours of men and women and the peculiarities that are at once recognised as universal. It implies a lack of pretension – the author gets no particular credit for portraying it well. The Human Condition, on the other hand, implies a personal sense of where life is significant, of where humanity suffers especially or feels intensively; of unusual violence and unusual modes of feeling; of interesting development or of illuminating decay. The subject matter may even be the same, but those who write about the Human Condition take an attitude towards it.

Whole books have been written about the concept of Nature to which John Bayley attaches so much importance in *The Characters of Love*. It is a concept which has evolved and changed over the centuries, but until the nineteenth century it was always an important part of the intellectual and emotional complex of attitudes that a man brought with him when he tried to understand the world. Now, nobody has much time for it. The word is used to describe or excuse bad behaviour, tolerable because 'it's only natural' and 'Nature will find a way'. So the word has come down in the world. Has the concept that lay behind it been brought down as well, or does it still influence human behaviour and methods of representing human behaviour in fiction? Bayley's book tries to answer this question by showing how three great English writers (Chaucer, Shakespeare and Henry James) acquired access to 'natural' ways of responding to the world. I have discussed Bayley's application of his critical method to James's *The Golden Bowl* in Chapter 4 above.[1] The fact that, in my view, this is a misapplication does not invalidate the usefulness of the method itself, nor of the emphasis he places on the concept of Nature which is so important a part of it. I agree with Bayley that many of the greatest works of English literature are supported by a feeling for what is 'natural', much as he describes it. I should say, for example, that modern writers like Bennett and Naipaul are much closer to naturalism of this kind than to the naturalism of the French authors Bennett admired so much. At their best, they do observe the 'almost involuntary fidelity to what is constant in human types and human affairs' which is typical of the approach.

Bayley opens his argument by describing three approaches to writing about the world which he believes are in some way deficient. The first he calls 'the dogmatic tradition', which he associates primarily with French writing and which seeks to impose an inflexible system of rule and generalisation on 'the hopelessly competitive plurality of our experience'. Novelists like Stendhal and Proust seem to believe that to perceive and to analyse the workings of love is to convey to us what love is actually like. They confuse an intellectual demonstration with an expressive picture of life, and in organising the demonstration they neglect to make any direct appeal to the reader's feelings. The second defective approach is one that Bayley refers to as 'the whole truth'. This is more difficult to explain than the dogmatic tradition, but it has to do with the author's conferring on his vision of life a special status which he, but not the reader, identifies with the truth. The most obvious example is that of William Gerhardi's lovers in the moonlight who are suddenly made aware of the smell of burning fishbones. Extremes of romance and reality, idealism and expediency, are aptly contained in a single scene. The author is insisting that this is what life is really like, and his insistence is noticeable, the emphasis on congruity and dissimilarity mechanical. My own view is that this device also

[1] See above, pp. 115 ff.

(it *is* a device, not a relaxed habit of seeing and taking in) is typical of French fiction. The most celebrated, and mechanical, example of it I can think of is the *comice agricole* scene in *Madame Bovary*, with its innumerable offspring scattered through the pages of Ford's Tietjens books and petering out in the early chapters of Rebecca West's *The Birds Fall Down*, which brings into startling conjunction two conversations in a compartment of a train speeding through northern France. Lastly, the third defective approach Bayley calls the Romantic. Here, the writer takes over the world and by sheer imaginative power convinces his readers that his attitude towards it, his interpretation of its structure and principle of being, is exclusively 'right'. Where the writer of the 'whole truth' approach leads us to believe he understands all about the world by inserting 'typical' situations in the fabric of the narrative, the Romantic writer makes everything in the narrative depend on his intense, private vision of reality. Then the intensity of his vision makes us forget how private it is. We are hypnotised, for the time being, by the writer's imaginative conviction. Only later do we discover that the vision was incomplete, its intensity achieved by a rigorous process of exclusion – exclusion of other approaches and other possibilities. It is not surprising that D. H. Lawrence is put forward as a good example of this approach. We might add the names of John Cowper Powys and L. H. Myers, among other English writers in the 1920s and 1930s.

What alternative does Bayley propose? It is what he calls a 'neutral' approach. The writer doesn't take up an attitude. His novels (or plays or narrative poems) are not organised in such a way as to persuade, convince, or even impress the reader. Instead his gifts are employed in the service exclusively of the characters. His business is to liberate them from any demand that might be made on them to represent or to mean rather than to *be*. This is a supremely difficult task, so much so that Bayley comes back again and again to just five or six writers who, he believes, succeeded in it. Dickens, Joyce, Proust, all are found wanting against this almost impossibly elevated standard, and we are left with Homer (I think), Chaucer, Shakespeare, Tolstoy, James and the author of the Japanese *Tale of Genji*. The reason it is so difficult is that success depends on the writer's ability to combine an enormous understanding of people with an equally enormous ignorance of the enormity of his understanding. He has to unlearn the fact of having learned what he has learned as soon as he has learned it, or indeed whilst he is learning it. If he does not do so he may be found guilty of exploiting his gift, of distracting the reader's attention from the characters as achieved individuals to the novelist appropriating the achievements as his own. This neutrality is quite different from Flaubert's, as he described it in his letters and tried to make it work in his novels, because Flaubert mistook neutrality for disinterested observation of the characters *as other people*. But, Bayley says, 'The great author can make us see his characters both as we see ourselves and as we see other people'. It is this 'freedom of the inner and outer vision' that was lacking in the whole realist tradition, and in the stream-of-consciousness novelists who tried to extend it. The supremely great neutral artist starts with the fact of consciousness. He does not try to go beyond this to describe its appearance, to investigate its machinery, for that would be to take up a deliberate position outside the consciousness of the character. But on this view of character creation there is no inside and outside. In this respect novels are unlike life, because they enable the reader to experience people – Chaucer's Criseyde, Tolstoy's Stiva Oblonsky – 'from the standpoint of [their] own consciousness', as, simultaneously, the subject and the object of their perception. 'In the hands of the master their existence enables us both to see them from outside and to feel what they are feeling, both to be aware of love as a phenomenon and to experience it precariously in ourselves.'

It is important that 'love' is referred to as the emotion which the reader simultaneously experiences and is made aware of. After all, Bayley's book is called *The Characters of Love*, and with good reason. 'Love' is the mysterious power which enables the writer to learn without knowing he is learning what he needs to know in order to make the characters of his book real. And it might be claimed that love is the condition we are in when, in real life, we respond to another person as both the object and the subject of our attention; when, that is, we fail to distinguish between that person's otherness and our instinctive knowledge of what it is like to be her. Significantly, love cannot consciously be learned. Unlike sex, it appropriates to itself neither techniques nor methods. Realist art is very largely an art that depends on methods

– methods as aids to becoming aware, and of communicating that awareness to others, to the readers. But awareness immediately makes over the characters into 'others', into objects of attention which, however well understood and finely analysed, are stuck in the category of otherness. As Bayley says near the end of his book, 'It is a paradox of modern society that we do not understand each other because we are always trying to be *aware* of each other'. I suppose the word 'awareness' has come even more into vogue since he wrote that sentence in 1960. I doubt whether in the decade that has elapsed since then we have grown to understand each other any better.

Bayley seems to have predicted the attack on the characters of fiction which, in different ways, I have associated with Kermode and Josipovici. The concern with fiction, consciousness, and the connections they establish with each other, has led to grave suspicion of the 'straightforward' representation of character. Bayley and Josipovici both accept that the modern novel embraces solipsism as, in Bayley's words, 'its necessity and its creed'. This must be so where consciousness occupies the foreground of the novelist's field of vision. He has admitted that the only way he can explore other people is by exploring himself, that 'consciousness begins and ends at home'. Three different courses are open to him. He can be enthralled by the patterns consciousness creates for itself, bringing them into fictive relationships with what may or may not be the truth. He can expose these patterns for the fictions they are, and in doing this, in a negative way, he can suggest something about the truth which consciousness itself cannot touch. Or he can take the machinery of consciousness as his subject, delighting in the description of its operations rather than in the ends it serves or the fictions it creates. There you have a brief but crude formulation of the positions occupied by Kermode, Josipovici and the apologist of the stream-of-consciousness school. Bayley is trying to get out of the trap which this emphasis on consciousness, the narcissistic delight of the imagination in itself, has constructed. And 'Nature' is the lever he is using to prise it open.

Nature has a great deal to do with the 'assumption of common ground', the sort of easy familiarity that was presumed to exist between author and reader in the early eighteenth century. Then, Nature was 'a kind of tacit agreement':

'The very bank and capital', in Burke's phrase, of civic reason;
and a trifling instance of this unanimity would be Hume's point
that all men agree to tread on the pavement instead of upon
their fellows' toes. Does such an agreement still exist? In life
obviously it does: for purposes of daily convenience we still
agree not to tread on each others' toes, but is there any com-
parable agreement in the world of the writer? Do we and
Proust tacitly agree that toe-treading is wrong? On the contrary, it is an article of faith to-day that nothing shall be taken
for granted between reader and author; we must submit ourselves to the purity of his insight and accept or reject it in the
isolation of our own responses. Tolstoy needs to *persuade* us
of very little, but we have to place upon Proust the burden of
each separate and individual proof.

No wonder modern novelists find it more difficult than Fielding
or even Thackeray did to take for granted the reality of people
and the indifference of people to themselves. Romanticism has
totally exposed the assumptions about reality that lay hidden
from view in the Natural world. According to Josipovici, it made
the habit of Natural vision unrespectable as well as untrue. So
the reality of the world is now made the object of a quest, and,
in one way or another, the novel, the fiction, *is* the quest. Usually,
as Josipovici shows, the novel is also its own discovery. It succeeds in drawing attention to itself. But what is it? Another object
added to the world. It seems a high price to pay for getting rid
of bad habits.

Many of our most precious possessions are, ultimately, fabrications. As Bayley points out, this was one of the things James discovered, and explained in his biography of Hawthorne. So much
of the substance of life, not just as it is lived in novels but as it is
lived outside of them too, is not 'real' in the puristic sense in
which contemporary philosopher-critics use that word. But it is
what we sense as real, what we have made real to ourselves. The
dense network of connections and relationships James found in
England and Europe has nothing to do with a philosopher's reality. Neither has the equally dense network of temperamental
conventions and habitual modes of expression and behaviour. As
these inner and outer conventions interlock at many different
levels, a substantial world is built up which we are familiar with,

which allows us to acquire a sense of ourselves. This is the world
which the great novelists have endeavoured to reproduce in their
fiction. It is not self-supporting, free-standing. It depends on there
being understandings, tacit understandings, between the writer
and reader. In this respect I believe Josipovici is right. The ambition of the realists to cut off the novelist not merely from his
characters but also from his readers was highly artificial. But I
attribute more importance to the fact that it expelled the sense of
agreement and committed the writer to building up brick by
brick the whole edifice of his imaginary world. A house, especially
a transparent house, where you can see straight through the walls
to the bricks it is made of, is not a world. It is certainly not *the*
world. It is a part of the world artificially separated from its
total environment – surveyed, staked out and laboriously built
over. What is produced is a prison. With all its elegance, proportion and perfection of detail it is not even real; and our knowledge that it is not real does not console us.

Bayley suggests that, though our feeling for Nature is diminished, and our commitment to personal attitudes towards the
world correspondingly enhanced, we still have 'love' to fall back
on. Love is our road back to Nature, back to acceptance of reality
as we can be made instinctively to sense it to be. 'The concept of
Nature assumes and balances the claims of these inner and outer
selves; recognising the interpenetration of consciousness and external appearance, of "realism" and the subjective feelings.' That
is what happens, also, when we love. It is what happens when
an author loves his characters, when he represents them not as
quantities to be known but as quiddities to be left for ever mysterious. Our own lives are mysterious to us, an odd combination
of what it feels like to be us, and what other people tell us we are.
The characters of fiction should partake of this same peculiar
mixture of subjective and objective identity. That is Bayley's
view, stressing the conventionality and constancy of our ways of
responding to the world and committing the writer to the conventions in a manner which is, as I have shown, totally at variance
with modernist thinking about fictions generally.

One thing that is constant in human affairs is the urge to
attribute value to them. We call this morality. It has been a con-
spicuous fact of modern life, as it is lived and as it is written

about in books, that morality has ceased to be conventional, it has ceased to be 'Natural'. Those growing-pains of the last chapter were caused by the attempt by one novelist to substitute a Romantic morality, a morality of the Human Condition, for a morality of Nature; and the decision of the other to draw back at the line where impulse issues in moral action. Ursula Brangwen's dissatisfaction with Skrebensky in *The Rainbow* takes place at a level far below moral formulation, but her decision to break with him is a moral decision and Lawrence's opinion about it is a moral opinion. Augustine's love for Mitzi in *The Fox in the Attic*, on the contrary, has no moral significance, and Richard Hughes does not foist one on to it. What interests us about Augustine is the way an impulse forms itself and becomes self-aware, not at all how it is valued. Both Lawrence and Hughes are Romantic writers. But just as Bennett transcended the realistic preoccupations he started out with, so Hughes transcends his own Romantic preoccupations. He does not imprison himself in an idosyncratic morality of the Human Condition, because he takes over the Romantic concern with growth and development and accepts it as something to be contemplated from a position far outsides its own uncertainties and dogmatic assertions. It is neither vicariously experienced nor morally valued. Lawrence was much more impetuous. He was not willing merely to contemplate. He had to grow painfully into a new moral health which he felt could be achieved only by experiment, assertion and then again assertion. Whether he escaped from or into a prison is something each of his readers will decide for himself. I believe that the door finally closed on him about half-way through *The Rainbow* and that the only freedom he enjoyed after that time was the freedom of some of his tales and travel books. In their different ways, however, the novels of Hughes and Lawrence are individual responses to a common situation, and that situation was created by Romanticism.

I have been arguing that the pictures we have in *The Fox in the Attic*, of Otto in his study and Tascha on the Odeonsplatz, refute the charge of special pleading, of being put into the service of an author's intentions which transparently and systematically reach beyond them; just as Bennett's pictures of Constance in the Baines draper's shop and Sophia at Frensham's refute the charge of disinterested and unconcerned demonstration. In their different ways, Bennett and Hughes give up their 'interests' to Nature, though I do not think their success can be attributed entirely to this fact. Is it possible, though, to get back to Nature from the traps of realism or late Romanticism, not as Bennett and Hughes have done, but in a morally responsible and responsive manner? If it is possible, what language shall the novelist use to describe what he finds on his way there and, to be optimistic, when he arrives?

Iris Murdoch has come close to evolving such a language. By this I do not mean that in her novels we find more satisfactory descriptions of 'what is constant in human types' than elsewhere in contemporary English literature – both V. S. Naipaul and Brian Moore have written novels of incomparably greater human 'density' than Miss Murdoch has ever done. What I mean is that when we read her novels we are persuaded into making use of a more sophisticated vocabulary to understand what is, morally, 'going on' in them. Behind the vocabulary there exists a range of concepts far wider than the one most of us have at our disposal when we try to understand what is involved in the common occurrences of life – in so far as those occurrences attract our moral attention. This is because Iris Murdoch insists that human behaviour, in its moral aspect, is more complex and more substantial than our inherited presuppositions about it have led us to believe. We have to rediscover the richness of the human personality which has been lost during two centuries of Romanticism, when the 'Human Condition' replaced 'Nature' as a basis for understanding what man is and how his acts are to be described.

In our own time Romanticism has taken two different forms, which are discussed in Iris Murdoch's essay 'Against Dryness'. In this country, she argues, linguistic analysis has delivered to us a picture of man which is described most lucidly in Stuart Hampshire's *Thought and Action*. Hampshire takes the view that man is 'rational and totally free except in so far as, in the most ordinary law court and commonsensical sense, his degree of self-awareness may vary':

He is morally speaking monarch of all he surveys and totally responsible for his actions. Nothing transcends him. His moral language is a practical pointer, the instrument of his choices, the indication of his preferences. His inner life is resolved into

his acts and choices, and his beliefs, which are also acts, since
a belief can only be identified through its expression. His moral
arguments are references to empirical facts backed up by decisions. The only moral word which he requires is 'good' (or
'right'), the word which expresses decision. His rationality
expresses itself in awareness of the facts, whether about the
world or about himself. The virtue which is fundamental to
him is sincerity.

In France this description is replaced by that of the existentialists,
in which:

Again the individual is pictured as solitary and totally free.
There is no transcendent reality, there are no degrees of freedom. On the one hand there is the mass of psychological desires
and social habits and prejudices, on the other hand there is the
will. . . . Again the only real virtue is sincerity.

The result in both countries is that:

We have suffered a general loss of concepts, the loss of a moral
and political vocabulary. We no longer use a spread-out substantial picture of the manifold virtues of man and society. We
no longer see man against a background of values, of realities,
which transcend him. We picture man as a brave, naked will
surrounded by an easily comprehended empirical world. For the
hard idea of truth we have substituted a facile idea of suavity.
What we have never had, of course, is a satisfactory Liberal
theory personality, a theory of man as free and separate and
related to a rich and complicated world from which, as a moral
being, he has much to learn. We have bought the Liberal
theory as it stands, because we have wished to encourage people
to think of themselves as free, at the cost of surrendering the
background.

The 'spread-out substantial picture' is the picture 'Nature', in
Bayley's words, delivered. The lack of it has been disastrous for
the twentieth-century novel. Without 'a background of values, of
realities which transcend him', the writer discovers that there are
only two kinds of novel he can write, what Iris Murdoch calls
the 'journalistic' and the 'crystalline'. Most modern English
novels do seem to fit into one of these two categories. I want to

look at the work of one, to my mind, interesting example of each, to test Iris Murdoch's judgement against the evidence of the novels.

A 'journalistic' novel is 'a large shapeless quasi-documentary object, the degenerate descendant of the nineteenth-century novel telling, with pale conventional characters, some straightforward story enlivened with empirical fact'. A number of candidates suggest themselves as examples of this category. C. P. Snow's *Strangers and Brothers*, Anthony Powell's *The Music of Time*, Angus Wilson's *The Middle Age of Mrs Eliot*, each in its different way a descendant of the nineteenth-century novel, each replete with conventional characters, each enlivened with empirical fact – though readers will differ in their views about the degree of straightforwardness in Anthony Powell's books. I chose *The Beginners*, by Dan Jacobson, because it is a book which does try to evolve a 'Liberal theory of personality' and it does try to use a 'spread-out substantial picture of the manifold virtues of man and society'. In the end I think it fails. The moral and political vocabulary is unsatisfactory and the conventional manner of representing the world is inadequate. The characters themselves are aware of what they lack – transcendent reality, a reality which is 'given', and within which they can realise their public and private selves.

> Even the older characters lack confidence in themselves: as we imagine people might have been confident when they believed in God, for example. Or when they believed the world was a place which changed slowly, if it changed at all. Or when everybody thought he'd been given a self or a soul which he could learn to know and struggle to improve. . . . We know that that old self no longer exists. It's dead. . . . We're simply the first, among the first, to recognise what has happened.

Jacobson endeavours to recognise what has happened, along with his characters, and then to use his recognition to give them back themselves – not the old selves of the believers, but the new selves of the Liberal South African Jews who populate the pages of his novel. One of these, Malcolm Begbie, is himself a novelist. He agrees with a university colleague that 'if you want to read about present-day South Africa the only place you can do it is in the nineteenth-century novel'. After all, they have the space, the landowners, the peasantry, the intellectuals. 'All we need', says Joel, the principal character, 'are the Gogols and the Turgenevs.' It is Jacobson's own sentiment. After all, looking back to his earlier work, isn't there something of Gogol in the humour of the excellent *Price of Diamonds*? And don't the two well-meaning but incompetent students who form the inner plot of *A Dance in the Sun* have something in common with Turgenev's passive observers – Shubin and Bersenyev in *On the Eve*, or even Arkady in *Fathers and Children*? *The Beginners*, though, is on an altogether larger scale than any of these. Jacobson is aiming for a Tolstoyan breadth and movement, what Christopher Ricks, in a glowing review of the book, called the ability to give us 'profound access' to a great many characters. I disagree with Ricks that Jacobson succeeds in his grand ambition, basically because Jacobson's Romantic disengagement from habit, his exploratory and deeply personal investigation of his characters, prevents him from being at ease with them, or, as Bayley would put it, from taking them sufficiently for granted.

What Ricks admires most about *The Beginners* is its populousness. The 'medium' in which character discloses itself – family, class, race, nation, etc. – is vividly evoked. In this respect it has something in common with what the Victorians accomplished, the virtues I myself find most vividly apparently in Naipaul's *A House for Mr. Biswas*. But Jacobson's achievement is all the more remarkable because of the handicap the society he writes about imposes on him. The medium which was so stable and unproblematical for Victorians has 'widened' and 'dissipated' in the twentieth century: 'where for George Eliot the society of *Middlemarch* was a web, for "the beginners" there are so many webs: life is nomadic, restless, peremptory, bored, cosmopolitan'. Relationships in the contemporary situation must be different. They will be much shorter-lived and more intense, 'fiercely influential for all their transitoriness'. They will show 'an understanding of the sporadic and the piecemeal'. Jacobson's strength lies in his ability to accept this change and to represent in his fiction the density as well as the uncertainty of these unsettled and oblique relationships. Just as the Glickman family breaks up, re-knits, scatters and re-forms itself at different times and in different places, so its separate members lose and rediscover themselves. Sometimes these actions are dramatic and final. More often they repeat themselves over and over again. Each part of the family is a sort of Levin or Pierre, searching for a significance in his life, finding and losing provisional orders and temporary arrangements. Rachel, the conventional daughter, settles for the husk of an ordered existence with a man whose ambitions she has constrained and who leads her a life of quiet misery and boredom. David begins as a rebel and ends as an Orthodox Jew in Israel. Joel lives out his author's own search into the possibilities of living. At the end of the novel 'His own life, his own actions, still seemed to him haphazard and disconnected, entirely accidental . . . he was as far as ever from knowing with any certainty what he was living for'. Joel's progress through *The Beginners* brings us most directly into contact with his author's attitude towards the world's demands and the ways men rise to meet them. It also exposes certain weaknesses in Jacobson's method which are intimately related to his way of looking at the world.

A little more than half-way through *The Beginners*, Joel reflects on the meeting he has had with his cousin Yitzchak. Yitzchak has just been telling the story of his escape from the Germans in Lithuania during the war. Joel is horrified, and amazed that at the end of his experiences Yitzchak wants nothing more than a good job, a car, 'some order and privacy in his life'. That is what the holocaust has taught him. Joel is trying to break out of privacy and limitation. Yitzchak is trying to break in. Even so, Joel and his cousin have one important thing in common. They are both beginners: 'The human capacity to lose and suffer seemed to be equalled only by the capacity to begin all over again the search for what had been lost in suffering, torn away, blown away, turned to smoke and ashes.' The difference between them is that Joel is searching not for 'what had been lost' but for something he never had – the certainty his brother David has discovered, but without the external sanction of a conventional religious faith. It is in this sense that he is like Levin in *Anna Karenina*. He is also like Mr Biswas, in his passage through a never-ending sequence of expectations and disappointments. This passage, for example, could just as well describe Mr Biswas at one of many stages in his later life:

Twenty-seven! It seemed an immense age to him. And the worst of it was that as he grew older the pace of time appeared to

increase, each year went by faster than the one before. Instead
of time somehow accumulating, thickening, as he had imagined
it would, so that it could be moulded into firm, known shapes
which would be his life, time was more elusive than ever, it
escaped any grasping, it left him dissatisfied and empty-
handed. . . .

Later 'he felt that his own past, all that had gone before, was as
unknowable to him as what he was going to do or become; the
present was always ceaselessly altering the past, making another
unexpected order or disorder out of it. And so it would be, until
the end.'

But to say this of a character, or have a character say it of
himself, is not enough. That sequence of expectations and disappointments, of compromises and self-deceptions, must be embodied throughout in the character and the medium he moves in.
Densely populated as *The Beginners* is, is it true to say that
Jacobson has succeeded in convincing his readers of the inter-
relatedness of human lives, in providing for us the 'profound
access' to his characters that Ricks says is the prerogative of
genius? I think not, or rarely. Unfortunately, according to Ricks,
I have no way of proving it, because 'of all the means in which
such a novel must be effective, a sense of living characters is at
once the most important and the most unamenable to argument. If you don't find the characters alive, it is hard to see to
what substantiation we could appeal.' It is very difficult, as we
found Dickens admitting to himself,[1] to see to what substantiation
we can appeal. But in the present circumstance, does not Ricks
himself hint at what is wrong when he says of Joel that he is
'more speculation than achievement, more an anxiety about what
he will become than a being somebody?' A 'being somebody'
is precisely what the most satisfying fictional characters are. It is
the greatest achievement of a novelist to have created such a
character. There are, of course, degrees of success, and Joel
Glickman is not a completely lifeless character. But something has
got between Jacobson's understanding of Joel, his sense of Joel's
character, and his ability to realise it substantially in the novel.
I believe that what has done this is the author's Romantic
commitment to consciousness, and to the representation of the

---

[1] See above, p. 27

machinery of consciousness. This is inseparable from his ambition, but where it is not transcended it must make of that ambition something impossible to satisfy.

Jacobson's failure has to do with the medium in which his characters are compelled to exist, and which is described for us by Malcolm Begbie and his friend Swanpoel near the end of the novel. They are discussing the position of modern novelists as 'guardians of what is essentially private in human experience'. For Begbie the most important feature of the cosmopolitanism which counts for so much of the texture of modern living is an uncompromising will to individuality. He has already commented upon the uniform process of production, consumption and disposal in which most people want to be absorbed. Individual consciousness is a 'burden' they will be glad to be rid of. Swanpoel disagrees with him. It is a fact that 'the process of process' is taking over, 'but the result is that we're all being forced into our own individuality more than people have ever been before; intolerably so'. Therefore our responses to the world are unprecedently relative: 'No absolutes for each of us outside our own feelings; no scale of time even imaginable outside the passing moments of the process.' People are faced with a choice between being 'taken over' by the process or taking the risk of working with it without sinking into it. To take the first choice is to opt for sheer mindlessness, the status of being nothing more than a cog in the social machine. To take the second is to opt for a life of vigilant effort and intellectual strain. The context of living no longer affords people the opportunity of taking the world at its face value and, by doing so, extending the self without undue self-preoccupation and self-consciousness.

Joel is the person who, more than anybody else in *The Beginners*, has taken the risk, has made the second, more difficult choice. Most of the other characters lose their sense of themselves as individuals whose experience is 'essentially private' in a way that Joel does not. 'Everybody is a self to himself', he says, in one of his most pompous moments, and he is right. But it is the business of the novel to convince us that he is right, not by insisting on the words but by attending to the facts, the appearances. What are these selves like, as they flounder in the processes of cosmopolitan twentieth-century life? The burden of proof, indeed of evidence, is too great for Jacobson to bear. The more his characters insist on the facts of differentiation, of the persistence of the self, the more they are inclined to disappear behind the effort their insistence has cost them.

Jacobson's problem in *The Beginners* is not unusual. It is the problem all 'intellectual' novelists have to confront, aggravated in his case by the particular conclusions his intelligence has delivered to him. The task of the modern novelist is to return to people a sense of self and consciousness as 'individual affairs'. Jacobson tries to do this by presenting characters struggling with the burden of their own self-awareness and privacy. But the tactics he uses are misconceived. In Levin, Tolstoy got away with a profound and extensive study of self-conscious intellectuality acquiring an understanding of its potential and its limitations. But Levin is a rare achievement. Too little of Joel's intellectual progress is seen to connect, as Levin's is seen to, with his straightforward experience of the world. To take an example, it is difficult to see what Joel was hoping to achieve by taking a walk on the Israeli border with Jordan immediately before he is shot down. His compulsion to take the walk might follow comprehensibly from what we have been *told* is his state of mind at the time, but his state of mind is such a ghostly thing; and going for a senseless walk in dangerous country is so decisively real. The link between the two different kinds of awareness is not established, as it is, for example, in Conrad's lonely and impulsive heroes – Lord Jim before the jump from the *Patna*, Decoud on the Great Isabel in *Nostromo*. Malcolm Begbie is another problem. He is a writer and a theorist, and he is the husband of another important character in the book. But neither of these Begbies has much connection with the other. They do not appear to be parts of a continuous and developing personality. The space between a character formulating ideas about the world, and the same character experiencing the world prior to formulating ideas about it, is infinite. The characters themselves are often embarrassed by the separate roles they have to play. They are uncomfortably aware that they are 'proselytising' or adopting ironic, defensive 'attitudes' towards their fellow-characters and, one suspects, the reader.

Ideas grow out of and turn back into conduct and experience. Jacobson knows this, but he has great difficulty representing it. That is why Joel is 'more an anxiety about what he will become than a being somebody'. Jacobson fails to establish a firm connection between ideas and lives. Also, he fails to convey the impression of life as it is lived at a non-intellectual level. This is important because it tends to diminish the reality of conventionally unambitious characters. Take Joel's sister Rachel. Her lack of reality contrasts strongly with its presence in Mr Biswas's Shama. Shama is another thoroughly conventional character. Nevertheless, at the end of Naipaul's novel we discover that she has acquired an importance out of all proportion to what we might have expected, given the impression she has made on us in most of the several scenes in which she has been present. In *The Beginners*, scenes like those in which Rachel, as a schoolgirl, pokes fun at Jewish rituals and the war, make their point, and they connect logically with later incidents she is involved in: the party where she makes a big fuss over a Nazi armband Joel has brought back from Italy, for example. But they have the air of demonstrations rather than the conviction of facts arising naturally out of the situation.

There are other ways characters fail to convince us of their reality. One of them is the discrepancy we often sense between the impression a person is said to make on other people and the impression he makes on us. The status Natalie enjoys in the Zionist group at the *hachsharah* is a good example. We are told she is bored with intellectual discussions and can be mutinous about having to do work she doesn't want to do. Even so, her position in the group is 'a special one'. She is regarded by the others as 'their touchstone, their flagbearer, almost as their saint, as if she had given up more, and would never hesitate to give up more than anyone else, to become and remain a member of the group'. Jacobson tells us that the way this happened was 'curious' – 'in some way'. Those four words are not enough to account for, let alone give body to, the mystery. When Natalie defects (in the end she settles in Rhodesia), we do not experience the mixture of surprise and self-correction that seems to be expected.

Another flaw in the method is Jacobson's tendency to let reportage get the better of his novelist's discretion. Early in *The Beginners*, Jacobus, one of the Glickmans' Negro workers, leaves his reading lesson, runs into the centre of the town, and catches 'one of the "non-white" trains to the Observatory'. Later Joel has to wait for an hour at a bus-stop outside the *kibbutz* where he is working in Israel: 'in the meantime almost everyone at the

stop begged frantically for a lift from every vehicle that passed
by – begging in a desperate, beseeching, bent-kneed manner, with
both hands cupped and dangling, that Joel had seen in no other
country'. Both incidents tell us something about the transport
system and, through it, the social structure of a country. They
also, by virtue of the fact that they do this, set the characters in
them at a distance from their own experience. Jacobus would
never have noticed it was a 'non-white' bus he had caught: it
would have been second nature to him. Joel knows by this time
what goes on at an Israeli bus-stop. In each case the author is
putting what he supposes is the reader's demand for information
before a credible record of his character's responses to what happens. The presence of the characters is subordinated to the facts
the novelist believes it is his duty to communicate. The reality
of what happens is correspondingly diminished.

These are some of the minor errors of tact and emphasis. All
of them spring from Jacobson's failure to connect the theoretical
discoveries the characters make with the detail of the lives from
which they should be seen to grow. They enter the substance of
the novel as so many barriers erected around the pull and push
of living that is supposed to be its subject. When Joel visits his
mother- and father-in-law for the first time and sees how oddly
his wife behaves in their presence, he muses to himself: 'What
different people we were – not merely from one another but from
ourselves at different times.' So we are, and so we should be
represented in fiction. But to do this the novelist needs to move
beyond the position Joel occupies at the end of *The Beginners*.
My feeling is that Jacobson has not done so, and that he has
reconciled himself to not doing so. In Iris Murdoch's terms, the
author has encouraged both himself and his principal characters
'to think of themselves as free'. They exercise this freedom, with
much anxiety, care and circumspection, at the expense of that
'background of values, of realities, which transcends them' to
which she attaches so much importance. They seem to understand
this, and often they regret it. Nevertheless, the writer's sincerity
commits them to being as they are represented in *The Beginners*.
They are the documentary inhabitants of a Romantic novel. The
extremity of their creator's vision, its commitment and its intellectuality, place the Tolstoyan spaciousness and physicality, which
he would have liked to have emulated, far outside his range.

Iris Murdoch's equally depressing alternative to the 'journalistic' novel is the 'crystalline'. This is 'a small quasi-allegorical
object portraying the human condition and not containing "characters" in the nineteenth-century sense'. Again, the names of
several candidates suggest themselves. Most of the novels of
Robbe-Grillet that I considered in Chapter 3 would qualify, or
in this country novels like *Travelling People* or *Trawl* by B. S.
Johnson. I have chosen Muriel Spark's *The Mandelbaum Gate*
because it offers interesting contrasts with *The Beginners* and
because it is one of the more intelligent varieties of those not
so uncommon 'crystalline' novels which are very much aware
of the fact that 'crystalline' is what they are. Writing about
Robbe-Grillet, I emphasised the way his novels offer themselves
as irresponsible products of the writer's imagination, complex fabrications that are built out of the writer's recognition that this is
the most important thing about them – that they are no more and
no less than fabrications, fictions. In their witty and astringent
way, Muriel Spark's novels tend to do the same thing. They are
often to be found commenting on their own dangerous artificiality. Most of them contain at least one novelist, whose awareness of
the mischievous role he is playing varies from book to book. In
The Ballad of Peckham Rye he is visibly the agent of a Satanic
plot against the other characters. One of his shoulders is higher
than the other and he has bumps on his head where the horns
have been. Usually, though, the novelists and plotters of Mrs
Spark's novels are at a further remove from their evil progenitor.
Often they are quite unaware of the power they exercise.

The short stories offer numerous examples of such novelists and
novelists *manqués*. One thinks of Needle, in 'The Portobello
Road', exercising in death the deplorable but fascinating talent
she failed to exercise satisfactorily in life. 'When I fail again and
again to reproduce life in some satisfactory and perfect form,
I was the more imprisoned, for all my carefree living, within my
craving for this satisfaction.' Now, as a ghost, she is able to
determine the life (and death) of the man who killed her, in a
way she could never do, even to the characters of her fictions,
when she was a corporeal creature. George, her friend and murderer, has become simply a character in a living novel. Or take
the nurse in 'A Curtain Blown by the Breeze'. She and her friends
have transformed the absurd Mrs van der Merwe into a 'character'

in real life. Her presumption in doing this rebounds on her when Mrs van der Merwe's new character turns out to be so effectively composed as to disrupt violently the lives of those who created it. There are many other examples of irresponsible novelists, wantonly interfering with the lives of those around them as if they were characters in their books. Ralph Mercer in 'The Go-Away Bird' is probably the most closely observed, in spite of his late arrival in this excellent long story. But at the same time as Mrs Spark acknowledges the dangers of being this kind of novelist, she is almost hypnotically drawn to write similar novels of her own. The fact that they are *about* what they *are* offers a sort of loophole, the same sort of loophole Robbe-Grillet produced when he framed his story of the soldier and the brown-paper parcel with the description of the attic room in *Dans le labyrinthe*.

The ideal novel of this kind would be like the body of the seraph in 'The Seraph and the Zambesi'. The most noticeable thing about this, we are told, is its constancy. When the teller of the tale moves towards it (it has appeared on the stage where a nativity play is about to be enacted), no change is observed in its size. It does not conform to the laws of perspective. Unlike other forms of life 'it had a completed look. No part was undergoing a process; the outline lacked the signs of confusion and ferment which are commonly the sign of living things, and this was also the principle of its beauty.' At least a part of the novelist's business, Mrs Spark would agree, is to respect and to reproduce those 'signs of confusion and ferment which are commonly the sign of living things'. At the same time I think she would also agree that she has a great respect and admiration for what is 'complete', for what is saved from the process. But nothing is saved from the process except as God sees it, and Mrs Spark (unlike Flaubert or Joyce) has too much respect for God to feel comfortable about usurping his position and creating a world which has the appearance of being viewed *sub specie aeternatis*. She is a creature in God's world, not a rival for his power. Furthermore, the Counter-Reformation Catholicism she subscribes to does not make it possible for her to see the world as a book which she is at liberty to reproduce in her own books, sharing in God's power whilst taking away from him no particle of it.[1] None of this,

---

[1] See my comments on Josipovici above, pp. 13 ff.

however, detracts from the beauty of the seraph. It is a dangerous beast. It burns down the building in which the play was to be performed. But, having been seen and admired, it is in danger of being emulated. Mrs Spark recognises the danger. I am not sure how far she avoids it.

Her first novel, *The Comforters*, demonstrates the sharpness of her recognition. Its heroine, Caroline Rose, is uncomfortably aware that she is being written about in a novel. Late one evening she hears a typewriter clicking somewhere outside her room, and several voices (or is it one voice imitating several voices?) telling a story about what is happening to her. 'I think it is one person', she says. 'It uses a typewriter. It uses the past tense. It's exactly as if someone were watching closely, able to read my thoughts; it's as if the person was waiting to pounce on some insignificant thought or action, in order to make it signify in a strange distorted way.'

There are two ways of interpreting Caroline's dilemma. One of these is suggested by the complementary dilemma of her old schoolfriend Eleanor Hogarth, whose whole life has been transformed, by herself, into an 'act' or 'performance' – rather like Mrs van der Merwe's in 'A Curtain Blown by the Breeze', though without external assistance. Eleanor has been for so long in the habit of totally submerging herself in whatever role she is playing that she is in danger of succumbing altogether to a personality that is not her own. Or rather 'it was impossible to distinguish between Eleanor and the personality which possessed her . . . as well try to distinguish between the sea and the water in it'. To watch her was therefore like watching doom: 'As a child Caroline, pulling a face, had been warned, "If you keep doing that it will stick one day." She felt, looking at Eleanor, that this was actually happening to the woman. Her assumed personalities were beginning to cling; soon one of them would stick, grotesque and ineradicable.' This is a plausible and elegantly phrased observation about people, and Eleanor does have in common with many of Mrs Spark's characters this gruesome conflation of real and rhetorical selves. The spritely caricatures which emerge from such a conflation populate her novels and short stories as they do also, though I think less successfully, those of Angus Wilson. Both writers are brilliant mimics, somewhat shrill and caustic voices at play. Wilson has tried to 'place' the

skill which produces that mimicry in his portrait of Margaret
Matthews, the short-story writer of *No Laughing Matter*, just as
Mrs Spark has done in the teasing play with levels of reality in
this novel. However, Caroline Rose does not really have much in
common with Eleanor. The level of reality on which each of them
exists does not, in the end, allow any comparison to be made.
For Caroline's knowledge of what she is affects what she is as
Eleanor's importance cannot do. Being a character in a novel,
Caroline aspires to influence the role she is playing, to have a say
in the character she is about to become. She cares about her
destiny, and refuses to identify it with the *peripeteia* of an artificial plot. She intends to stand aside from this 'and see if the
novel has any real form'. We might be puzzled about this dis-
tinction between the alternative structures of the novel if we
did not remember two things about Mrs Spark and her character:
both of them are theoreticians of the novel; and also both of
them are Catholics.

We are persuaded to attribute more importance to a second
way of interpreting Caroline's dilemma, not in the psychological
terms suggested by the comparison with Eleanor Hogarth, but in
terms which are first of all aesthetic, and eventually theological.
Frank Kermode, writing about *The Bachelors* in the *New Statesman*, quoted the crucial passage I have just quoted about the
distinction between an artificial plot and a real form; and went
on to point out that, given the complications of the plot, the
improbabilities, the writer's interference, it is difficult to see how
the novel can say anything true or interesting. At any rate, he
says, that is what Mrs Spark seems to be saying. Difficult, but
not impossible. Because 'even among the falsities of a novel, as
among the shapelessness of ordinary life, truth figures; and it does
so because the imagination, in so far as it is good, is bound by
categories which stand in relationship to absolute truth'. He
goes on to show how these categories manifest themselves in the
'atavism' of her plots. Actions seem to fall into a pattern or
patterns, suggesting the presence of a designing hand that un-
covers, behind the artifice of the plot, a picture of the truth,
which the plot alone is incapable of bodying forth. The point
Kermode is making here is a good one, and is unaffected by the
ambiguities which his approach to fictions generally imposes on
him. I want to proceed to investigate the effect of Mrs Spark's

beliefs, about the relation between truth and fiction, on *The Mandelbaum Gate*, her longest and most substantial novel to date.

The Mandelbaum Gate is a very complex novel, subtle in its plotting, deft in its control of the point of view and the time-shifts, and tantalising in its arrangement of detail. I have already said that it offers interesting contrasts with *The Beginners* – in its use of an exotic setting, its incorporation of political and ideo-logical material, and the central position occupied in it by some-one (Joel Glickman in *The Beginners*, Barbara Vaughan here) who is undergoing a crisis of identity, a discovery of the self. I hope I shall not be accused of prevaricating when I say that, in spite of these obvious points of comparison, *The Mandelbaum Gate* does not read much like *The Beginners*. Instead it reminds me of nothing so much as another, earlier novel with an exotic setting, written as much out of the hope that is proper to unbelief as this is written out of the hope that is proper to belief. I refer to E. M. Forster's *A Passage to India*. Freddy Hamilton is a Catholic novelist's version of the humanist Forster's Mr Fielding. Barbara Vaughan is her Adela Quested. Abdul and Suzi Ramdez share some of the character traits and situations of Aziz – though here the differences between the two novelists' beliefs render the comparison, on its own, a little far-fetched. In fact, the mixture of understanding and misunderstanding between Fielding and Aziz is better reproduced in the friendship between Freddy and Alexandros, the antique dealer, in *The Mandelbaum Gate*. But in both novels an expedition to a strange place occupies a crucial position in the plot, and in both cases a somewhat distant relation-ship between two members of the English community in a foreign country creates a disturbance which has a visible and disruptive effect on the social groups from which they have, temporarily, withdrawn themselves.

I believe we can take the comparison further than this. Both novels are highly patterned and carefully constructed in order to bring to the reader's attention very subtle and suggestive links betwen one block of narrative and another. For instance, the attitude to wasps of several of the characters in *A Passage to India* might be compared with the attitude to wild flowers of several of the characters of *The Mandelbaum Gate*. The thematic link between Freddy's burning of his letters to England and of the decoded transcript of another letter, from an English diplomat's wife to the Egyptian authorities, has its analogies in *A Passage to India*. So does the play with, not the image of an idea, but its structure in the design of parallel incidents. In *A Passage to India*, the confusions of the 'Temple' scenes reflect intriguingly on one another and on the earlier confusions of the main action of the novel. In *The Mandelbaum Gate*, important aspects of the drama turn on mysterious connections that are established between knowing and not knowing. Both novels concern themselves with confusions or muddles of one sort or another, and both try to extract a significant truth about life from them. In *The Mandelbaum Gate* the confusion arises, in large part, from the establishment of those connections between knowing and not knowing that I have just mentioned. I should like to turn now to the forms they take in the detail of the novel.

When Barbara Vaughan's vindictive and interfering friend Miss Rickson tries to prevent her from marrying the non-Catholic divorcee she loves, she fakes a birth certificate (in fact a photocopy of a birth certificate). But owing to an oversight the certificate turns out to be just what Barbara requires because in a roundabout way, from a Catholic point of view, it invalidates her future husband's previous marriage. Miss Rickson, in later life, is in the habit of asking Catholic priests what is the status of a Catholic marriage based on evidence which both parties to it believed to be true, but which in reality was faked. She receives the reply that 'if both parties remain in ignorance and the Church is satisfied, then it's a valid marriage'. But we know that Barbara will marry her divorcee anyway, and that she has a shrewd idea that, Miss Rickson being what she is, the certificate might well not be what it claims to be. Her position is similar to that of Suzi Ramdez when she watches Freddy Hamilton burn the decoded message. He tells her that what he has burned is a poem dedicated to her and recites it from memory. She recognises that what he has recited is a translation from Horace (Suzi is what Bertie Wooster would call a 'brainy bird') and he counters her recognition with a flattering explanation. Eventually Suzi agrees to know and not to know what was really written on the paper, just as Barbara agrees to know and not to know that the birth certificate is a forgery. Both are fictions that are truer, given the positions they occupy in the total pattern of activity in the novel, than the facts they have been made to replace. They answer to a higher truth, the truth of 'real form', as distinct from the lesser truth of the 'artificial plot'. So the plot is adapted to the form and the characters are delivered into their true selves. These selves will not be constrained by the accidental presence of contingent events. Instead the events are often miraculously made to subserve the requirements of the selves.

The selves in question belong to Barbara Vaughan and Freddy Hamilton. But they are not their common-or-garden selves. At the beginning of the novel both Barbara and Freddy are trapped in conventional images of themselves: Barbara with her torments of conscience over whether or not she will marry her archaeologist; Freddy with his routine work at the embassy, his routine visits to his friends in Jordan and his routine letters to his mother and her lady companion at home. But neither of these conventional selves is real. Each is built on a foundation of deceit which makes over reality into a very much more sober and secure condition than it really is. Barbara's love for her archaeologist is muffled by the deadly veneer of respectability she presents both to herself and to other people. Freddy's secure little office harbours at least two spies; his real friend in Jordan is Alexandros, who expands his horizons, not the Cartwrights who contract them; and the domestic tiff he envisages between his mother and her lady companion is in fact the prologue to a bloody murder. Until they meet in Jordan, Freddy and Barbara present to each other their conventional selves – the dull diplomatist, the Jewish–Catholic schizophrenic. The danger to which Barbara's presence in Jordan exposes them miraculously releases them into their true selves, and the complicated patterns of the plot, together with Mrs Spark's elliptical manner of unfolding it, support this sense of release and augmented life. The background of pilgrimage across the symbolic stations of Christ's teachings and sufferings on earth enforces the suggestion that what Barbara, at any rate, has undergone is a transfiguration, a release into identity made possible by Freddy's encouragement for her to 'be a sport'. Like Freddy's rhymes in his letter to a friend at All Souls, her actions are 'disinterested and dutiful'. 'It was possible to do things for their own sake, not only possible but sometimes necessary for the affirmation of one's personal identity.' Freddy's liberation is most vividly caught in the description of his dinner with Alexandros, when he is 'perfectly at ease with his own self-awareness' which 'harmonised at the back of his mind with the immediate subject of their conversation' (i.e. Barbara). But in his case it doesn't last. Back in the Israeli sector of Jerusalem, his mind blots out the events of the past two or three days. Gradually the memory of them returns, and with it the practical effects associated with the arrest of his colleague Gardner. Like Miss Pinkerton's apocalypse in the story of that name, the adventure with Barbara is an aberration that has important consequences. The pilgrimage may have been a sort of game, a fiction made substantial by the unaccountable fact of Freddy's and Barbara's presence in it, but an odd assortment of truths have been unearthed during the time it was played out. 'With God all things are possible', Barbara reflects. ' "And", she thought, "we must all think in these vague terms: with God all things are possible; because the only possibilities we ever seem to be able to envisage in a precise manner are disastrous events; and we fear both vaguely and specifically, and I have myself too long laid plans against eventualities." '

A dramatic contrast with the fiction, the pilgrimage that is undertaken by the principal characters, is provided by Mrs Spark's description of the Eichmann trial. The man in the glass box occupies the centre of the novel. Barbara had attended the trial, briefly, before her visit to Jordan. She entered the court during a 'dull phase' of the proceedings which, in spite of its 'dullness', was in fact 'the desperate heart of the trial'. What Barbara notices is the contrast between 'the dead mechanical tick' of the discourse and the living agony of its subject. The sensation it gives her is 'the one that the anti-novelists induce'. 'She thought, repetition, boredom, despair, going nowhere for nothing, all of which conditions are enclosed in a tight, unbreakable statement of the times at hand.' Eichmann himself does not appear to be answering for his own life, 'but for an imperative deity named Bureau IV–3–4, of whom he was the High Priest'. What happens in the court, the facts of the massacres expressed with unimpeachable statistical accuracy, gives no idea of the truth it is the business of the court to establish. The trial fails to represent the truth to anybody but a lawyer's satisfaction because it has no plot. This is to say that the meaning of the events it is concerned with fails to emerge from the evidence. Every claim, every counter-claim, made at the Eichmann trial is tested and weighed in a scales of justice. Slowly and surely, what is fact is sifted from what is probability, what is possibility, and what is mere fiction. But as the amount of verifiable and verified fact grows larger, the truth of the situation the facts have to do with grows less. Barbara learns more about the truth of her life through the confusions and uncertainties of her pilgrimage among the holy places of Jordan than she or anyone else learns about Eichmann and the death camps through the laboriously established certainties of the trial. The truth has no plot and it has no form. Indeed, without a plot it cannot have a form, though a form is not the same thing as a plot. It is at this point that I come up against some awkward obstacles to my response to Mrs Spark's novel. Unlike the Eichmann trial, *The Mandelbaum Gate* has a plot which assembles the events of several narratives in such a way as to create from them a significance which, though both the principal characters acknowledge it to be artificial, nevertheless they feel to be real in a more important sense. It sets their lives in order, an order which is reproduced in the patterning of events in the novel we read. But Mrs Spark goes further than this. By attaching the significance she does to the mysterious quality of 'form' (I continue to use the word she used in *The Comforters*) as something which arises out of plot but which has a higher status than plot, she provokes a correspondence between plots and those real and subsistent truths of which they are held to be the fictional analogues.

Not far from the end of the novel, Barbara explains to Suzi Ramdez what I take to be Mrs Spark's own point of view:

> . . . either religious faith penetrates everything in life or it doesn't. There are some experiences that seem to make nonsense of all separations of sacred from profane – they seem childish. Either the whole of life is unified under God or everything falls apart. . . . . She was thinking of the Eichmann trial, and was aware that there were other events too which had rolled away the stone that revealed an empty hole in the earth, that led to a bottomless pit. So that people drew back quickly and looked elsewhere for reality, and found it, and made decisions in the way that she had decided to get married anyway.

What seems to be suggested here is a system of symbolic correspondences between sacred truth and profane facts. Even where the facts are wanting, the truth must subsist. From a certain point of view the facts can be adapted to the patterns of truth – papers burnt, marriage certificates forged – and the duplicities of men may be recognised as manifestations of the harmonising power of God. Kermode's comment on all of Mrs Spark's novels is peculiarly suited to this one. 'Such novels', he writes, 'assume the reader's sympathetic participation in muddle, they assume a reality unaware that it conceals patterns of truth. But when an imagination (*naturaliter christiana*) makes fictions it imposes patterns, and the patterns are figures of the truth.' So the imagination penetrates the confusion of reality and extracts from it patterns of truth which happen to be vouched for by the Catholic faith to which this novelist has committed herself. The pattern in the confusion mysteriously reflects the transcendent pattern established outside it by God. The non-Catholic reader is left with a strange story oddly and fortuitously falling into a pattern he knows the novelist is ultimately responsible for. But for the Catholic reader it is very much more. It is a statement of truth built into the shape of the fiction, but not dependent on the fiction for its reality. This makes it difficult for me to understand what Kermode means when he continues with the statement that 'none of it would matter to the pagan were it not for the admirable power with which all the elements are fused into the shapes of self-evident truth'. Self-evident coherence and consistency in the patterning of the narrative, yes. But self-evident truth in the design of the fiction I should have thought was more than a pagan could be expected to acknowledge. Mrs Spark's confusion is shaped into a brisk and intricate design, and it is a design we can accept is held to be peculiarly appropriate by the characters. It renews their sense of themselves. Further, this sense of themselves may be consistent with Catholic doctrine; but the link between the one thing and the other will be made or not made, as the case may be, by each separate reader. If he shares Mrs Spark's faith he will make the appropriate connection. If he does not, I can see nothing in the crystalline structure of the fiction to persuade him that he must.

These, then, the journalistic and the crystalline, are the alternatives Iris Murdoch proposes the contemporary novelist is bound to choose between. Both are inadequate to deal with the world as a novelist should deal with it. For we are not, as these types of novelists in their different ways would have us believe, 'monarchs of all we survey', though contemporary philosophies of freedom might lead us to suppose we are. Instead, we are 'benighted creatures sunk in a reality whose nature we are constantly and overwhelmingly tempted to deform by fantasy'. This is as true of Mrs Spark as it is of Dan Jacobson, although Jacobson is more worried by it. He is as much aware as Iris Murdoch that we require 'a renewed sense of the difficulty and complexity of the moral life and the opacity of persons'. But he is prepared to blunder along with the old liberal and Romantic concepts which she believes are no longer adequate 'to picture the substance of our being'. Mrs Spark, on the other hand, does not appear to be much concerned with the moral life. Her Catholic beliefs, and the relationship with her fictions they have allowed her to create, have encouraged her to detach herself from the messy, unfinished and inelegant surface of a word without a destiny. All the more surprising, then, the Iris Murdoch's fiction should bear so much resemblance, in important details, to Mrs Spark's. In an interview with Frank Kermode in 1963 she said that she started writing a novel hoping that 'a lot of people who are not me are going to come into existence in some wonderful way'. From what she has said about her respect for individuality and the 'opacity' of persons, this is no more than we should expect. But she admits to being unable to maintain this outward-looking delight in her creations. Instead, 'it turns out in the end that something about the structure of the work itself, the myth as it were of the work, has drawn all these people into a sort of spiral, or into a kind of form which ultimately is the form of one's own mind'.

This is the way we should expect a 'crystalline' novelist to behave. If it really were a satisfactory description of what Iris Murdoch's novels are like, the only difference between them and the novels of Muriel Spark would be that the form of Mrs Spark's novels is not that of her own mind, but that of reality as she endeavours to convince us God would see it. From the humanist point of view Mrs Murdoch would subscribe to, there is not much to choose, aesthetically, between a world ordered by God and a world ordered by the private imagination of a novelist. They are equally crystalline, equally turned in on themselves, creating a fantasy of organisation out of a reality of mystery and muddle.

Of course, what she is describing in her talk with Kermode is what she *believes* occurs in her novels, and then only 'often', not always. But I think it is a matter of almost universal agreement among those who have read her novels that they *are* highly patterned, sophisticatedly contrived, and not at all what one would expect from her theoretical pronouncements. Yet, in a curious way, they do give us a renewed sense of the difficulty and complexity of the moral life. In other words we find in her novels a strange combination of design or pattern, and an encouragement to flee the captivity which design and pattern are apt to impose on us. The shape of the fiction, whilst appearing to work against what the fiction is trying to say, turns out to be an unexpected support – more than that, the principal means by which Iris Murdoch's enrichment of concepts is able to take place.

One of the problems of writing about Iris Murdoch is that her own pronouncements on the novel have led readers to expect something very different in her fiction from what they actually find there. They have attached so much importance to what she has written about the 'opacity of persons' that they have tended to overlook the other important point she has tried to make about the enrichment of moral concepts. In fact, very few of the characters in her novels are at all 'opaque' in the sense in which she uses the word: that is to say, having the appearance of being mysteriously alive, and free from the novelist's ideological interference. On the contrary, they are the inhabitants of complex plots which are demonstrably more interesting than they are themselves. And these plots are the principal means whereby the novelist expresses her ideas about freedom, reality, goodness, truth – all those grand abstractions that have to be given a local habitation and a name in order that her second ambition, the enrichment of the concepts we use to deliberate upon the moral character of our actions, can be satisfactorily realised. Representation of the irreducible mystery of persons takes second place to a manipulation of concepts which will enable the reader to reacquire an understanding of that mystery, that opacity. The novels are attempts at habituating us to the use of those concepts in what is often a bewildering variety of situations and relationships. More than that, the intricate patterns of their plots are designed to reflect, in provocative ways, on the concepts the characters inside them spend so much of their time discussing.

The difficulty of writing about Iris Murdoch is made all the greater by virtue of the fact that the concept which dominates her fiction is that of the ultimate fallibility of concepts. She believes that though concepts are obviously of great value (if they are used properly), the time always comes when they are no longer necessary, when they must be allowed to fall into disuse. The trouble is that people often do not realise this. They continue to use concepts when they are no longer appropriate, with the result that the world they are being used to help interpret is transformed into a fantasy. At this point the concept is being abused. It is being converted into a means of evading reality, of 'consolation' (a key term in Iris Murdoch's moral vocabulary), of substituting an irresponsible freedom for a painful search for truth. In this way people sacrifice their sense of themselves and others as complex personalities living in a world of values and realities which are transcendent, which are unaffected by their fantasies and their false notions of freedom. The novels incorporate a wide variety of examples of this kind of abuse. Time after time a character is discovered transforming reality into a fantasy that his lack of concern for the truth has set him free to enjoy. Time after time the consequences of this freedom are meticulously documented in the complex web of activities the novel describes.

Reading the novels for the first time we might well feel as Hugh Peronett felt, in *An Unofficial Rose*, when he called on Emma Sands and Lindsay Rimmer: 'confronted with an entirely unfamiliar world, a world which seemed to have its own seriousness, even it own rules, while remaining entirely exotic and alien'. On the surface, the world of each novel is different. The picaresque narrative of *Under the Net* has little in common with the world of faithfully observed domestic detail of *An Unofficial Rose*, and neither of them has much in common with the fairy-tale world of *The Unicorn*. Also, the style and mood of each is different. *Under the Net* belongs as much to the world of the angry comedies of the 1950s as *An Unofficial Rose* belongs to that of Henry James, and *The Unicorn* to that of the mystery novels of Sheridan Le Fanu. In fact the closer we look at them, the more we shall discover that the philosophical patterning which is an attribute of Iris Murdoch's private temperament is co-extensive with another type of patterning which is not far removed from literary parody. The end of *Under the Net* inverts a motif (the song) from the end of Sartre's *La Nausée*. The story of Mars and Venus weaves its way in and out of incidents in the same novel. And an image taken from Wittgenstein's *Tractatus* is deployed in a variety of contexts that play with many of the concepts the philosopher was dealing with in that book.

If we are to isolate one preoccupation of these novels, in an attempt to discover some kind of order in their bewildering complexity, I should say that the one we must choose, the one that supports all the others and makes it easier for us to understand their significance, is that of design, of formal arrangements. This might appear unambitious. What about the grander concern with concepts like freedom, goodness, containment, imagination? All these are important. But I believe we can only understand them by attending to Iris Murdoch's handling of what I have called design, or pattern. She has a disconcerting habit of cutting off her characters' actions and their effects from any clear discrimination of their motives. Beyond that she has come to place greater emphasis on connections between characters than on relationships between them. As Randall says to Ann Peronett in *An Unofficial Rose*, 'it's odd how *connection* survives any real relationship', and Michael Meade to himself in *The Bell*, 'Our actions are like ships which we may watch set out to sea, and not know when or with what cargo they will return to port'. Michael comes close to disclaiming responsibility for the effects of actions set in motion by the self as a free agent, by cutting them away from any control our intention likes to think it can continuously exercise.

Patterns are made up of actions, not motives or intentions or consciousness. If actions, if effects, cannot be controlled by the intention of the person who causes them to come into existence, they will develop a momentum of their own and create their own random connections and disconnections. In fact Iris Murdoch does not go so far as this. Action is never entirely mechanical and automatic in her novels. It does take its basic direction from its source in the kind of person from whom it issues, but its specific route is rarely predicated by that source. Indeed, the person often finds it difficult to trace any connection between the purpose for which an action was performed and the identifiable consequences of such an action. This is very disconcerting. Men require the illusion that there are predictable connections between what they intend and what comes of what they intend. They need to be 'consoled'. And so they create fantasies. They invent connections which impose a pattern and design on what is of itself not patterned or designed. Then they go on to convince themselves and one another that these patterns, these designs, these *plots*, are inherent in the actions themselves. They convince themselves that they really exist. To do this, they need to be inhabited. So the characters in Iris Murdoch's books find themselves living in an artificial world that has been imposed on them and constructed around them by their own inventive imaginations, by the need they feel to console themselves. Gradually the artificiality, the fantasy, becomes so complex and so substantial that it is difficult for anyone to think it is not real. Some characters make deliberate use of their knowledge that this is so. Others fail to recognise the illusion their lives have come to be made of and are committed for ever to a world of fantasy. Others break out of the pattern: they have come to realise that it does not really exist. This last group is usually composed of the characters the author most admires. For Michael Meade, for example, the discovery that there is no pattern is only a beginning of a new, more clear-sighted spiritual struggle than the one that preceded it. And Ann Peronett, looking back on her last interview with her lover, Felix Meecham, feels that it had all been a muddle. 'Yet deep in the muddle there was, there must be, some decisive form.' 'It was as if what she had done was plotted on different and incongruous maps, which made it seem to her sometimes that different levels of conduct must have co-existed, and sometimes what she had really done was some yet other indiscernible thing.'

Iris Murdoch's scepticism about patterns and plots has led her to take the view that intention and action and the effect of action are not so directly related to one another as most earlier novelists had led us to believe they were. She does not believe that motive and consequence, cause and effect, are as firmly connected with each other as they have usually been represented in fiction. Therefore her attitude to character and her method of representing it are very different from the conventional attitudes and methods of earlier fiction. At the centre of each of her novels is a character's discovery of his identity, his reality. There is nothing very unconventional about this. It is the way he makes the discovery that is unconventional. For he does it by discarding the role he has been manoeuvred into playing within a dense network of plots – plots constructed by himself and plots constructed by other people. The network is gradually revealed (to the reader as well as to the character) to be an artificial environment. It is unreal, and its unreality tends to diminish the character's sense of his own reality as well as that of other people. Looking in on the arrangement of the plot from outside, the reader is encouraged to move *from* the action *to* the characters; not, as is more usual, the other way about. As the characters try to understand the nature of the plots in which they are involved (some are busy making them up, and others are busy consoling themselves with what they falsely suppose is the reality of the plots they are hatching), so, from his different point of vantage, the reader is trying to understand the bearing of each separate plot of the novel on the others. He can understand how a character is to be judged, how his attitude to the world is to be 'taken', only by the position he occupies within a plot which is constructed out of many plots – those that have been contrived by the characters for one another to inhabit. As the action of the novel gets under way, the source of the contrivance gradually becomes clearer. And as the source of the contrivance becomes clearer, so the positions the characters occupy, as distinct from the positions they *think* they occupy, become clearer also. This enables the reader to formulate opinions about them, to apply to them concepts which the structure of the novel suggests are appropriate. As Jake Donaghue puts it in *Under the Net*: 'We all live in the interstices of each other's lives, and we would all get a surprise if we could see everything.' Iris Murdoch places her readers in a position from which they can see everything. But they do not see everything all at once. Only gradually are the links between the different plots, and therefore the bearing of those plots on one another, allowed to disclose themselves. What the reader sees, intriguing though it usually is, hardly adds up to a dense and substantial world of fiction such as the Victorians and the Russians created.

It is a world that has been invented as if in play. Each of the novels is like a game. The pieces can be assembled in different ways and make different sorts of sense. Most, if not all, of these are non-sense. They are fantasies possessing the air, but not the substance, of sense. When, at the end of the novel, they slot into their final positions, the pattern they contrive to make is probably still false. But it may be that in the movement of the pieces we have caught a glimmering of what the design that would make sense would be. Bringing the pieces to life, at last, as the characters they represent, we may discover that one or more of them, too, has caught a sideways glance at the design into which he could most comfortably fit, the shape his life should take. I propose to move on, now, to see how such characters occupy a variety of positions in the plots to which they belong. First I shall be looking at *Under the Net*. Then I shall move on to *A Fairly Honourable Defeat*. In this way I hope to be able to demonstrate the consistency, as well as the development, of Iris Murdoch's handling of her medium from her first novel to one of her most recent. Both seem to me to represent Mrs Murdoch at her best.

The central theme of *Under the Net* is Jake Donaghue's acquaintance with Hugo Belfounder. Jake, the narrator, as well as the hero of the novel, says so, and it is a fact that the picaresque plot turns on the axis of this relationship between the two men. Hugo is a wealthy businessman who has made his money out of fireworks. He inherited the family armaments business but, being a pacifist, converted it into something less repugnant to his principles. Jake first meets him at a clinic, where both men are voluntary patients acting as guinea-pigs in an experiment to cure the common cold. He is immediately impressed by Hugo, to whose objectivity and attachment he is powerfully drawn. Hugo does not so much enunciate, as embody a philosophy of life which Jake finds very attractive. What it amounts to is, I suppose, an extreme scepticism about language and communication generally, coupled with a consuming interest in everything language is supposed to have been evolved to grapple with. He believes that everything has a theory but that there is no master theory: 'Hugo held no general theories whatsoever. All his theories, if they could be called theories, were particular.' I think it is important that this book is dedicated to Raymond Queneau, who was as responsible as anybody for inventing the dada-science of pataphysics. Pataphysics, the science of the particular, was very much in the air in 1954, when Mrs Murdoch published *Under the Net*; and, so far as I can make out, Hugo's philosophy of particular theories is fundamentally pataphysical. The fact of the dedication, coupled with the relevance of Queneau's work (picaresque novels like *Zazie dans le Métro* as well as the pataphysical essays) to the beliefs of one of the central characters of the book, emphasises the importance the novelist attaches to the philosophy to which, we are told, Hugo subscribes. The consequences of this philosophy are startling, and in a way absurd. Hugo enjoys his long conversations with Jake as much as Jake does. Yet those conversations are about the uselessness of conversation. 'As soon as I start to describe, I am done for', says Hugo, because 'The whole language is a machine for making falsehoods'. ' "I know myself," said Hugo, "that when I really speak the truth the words fall from my mouth absolutely dead.' " Jake is duly impressed: 'it was as if his very mode of being revealed to me how hopelessly my own vision of the world was blurred by generality'. Hugo's theories eschew classification. He notices only detail, and sees everything as absolutely unique. No wonder, then, he despises language, with its inherent generality, its habit of abstraction from experience. Hugo's philosophy is directed to the same end as Miles Greensleave's poems in *Bruno's Dream*, those descriptions of the anemones with which this book opened. The end, in each case, is typically modern – an escape from unreality into silence.

When Jake writes up the conversation he has had with Hugo, in the form of a philosophical debate between two fictional characters, he calls the book they comprise *The Silencer*. In it Annandine enunciates Hugo's philosophy of silence, using the image in the title of Mrs Murdoch's book to clarify his meaning. The movement away from theory and generality, he says, is the movement towards truth: 'All theorising is flight. We must be ruled by the situation itself and this is unutterably particular. Indeed it is something to which we can never get close enough, however hard we may try as it were to crawl under the net.' Now it has been pointed out by several critics of this book that the net referred to here and in the title is the same net Wittgenstein referred to in his *Tractatus* (6.341 etc.). There the image of a net is used to signify any arbitrary linguistic device which 'brings the description of the surface [of a thing] to a unified form'.

Laws, for example, including laws of causation, 'treat of the network and not of what the network describes'. John Passmore explains this as follows:

> If we think of science as an attempt to describe the world by means of a fine mesh, *a priori* laws, Wittgenstein says, are not part of the results at which we thus arrive: on the contrary they are the characteristics of the mesh (although it *shows* us something about the world, Wittgenstein thinks, that it can be described in such-and-such laws).

The net is a metaphorical representation of the concepts we require 'to picture the substance of our being'. Our interest in it is not in respect of what it is in itself, but as a way of describing what lies underneath it, which is the unclassifiably particularised universe we discover in Queneau's novels.

The central issue to be explored in any interpretation of *Under the Net* must be the importance we attach to Hugo Belfounder and his ideas. As I have pointed out, in important respects his philosophy is similar to that of the writer to whom the book is dedicated; and the dominating image Jake uses to explain it is borrowed from Wittgenstein, a philosopher whom we know Iris Murdoch admires. Furthermore, Jake, the hero of the novel, is impressed by it. *The Silencer* seems to have been written by him in order to provide as nearly a systematic explanation of Hugo's philosophy as the nature of that philosophy will permit. There is, in other words, a considerable body of support, from within the text, for the view that the picture of the world which *Under the Net* proposes is consonant with the picture of the world that is proposed in Hugo's conversation and in Jake's book. However, it would be extraordinary if this were really the case. After all, Hugo's philosophy is essentially Romantic, extremely modern. The emphasis it places upon the particularity and uniqueness of things, the absurdity of classification, the poverty of language, is consistent with the attitude towards art and communication we found expressed by Gabriel Josipovici in his book on the novel. As I pointed out in Chapter 1, similar Romantic views to these led Josipovici to a belief in art as an articulation of silence. And as I pointed out immediately above, the title of Jake's book is *The Silencer*. But as soon as I have made these points I am reminded of two things. The first is that

Hugo's philosophy is not itself a philosophy of silence. Though he believes that language distorts reality and that we make too many concessions to the need to communicate, he never commits himself to silence. Nor does he enjoin silence on others. It is Annandine, Jake's dramatised version of Hugo, who expresses the belief that for most of us truth can be attained, if at all, only in silence. And even he believes that 'the strongest' can resist the weight of theory with which all expression is encumbered. The second is that what we hear about Hugo's philosophy is mediated through Jake, whose memory of his conversations at the clinic is imperfect, and is in any case affected by his transcription of them in *The Silencer*. This transcription is from notes he made some time after the conversations actually took place. When he looked at the notes again he found that they 'didn't make sense', so he 'added to them a bit', 'polished' them up, made them look more 'intelligible'. This combination of first-person control over the information disclosed, and the link between Hugo's philosophy and Jake's grasp of that philosophy, suggests one very important thing: we never come directly into contact with Hugo's philosophy. All we hear about is Jake's version of Hugo's philosophy, which is not the same thing. The first time we meet Hugo in person, at a political rally in his film studio, we have no opportunity of hearing him express his views. The second and last time we meet him, at the hospital where Jake is working as an orderly, he has nothing of a philosophical nature to say. So we have to rely on Jake's account of Hugo, written up long after the publication of *The Silencer* and some time before the facts about Hugo's involvement in Jake's life have come to the surface (of Jake's mind as well as ours). The most interesting aspect of this account is that there is an enormous difference between what Jake says about Hugo and what Hugo says about himself. Jake's comments on Hugo are full of superlatives, bristling with approbation. Hugo's part of the conversation is tolerably interesting, but hardly as exciting as Jake has led us to believe it to be. Certainly it is not as impressive as the polished reproduction of it we are given in *The Silencer*.

Iris Murdoch is committed to a belief in and a respect for what she has called the 'opacity of persons'. She is further committed to the view that we need a new vocabulary of moral awareness, a new set of concepts with which to picture man's situation in the world. In *Under The Net* she presents to us a philosophy of life which incorporates one of these beliefs and expels the other. Only by relinquishing a vocabulary of any kind, only by eschewing the need for concepts, is it possible to come into contact with that dense aggregate of particularities which make up the mysterious identity of each of the things that are in the world, including individual persons. At this point the connection with Wittgenstein's philosophy is broken. For Wittgenstein the net was a necessary instrument in our attempt to make sense of the world. The error lay in misusing it, or making the mistake that what it was and what it described were one and the same thing. To 'crawl under the net' is to commit oneself to ignorance. In fact, in spite of what Annandine says in *The Silencer*, no character in *Under the Net* (Anna Quentin comes closest to it) takes the view that one should try to do this. To crawl under the net is one of two major philosophical errors which are embodied in the narrative of the book. The other error is 'to treat of the network and not of what the network describes'. The pattern, or plot, of *Under the Net* is formed by the combination of these two errors as they are manifested in the lives and actions of most of the characters.

The second error is treated at length, and accounts for most of the permutations of the plot. But it would not be able to exist, and the plot would not be able to function, were it not for the presence of the first. This is revealed most conspicuously in the person of Anna Quentin. Her mime theatre in Hammersmith is a visible expression of the Romantic respect for silence. Its rooms are filled with a chaos of exotic objects, reevaling Anna's love of contingency and hatred of order, of system. Furthermore, the very activity of mime casts doubt on the efficiency of the most systematic form of communication we possess – that of language. The most profound form of communication dispenses with language altogether. Anna feels the same about love. 'Love is action, it is silence', she says, just as Hugo had said that he supposed '*actions* don't lie'. But even here, in the contingent world of Anna's dressing-room, with its jumble of glass balls, toy animals, Paisley shawls and a multitude of other fabrics and bizarre objects, Jake feels he is seeing someone in the grip of a theory. He is right in more ways than he knows. Not only Anna but he himself is in the grip of a theory. Anna's theory is that no theory will account for the multifariousness of reality and that silence is therefore enjoined upon those who seek to know reality. It is, we are to learn later, a variant of the philosophy Jake attributes to Hugo Belfounder. Jake's theory is that Anna can subscribe to such a theory only as a result of Hugo's having explained it to her, and that therefore a relationship between Anna and Hugo exists which must be of a particular character, which he goes on to define and make real to himself.

The narrative of *Under the Net* comprises Jake's discovery of how far he is right and how far wrong in making these suppositions about Anna and Hugo. He has to find out if what is real to himself, what determines the nature of all his actions, is real for the world in which those actions occur. And we have to remember that, whether his beliefs are right or wrong, the actions which arise out of them do themselves add something to the world. Error makes up a large part of the substance of reality since, on the evidence of this book, a large part of what we believe to be true bears little relationship to the facts – in so far, that is, as what the facts are can ever be determined.

Also, the narrative of *Under the Net* is Jake's narrative. As A. S. Byatt has pointed out, this is very important, because it means that Jake's explanations, Jake's summings-up of events, are taken by the reader at their face value, as being appropriate or correct, when they may later be revealed to be nothing of the kind. In Mrs Byatt's words, the convention of first-person narrative 'allows us to suppose that if the narrator says "I saw that it was not Sadie that Hugo loved, but Anna", this is in fact the case'. For Jake, in other words, his own interpretation of what is real *is* what is real, and because his interpretation is conveyed through first-person narrative, it becomes what is real for the reader too. The net of language is being confused with the reality it is the business of the net to describe. The same is true of Iris Murdoch's next novel to use the first-person narrative, *A Severed Head*. Here too the narrator (Martin Lynch-Gibbon) makes such fascinating patterns as he casts his net, that our eye fastens on the net itself and ignores the reality it should have been deployed to catch. Reality is usually the one that got away. The more the net fails to catch it, the more the motions of the net tend to hypnotise and fascinate. This occurs at greater and greater expense to our understanding of what should lie beneath it – beneath, that is to say, the false interpretations of the narrator's first-person account.

As a matter of fact the real events of *Under the Net* are very simple and very obvious. Sadie Quentin is fond of Jake. She says so. Sadie is afraid of Hugo. She says so. Anna is in love with Hugo. Her activities at the mime theatre proclaim it. Hugo does not love Anna. If he did, he wouldn't be pestering Sadie. Once these simple and obvious facts are understood, everything else falls into place. But Jake cannot afford to understand this because he is in love with Anna and he is not very fond of Sadie. Also, his understanding of Hugo does not extend to his being able to see how Hugo could possibly be in love with Sadie, or Anna with Hugo. For Jake, Hugo must be in love with Anna, not the other way about. Contrary to Jake's requirements, however, reality is usually what it proclaims itself to be. What *is* is usually 'of the surface'. The apparent facts are usually the real facts. This also is Wittgensteinian, though this time we have to refer to the Wittgenstein of *Philosophical Investigations*:

> Philosophy simply puts everything before us, and neither explains nor deduces anything – since everything lies open to the view there is nothing to explain. For what is hidden, for example, is of no interest to us. . . . The aspects of things that are most important for us are hidden because of their simplicity and familiarity. (One is unable to notice something – because it is always before one's eyes.) (126 and 129)

Jake is living proof of the fact that what is hidden is by no means uninteresting to us. On the contrary, it is the stuff of which consoling fantasies are made. Sooner or later truth breaks through. In *Under the Net* we have to wait for Hugo's explanation to Jake at the hospital, which forces Jake to concede: 'I was in on it. . . . I knew everything. I got it all the wrong way round, that's all!' By this time his error, his fantasy, has added a great deal more reality to the world which is in its turn subect to the fantasies and requirements of others: Madge in Paris, Sadie in London, even Dave Gellman, the utilitarian philosopher in his flat in Notting Hill Gate, are drawn into the web of fantasy and fiction that Jake's interference with reality has created.

As a result of his many failures of understanding, Jake learns two things. For a start, he learns that what Hugo is, what he represents, cannot be imitated or reproduced. His book, *The Silencer*, and Anna's mime theatre are both imperfect embodiments of what each admires in Hugo. Hugo is, in a way, a living proof of the correctness of what, between the lines, we might take his theory to be. Every body and every thing is essentially different, and this difference is to be respected, even loved. Certainly Jake feels this about Anna. At the end of the book he releases her from his possessive desire into a freedom – the freedom to be *other*, that the lover confers upon the person he loves. She is made free of the pattern he has constructed around her. She is allowed out of the plot in which he has forced her to enact a wholly inappropriate fictional role. Now Jake realises that there is no pattern, of the kind he had pretended there was. But does that mean that there is no pattern, that what Annandine said in *The Silencer* is true and that we are committed to a world of rich and exquisite particularity, but no meaning, no design, no plot at all? Must we crawl under the net, or can we make intelligent and responsible use of it from above? The answer to this question is the second thing Jake learns in the course of his adventures.

In her conversation with Frank Kermode, Iris Murdoch said of *Under the Net* that 'It plays with the philosophical idea. The problem which is mentioned in the title is the problem of how far conceptualising and theorising, which are from one point of view absolutely essential, in fact divide you from the thing that is the object of theoretical attention.' So far my description of the roles played by Anna, Sadie and Hugo in what I have called Jake's 'plot' has emphasised the fact of division: the gap between the reality of the situation between Anna and Hugo and Hugo and Sadie, and the unreality, the fiction, of Jake's elaborate misunderstanding of that situation. Now I have to go on to explain the point of view from which conceptualising and theorising – those activities of the mind which impose plots and patterns on our experience of events – may be held to be 'absolutely essential'.

All Iris Murdoch's novels are concerned with the relationship between freedom and reality. Many of her characters have a highly developed sense of their own destinies, which is apt to take the shape of a pattern they will upon reality and hope to develop and enlarge through the exercise of their freedom. Others among them are aware of pattern and design in their lives. But they do not see this pattern as something that is willed, and consequently imposed upon a reality which may offer considerable resistance to it. The pattern Jake has imposed on the lives of those around him is revealed to be no more than a fiction by Hugo's disclosures about Anna and Sadie. Similar unexpected events have the same effect on other characters in later books. Michael Meade, for example, in *The Bell*, has his privately fashioned sense of order and design knocked from beneath him by Nick Fawley's death: 'The pattern which he had seen in his life existed only in his own romantic imagination. At the human level there was no pattern.' On the other hand there are characters like Michael's colleague at Imber, James Tayper Pace, whose respect for reality is so great that the idea of freedom is neglected altogether and replaced by a willing subservience of the individual to an order or pattern which is transcendent, unresponsive to private will. One of the most extreme exponents of this point of view is Gerald Scottow, the 'warder' of Gaze Castle in *The Unicorn*. He believes that 'freedom' has no meaning. 'There are great patterns in which we are involved, and destinies which belong to us and which we love even in the moment they destroy us', he says. 'The pattern is what has authority here, and absolute authority.' The rest of the novel demonstrates how this can be held to be true and how it can also be held to be untrue.

Jake Donaghue's progress through the events of *Under the Net* is a progress from the point of view represented by Michael in *The Bell* to the point of view represented by Gerald in *The Unicorn*. At first glance this seems ridiculous, since Michael is in many ways an admirable character and Gerald is in many ways a deplorable one. It may not seem quite so ridiculous, how-ever, if I add that what Jake eventually accepts as the pattern in which his life is irretrievably involved is, unlike that of Gerald Scottow, a pattern of his own making. It is the plot he recognises he really belongs to, not the plot that, throughout the novel, he has been busily constructing in order to evade the reality of the situ-ation. Like Mr Biswas or Constance Baines, though at a very different level of mimetic reality, he is what he has made himself, and it is true that what he has made himself has been largely, though by no means wholly, determined by contingent circum-stance. At the end of the novel, when he has decided to buy Mr Mars, the superannuated star of many animal films, for the price

Sadie has demanded, he explains that 'the formal properties of the situation left me with no choice'. He *has* to buy the dog. Long before this he had felt that the development of the relationship between himself and Hugo was 'inevitable', a matter of destiny. In the same way, his decision to stop translating the work of a best-selling French novelist and to start writing books of his own is the result of a vision he has had of his destiny 'which imposed itself on me as a command'. When he made this decision, and turned down the lucrative offer from Madge's new film company, 'I saw at last . . . the real shape of that which had before so obscurely compelled me'. Jake is indeed a man with a destiny. But it is a destiny which is not so much imposed from above, having nothing to do with the will of the person to whom it attaches, as created out of the combination of real actions with real results that such a person has himself performed. .

I have implied above that the link between intention and consequence in the activities of Iris Murdoch's characters is not always as clear as it is in those of the characters of most earlier English novelists. How is this consistent with the picture of destiny, and the freedom to choose one's destiny, which I have been saying occupies much of the theoretical foreground of her novels? I think Jake's ability to recognise his own destiny and apply himself to its accomplishment, after the various errors and misconceptions his conduct has exposed him to, is a sign of the position *Under the Net* occupies at the opening of Iris Murdoch's career as a novelist. More often in the later novels, characters who are in some sense admirable, who have escaped or never been caught in false notions of freedom, are not aware of the forms of their destinies. They sense obscurely, if at all, the appropriate forms of their lives, the indefinable but none the less effective links between what they are and the moral environment that is in large part the consequence of what they are. So the actions of a good person strangely, often indirectly, promote good. Those of an evil person promote evil. But the connection between the good or evil act and the good or evil person is rarely perceptible. Nevertheless it is real. It can only be seen from the novelist's playfully controlling point of view – the point of view the reader is gradually persuaded into accepting as the novel moves towards its end. It is in this sense, to return to the passage I quoted earlier from *An Unofficial Rose*, that Ann Peronett's conviction that, deep in the muddle of her relationship with Felix, there must have been some 'decisive form', is to be understood. The form Jake Donaghue sees clearly at the end of *Under the Net*, which in his case replaces those false consolations of fantasy he had imposed on events at an earlier time, is only obscurely present to Ann's comprehension. Nevertheless it exists. Her recognition of this fact, and her instinctive willingness to live her life in the knowledge of it, demonstrate both her respect for reality, and the inevitable limitation this imposes on her conduct. This is what I meant when I wrote at the end of an earlier chapter that Iris Murdoch's plots are extensions, in a more philosophical manner, of Henry James's concern with the 'contrivance of relations'. Like James's, Iris Murdoch's characters are compelled to an act of recognition. They have to recognise the reality of their destinies, the patterns they really belong to. The conventionality of their lives, where they succeeded in doing this, is also similar to that of James's characters. Maggie Verver's dull recognition of the forms, her dogged observation of the correct relations that obtain among the members of her family group, is very much like that of Ann Peronett in *An Unofficial Rose* or Maria Magistretti in *The Italian Girl*. All these characters submit to their destinies. In doing so they make themselves a trifle ridiculous, where they are not dull, to the other characters. Jake is never dull, because we take leave of him at the point where he is about to enter on his new destiny. Nevertheless, a book about writing a book (which is what he is about to do) would in all likelihood have been much less interesting than one about not writing a book (which is what *Under the Net* is). In one of Irish Murdoch's latest novels, *A Fairly Honourable Defeat*, the roles of the man who interferes with reality and the man who submits to it are clearly separated and duly apportioned to two of the principal, and in their different ways dominating, characters. I want to move on from *Under the Net* now, and see how the philosophical preoccupations we saw at work in that novel are deployed in the plot of this more recent one.

On a fine autumn morning in 1969, Rupert Foster, a respected civil servant, is found dead in the swimming-pool of his house in S.W.10. It is established that he died of drowning (but with a large dose of sleeping-pills and alcohol in his body) and it is presumed that he fell into the pool accidentally. The verdict at the inquest is death by misadventure. It is all reminiscent of Radeechy's death in *The Nice and the Good*, although that had been caused by a revolver shot, was definitely suicide (if it was not murder), and, more importantly, it happened at the very beginning of the book. Rupert dies at the end of *A Fairly Honourable Defeat*, and there is genuine doubt as to whether or not he has committed suicide. Whether this is or is not true, however, it is the act to which all the earlier actions appear to have been leading. What the novel is about is how far we can feel ourselves justified in supposing that those earlier actions really did produce this result. Is the appearance of inevitability substantiated by the collective detail of the actions the novel presents?

Rupert and Hilda have been happily married for twenty years. Their house at Priory Grove, with its courtyarded garden surrounded with roses and its diminutive swimming-pool, is a haven of peace and tranquillity for the odd assortment of friends and relations whose lives are objects of loving attention to the godlike pair. Their relationship is similar to that of Octavian and Kate Gray in *The Nice and the Good*. The only cloud on their horizon is the behaviour of their son Peter, who has opted out of his studies at Cambridge and is now living a life of total irresponsibility and petty theft in the company of his uncle Tallis. Even this is not disastrous, because Tallis's wife and Hilda's sister, Morgan, is due back from America, and she is known to have influence with Peter, and will probably manage to see him back safe in Cambridge. However, Morgan herself is something of a problem. Her marriage with Tallis broke up when she fell in love with Julius King, a man of mesmeric and potentially dangerous personality, who has now finished with her and not started anything else. Tallis, Julius and Morgan will all be in London at the same time. And this is not all. Rupert's younger brother, Simon, has set up house with his homosexual friend Axel, another civil servant and a friend of Rupert's and Julius's. With all this material at his disposal, Julius is not likely to remain at a loose end for long. The first three chapters of the novel are rather transparently assembled with a view to getting this information across. They are like the expository first act of a play by Shakespeare. With the arrival of Morgan in chap. 4, the play proper has begun.

It is not a fanciful comparison. *A Fairly Honourable Defeat* does have a great deal in common, in its narrative strategy, with a play by Shakespeare. I should guess that Iris Murdoch is conscious of this, that the similarity is a part of her strategy. In a radio interview with Ronald Bryden, given during the period in which she was writing *Bruno's Dream* and, no doubt, meditating her next novel, she confessed her love of Shakespeare, especially of his ability 'to combine a marvellous pattern or myth with the expansion of characters as absolutely free persons, independent of each other – they have an extraordinary independence, though they're also kept in by the marvellous pattern of the play'. The relationships between a person's independence and the part he plays within the pattern of a life or a play or a novel has been, as we have seen, a dominant theme in Iris Murdoch's own fiction. No wonder, then, that she should admire the multifarious demonstrations of it in Shakespeare.

In the same interview the conversation turned to the presence of little 'courts' in the novels. Ronald Bryden pointed out that in most of them the characters tend to fall into separate groups, usually within separate houses, or divisions in the same house. Remember the geography of Imber in *The Bell*, the cliques and factions revolving around Hannah at Gaze in *The Unicorn*, and the disposition of characters inside and outside Carel Fisher's rectory in *The Time of the Angels*. This also is like Shakespeare, especially the Shakespeare of the romantic comedies – the groupings in the crazy park at Navarre, for instance, in *Love's Labour's Lost*. Iris Murdoch's comment on this is interesting. She agreed that she did tend to make her characters fall into groups, but that she would like to do something different: 'What I would like to do . . . is to have a novel which hasn't got a court, which is much more scattered, where the people aren't really connected with each other. As if one could have a novel entirely composed of peripheral characters, with no main characters.' Well, in *A Fairly Honourable Defeat* there is a court, Rupert's court, but as the action develops we become less and less certain who really presides over it, who is king. Of course, the obvious candidate, after Rupert's fall from grace, is Julius, Julius *King*: it only requires a reversal of Christian and surnames to prove it. Julius clearly thinks he is king, most of the time. But he is wrong. His real name is Kahn, not Khan. He misses sovereignty by a misplaced 'h'. So who is king? Many of the characters are blind, blind to the forces that bind them and release them; and in the country of the blind the one-eyed man is king. Tallis is the only character with at least one eye open. If anybody has a right to the title he has. But he despises power. In the end we have to accept a court without a king; in fact at the very end there is no longer a court, only an empty house. All the characters *are* peripheral. The novel spans the length of time it takes for them to realise this.

Apart from Tallis and, perhaps, Hilda, all of them assume that they are at the centre of little dramas that are themselves at the centre of a big drama. This is partly true. The characters do put on the trappings of a little play-within-a-play straight out of Shakespeare's romantic comedies. Morgan becomes a boy dressed up as a girl dressed up as a boy in Julius's flat; Simon and Julius eavesdrop on Rupert and Morgan in a scene modelled on events that might have grown out of the situation created around Benedick and Beatrice in *Much Ado About Nothing*. The business of the misunderstanding between Julius and Hilda as to whether Peter or Rupert is Morgan's lover is also theatrically comic, and must have a prototype somewhere in Shakespeare. These are the 'little dramas'. Usually they take the form of some kind of misunderstanding or misinterpretation of the facts. The novel is riddled with information withheld and events misread: Simon doesn't tell Axel about his visit to Julius, which he mistakenly supposed was in aid of Axel's birthday; Morgan thinks Axel must have told Hilda about her and Rupert – there are dozens of these errors out of which the comedy is wrought. But a greater error is manufactured out of the lesser. False connections are made between constructions put upon events which are themselves false. Hilda tells Julius 'A lot of little things make one big thing', the sum is greater than its parts. Julius replies, correctly, that Rupert's misdemeanours – 'if they are such' – 'are quite scattered and probably quite momentary and random lapses. . . . These things should not be added up, it is far more just to see them as a series of impulses than as a deliberate policy.' But Hilda is not interested in the details. She prefers to complete her big theory at the expense of the little facts – like whether Rupert and Morgan have, really, made love to each other.

What is true of Hilda is true of most of the others. They invent dramatic identities for themselves and allot supporting roles to the rest of the 'cast'. Axel 'imagined' the affair between Julius and

Simon 'into existence with all the details and everything seemed to fit'. For Morgan, Peter is 'perfect' because he 'fits the role' she has allotted to him, because he is 'exactly what I need'. (As Julius tells her, 'You are always wanting other people to act in some drama which you have invented'.) Morgan has her own explanation for this. Shortly after she has bet Julius ten guineas that he cannot detach Simon from Axel within three weeks, she has a long argument with him about language. Julius believes that 'Language is a reasonably useful jumble with an in-built capacity to manoeuvre itself. These manoeuvrings can be watched. . . . But they are merely what they are. There is nothing behind them.' Morgan, who is a professional linguist of what seems to be a structuralist type, cannot accept this: 'Why should language be a mountain of accidents. Nothing else in the world is. Any theory tries to explain, or at least to display, multiplicity by conjecturing deep pattern.' We are back with Hugo–Wittgenstein's net of concepts and the uses to which it should be put. Is there or is there not a 'general structure'? If there isn't, how does Julius avoid chaos? If there is, can it be the kind Morgan conjectures, with all the attendant mistakes and fantasies that it produces? Can it be anything more than a subjective fallacy which does not connect, but collides, with the real world of acts and consequences?

One of the answers to these questions lies in Rupert's book, the book Peter and Julius destroy immediately before the party that is to be given to celebrate its completion. In it, Rupert has evidently tried to systematise the views he has discussed with Julius at various times in the past. Unlike Morgan and Hilda, Rupert chose to ignore 'the drama of his motives. He sought simply for truthful vision, which in turn imposed right action.' In doing so he was trying to answer Morgan's bewilderment about the distance that lies between an act and its consequence – like her meeting with Rupert and the effect it has had on her relationship with her sister. 'How can one live properly', she asks, 'when the beginnings of one's actions seem so inevitable and justified while the ends are so completely unpredictable and unexpected?' Rupert starts to answer this question from the position Theo (in *The Nice and the Good*) and Miles (in *Bruno's Dream*) attained only at the end of the novels to which they belong, and after much real suffering. Rupert has not suffered. Therefore his defences crumble as soon as any real demand is made on his capacity to suffer. The book opens with him telling his wife that he is sure love tells in the end:

> There are times when one's just got to go on loving somebody helplessly, with blank hope and blank faith. When love just *is* hope and faith in their most decided form. Then love becomes impersonal and loses all its attractiveness and its ability to console. But it is just then that it may be able to redeem. Love has its own cunning beyond our conscious wiles.

In the end this is proved to be true, but not by Rupert, and not *for* him either. Rupert is destroyed, easily, even unintentionally, by Julius, who holds distinctly contrary opinions.

Julius had talked to Morgan about 'watching' the manoeuvrings of life, as well as language, behind which nothing exists. Watching is as typical of him as lecturing is typical of Rupert. At the end of part 1 of *A Fairly Honourable Defeat*, an odd little incident takes place in a Chinese restaurant four of the characters visit. A Jamaican is being attacked by a gang of teenage hooligans as first Simon, and then the others, enter. Later Axel, one of the group, explains that all of them acted characteristically. 'Simon intervened incompetently, I talked, you [Julius] watched, and Tallis acted.' It is significant that Julius watched, just as he is later to be found looking through windows, searching for letters, eavesdropping on Morgan and Rupert, and (earlier this time) staring at Tallis when he enters Axel's house to find out about Morgan. Incidentally, I think this is mimetically very accurate. People upon whom characters like Julius are modelled *do* enjoy watching other people like this, just as many homosexuals behave like Axel and Simon. I mention this to alert my readers to the fact (which they are probably already aware of, but may be under the impression that I am not) that Iris Murdoch is well equipped with many of the conventional representational skills. However, Julius's watching is not just a matter of mimetic accuracy. Tallis also watches, notices things. The point about Julius is that he is watching from a position that appears to exist outside the action the other characters are involved in. His position there appears, both to the characters and to ourselves, to confer on him a kind of power, a mesmeric quality. He is an enchanter.

Consider Julius's role. Unmoved himself, he exists to move

others. The others are primarily Simon, and through him Axel; and Hilda, and through her both Rupert and Morgan. Those he moves are married, in Simon's and Axel's case figuratively, but not superficially, speaking. His plot to endanger Simon's relationship with Axel involves his having Simon overhear Rupert making love to Morgan. His plot to separate Rupert from Hilda involves the discovery of trinkets – letters – and a persistent train of indelicate suggestion operating upon events which in themselves are scarcely suspicious. Julius has no observable motive. We learn that he detests Rupert's book and the sentiments expressed in it; and, of course, in a sense Rupert has slept with his wife (in fact his mistress) Morgan. Where have we heard all this before? Surely in *Othello*. The only difference is that the part of Othello is shared between Rupert and Axel, and that Julius, the Iago figure, operates on the wife (Hilda and Simon) instead of the husband. The detail of the plot is derived from the comedies, but the shape of the whole is tragic. At the end of it Rupert, like Othello, kills himself. Like Othello, he is self-deceived as well as deceived by others. And Julius, like Iago, appears to be a 'motiveless malignity'. Also like Iago, his lack of motive is pictured not by an absence of that agency, but by too much of it. We can say of Julius what Iago says of himself: ''Tis in ourselves that we are thus, or thus.' Iris Murdoch agrees wtih this as a general principle: but she attaches a very different value to it from the one that either Iago or Julius does.

Julius accepts the other characters' appraisals of themselves at their face value. Morgan assigns Peter a role in her own play. Very well then. Julius will tell Morgan:

> Human beings are roughly constructed entities full of indeterminacies and vaguenesses and empty spaces. Driven along by their own private needs they latch blindly onto each other, then pull away, then clutch again. Their little sadisms and their little masochisms are surface phenomena. Anyone will do to play the roles. They never really see each other at all. There is no relationship . . . which cannot quite easily be broken and there is none the breaking of which is a matter of genuine seriousness. Human beings are essentially finders of substitutes.

If Julius is right, human beings are no more than puppets. That is what Julius says they are, and that is why he calls what Rupert

and Morgan enact in front of Simon a puppet show. But Julius
is not a puppet. He is the puppet-master. There was 'nothing
there' between Rupert and Morgan. But then the fact that they
supposed there was means that there was nothing there between
Rupert and Hilda, beneath the consoling fictions they invented
to keep each other happy. All three of them, and Axel and
Simon too, have been 'deceived by mere appearances and appari-
tions', chief among which is love – not a 'permission of the will'
and a 'lust of the blood' as it was for Iago, but a mixture of 'pity
and variety and novelty in an emotional person'. Julius provided
the mixing-bowl and, lo and behold, 'they . . . behaved predictably
to an extent which is quite staggering. . . . They really are puppets.'

It looks as if Julius has won the argument with Rupert. At
the end of the novel Julius is enjoying Paris in the last days of
autumn, and Rupert is dead at the bottom of his swimming-pool.
But he has not won it, because the argument was not really with
Rupert at all. Julius embodied what he spoke in a way Rupert
never did; because evil can speak itself in a way good cannot.
Rupert spoke the good but did not embody it. That was done by
Tallis, and Tallis is not destroyed. Furthermore, Julius does not
succeeded as he expected. Evil does come of evil – Rupert is
dead. But that evil is not the intended evil. I should argue myself
the same for *Othello*. Until Act III, Iago does not intend to destroy
either Othello or Desdemona. Forces beyond his control *make*
him do it. What makes Julius destroy Rupert? For as he tells
Tallis, he didn't really intend things to proceed so far: 'It all
rather got out of hand.'

What Julius fails to recognise is the fact that marriage – by
which it is possible to mean any relationship binding two human
beings together – is a condition, and as such is not entirely to be
accounted for by the sum of the separate personalities who compose it. This is most clearly exemplified in the retrospective scene
in which the coming together of Axel and Simon is described.
They met in the National Museum in Athens. There, in an
alcove, stood a marble *kouros*. Both men were attracted to it.
Their hands touched over the buttocks of the Greek god. Therefore, as Morgan (to whom the story is being told) suggests, a god
brought them together. There is that in their marraige which
exists independently of the two separate spouses. To interfere
with the god is to inflict unpredictable damage to the persons

in whom he has taken up his abode. There is a hint of the E. M. Forster of the short stories ('The Road from Colonus', for example) in this incident.

Possibly even more important, Julius fails utterly with Tallis. Remember that in the struggle with the hooligans at the restaurant, whilst Julius watched, Tallis acted. He acts again at the end of the novel when he finds out what Julius has done. Axel brings to our attention the fact that 'The only person about the place with really sound instincts is Tallis. He led Julius straight to the 'phone.' And Julius, for the only time in the book, meekly follows. The fact that Tallis is an unimpressive figure who can't keep his wife or stand up to his father or even prevent his flat from becoming a rubbish-dump simply confirms his goodness which, as Julius himself says, is 'dull'. Evil is exciting. It is much more interesting to play Iago than Desdemona. 'It is also very much more mysterious than good. Good can be seen through. Evil is opaque.' This is true of Tallis. Where Julius is, as Morgan says, 'so clever, and yet . . . mysterious and exciting too', Tallis is 'obscure and yet . . . without mystery'. In fact Tallis is everything the other characters are not. The muddle he lives in is made up of singly observed individual entities that compose no evident pattern or design. His 'dull holding on and hoping' to and for Morgan is an example of the love as just 'hope and faith in their most denuded form' that Rupert theoretically approved but failed to see in front of him when it presented itself in the form of his brother-in-law. Julius recognises this in Tallis and finds himself powerless before it. To Tallis's question why he has come to him to confess his plot against Rupert and the others, all Julius can reply is 'Oh you know why'. Indeed he does. For unlike every other person in the novel, Tallis sees Julius as a victim, not as a charismatic enchanter. He sees the concentration-camp number on the victim's wrist, just such a mark as Mischa Fox must also have carried in *The Flight from the Enchanter.* So in his final meditation on the events that have occurred, Tallis discovers a pattern that he does not show himself to be aware of as such, and cannot therefore make use of. The accident, he believes, 'was deeply the product of its circumstances'.

Tallis did not try to unravel these nor did he speculate about the guilt of any person, not even about his own. He grieved

blankly over something which seemed in its disastrous com-
pound of human failure, muddle and sheer chance, so like
what it was all like. It went wrong from the start, he said to
himself. But these were not his words and this was not his
thought, and he put it away from him as a temptation. Then
he tried just to remember Rupert and keep the memory clear
and feel the pain of it endlessly.

Tallis, then, vindicates the good and proves that the top of
Rupert's moral structure is not completely empty – as Julius had
argued it was. Rupert died, not because of Julius's scheming, not
because Hilda left him, not because Morgan despised him. He
died because he was what he was. Axel describes to Simon 'the
terribly tangled network of causes which led to Rupert's death
and how very little any of us actually knew at any given moment
about the whole situation and about the consequences of our
actions'. Once again, the network is not the substance. Once
again, the patterns we impose on reality are distinct, in action and
in thought, from reality itself.

Pattern and reality are distinct. Reality, in fact, has no plot –
unless, like Muriel Spark, the novelist can produce a God to
supply one. Yet we cannot help behaving as if there were a plot,
as if the activities of men and women were connected to one
another in such a way as to produce a pattern, which in its turn
implied a meaning. Because we behave like this, because we
manufacture fictive links between one action and another,
between cause and consequence, and between what we are and
what we do, we fill in the neutrality of what is real with the
exciting, vividly interesting partiality of what is false. This, in
turn, becomes real, in the sense that it becomes something that
has to be taken account of by everyone else who has to do with
us. In this way we construct a network of relationships which
form themselves into social, political and cultural arrangements.
They become the reality we have to work with, and in a very
little time we fail to notice the difference between this actual,
though fabricated, reality, and the inconceivably true reality
whose absence is either bewailed by philosopher-critics like Josipovici, or celebrated by aesthetes like Kermode – who use it as an
opportunity for constructing alternative worlds, superior fictions.

Iris Murdoch tries to discriminate between those patterns which are the products of her characters' fantasies, the grotesque outgrowths of their determination to be free, and those which are inherent in the acts they have performed and the positions which, in consequence, they discover they occupy. Like Ralph Touchett in James's *The Portrait of a Lady*, they learn to 'accept the situation', just as, we were told, Jake Donaghue accepted 'the formal properties of the situation'. The same could be said of Tallis in *A Fairly Honourable Defeat*, with the important difference that he learned to do so before the action of the novel ever began.

In a world where most people are for ever exercising their claim to be free, such behaviour is unlikely to be thought natural. In its essense it is natural, in the sense we found John Bayley using that word, but in its relationship to the Romantic world of free individuals that surrounds it, it is bound to seem eccentric. The form of Iris Murdoch's plots, and the positions occupied in them by these natural and eccentric characters, reveals the ambiguous position she finds herself in vis-à-vis the worlds of nature and of freedom. Intellectually, she escapes the trap this modern dilemma sets for her. But her very intellectuality narrows the scope of her work to an enrichment of the concepts by which we grow to understand reality; whereas one supposes, from what she has said in the interviews with Kermode and Bryden from which I have quoted, she would like to go further than this and be able to represent the opacity of persons, the mysterious fact of individuality, as a substantial presence in her fiction. However, her philosophical intelligence and her very highly developed sense of pattern, of design, prevent her from doing so. Her characters lack the 'extraordinary independence', the 'expansion', she admires in those of Shakespeare. This confinement in the splendidly imaginative myths she has constructed around them make them official, not unofficial, selves; however true it may be that the office they serve is so liberal, so tolerant, so concerned with the exercise of true freedom.

The novels by Dickens, Bennett, Hughes and Naipaul that I have tried to appreciate in the body of this book have in common a feeling for the substantiality of the world and of the vividness of the lives people live within it. The reality of the world, and the reality of those lives, is never in doubt. It is not a matter of philosophical concern. Each of these novelists is content to represent the world, to dwell lovingly and interestedly on its manifold appearances. On several occasions I have used the phrase 'saving the appearances'. I have meant by it urging upon the reader a respect for what appears to be the case, which is so strong, so enthralling, that it does not occur to him to inquire *what* they are the appearances of. There is much to be said for John Bayley's respect for Nature. In a sense, it is not very different from a respect for appearances. But, as Bayley himself would no doubt agree, it is not the whole truth. In the world at large, not everyone is responded to as a private, discrete and mysterious being, to be apprehended with reverence and love. We rarely experience people 'from the standpoint of their own consciousnesses'. Perhaps what I am saying is that there are limits to a novelist's capacity to love his characters, just as there are limits to our capacity to love in real life. The range of feeling between love and indifference, however, is very great. What I have tried to show is the ease or difficulty with which the novelists I have studied traverse the whole landscape of feeling. The death of Krook in *Bleak House* is the consummation and purpose of his fictional life. The life of Tulkinghorn doesn't entertain the idea of death as in any way appropriate to its character. It comes as a hideous surprise, a fictionally necessary aberration. Yet Tulkinghorn and Krook, as well as Skimpole and the Jarndyce family, rub along well enough with each other within the confines of the same novel. Or in Hughes's *The Fox in the Attic*, Tascha and Hitler, Wolff and Augustine, live altogether different lives, touching one another only in the geographical sense. In all other respects, their existences, their selves, are of a different character, and these different characters are not rounded off and smoothed down to get them to pretend they are the same sorts of being as all the others. Bennett and Naipaul achieve this multi-responsive representation of appearances in a less dramatic way. Nevertheless, their feel for the common strangenesses of life is unfussily and truthfully communicated. None of these writers is indifferent to the world. Their lack of indifference is evident in the novels they have written. They have kept up appearances which are scarcely distinguishable from reality. Of course, what they offer is possibly false, at best irresponsibly imaginative – in a word, unofficial.

Bibliography

Wherever possible I have avoided cluttering the text with footnotes providing references to books and articles consulted. Instead, I append a list of these here, under the appropriate chapter headings. All dates are to English first editions, unless otherwise stated.

Chapter 1: Nothing but the Truth

page

Frank Kermode, *The Sense of an Ending* (London, 1967)   5

——, *Continuities* (London, 1967).   5

Hans Vaihinger, *The Philosophy of As If*, trans. C. K. Ogden (London, 1924).   5

Aristotle, *Poetics*, trans. S. H. Butcher (London, 1894).   7

Wallace Stevens, 'An Ordinary Evening in New Haven', in *The Auroras of Autumn* (1950); reprinted in *Collected Poems of Wallace Stevens* (London, 1969).   8

Gabriel Josipovici, *The World and the Book* (London, 1971).   10

Roland Barthes, *Le degré Zéro de l'écriture* (Paris, 1953).   19

Franz Kafka, *Parables and Paradoxes* (New York, 1961).   20

Ian Gregor and Mark Kinkead-Weekes, *William Golding: A Critical Study* (London, 1967).   24

Chapter 2: Deaths and Entrances

Walter Dexter (ed.), *The Letters of Charles Dickens*, 3 vols. (London, 1938); see also for p. 40.   27

A. E. Dyson (ed.), *Dickens Bleak House: A Casebook* (London, 1969).   27

W. J. Harvey, *Character and the Novel* (London, 1965).   30

John Butt and Kathleen Tillotson, *Dickens at Work* (London, 1957).　　32

Anthony Trollope, *An Autobiography* (London, 1883).　　33

Henry James, review of *Our Mutual Friend*, in *Nation*, i, 21 Nov 1865.

F. W. Boege, 'Point of View in Dickens', *P.M.L.A.*, LXV (1950).　　37

E. M. Forster, *Aspects of the Novel* (London, 1927).　　38

Raymond Williams, *The English Novel from Dickens to Lawrence* (London, 1970).　　40

John Wain, '*Little Dorrit*', in *Dickens and the Twentieth Century*, ed. John Gross and Gabriel Pearson (London, 1962); reprinted in *Essays on Literature and Ideas* (London, 1964).　　41

F. Locker-Lampson, *My Confidences: An Autobiographical Sketch Addressed to My Descendants* (London, 1896).　　45

William Empson, *Some Versions of Pastoral* (London, 1935).　　45n

John Bayley, *The Characters of Love* (London, 1960).　　45n

V. S. Pritchett, *The Living Novel* (London, 1946).　　46

Nigel Dennis, *Cards of Identity* (London, 1955).　　49

Laurence Lerner, Introduction to the Penguin ed. of *Wives and Daughters* (Harmondsworth, 1969). For Lerner's views on other English novelists dealt with in this book, see *The Truthtellers: Jane Austen, George Eliot, D. H. Lawrence* (London, 1967).　　49

Stephen Ullmann, *Style and the French Novel* (Cambridge, 1957).　　53

David Daiches, *George Eliot: Middlemarch* (London, 1963).　　54

Frederick Greenwood, 'Conclusion: A Note by the Editor', *Cornhill Magazine* (Jan 1860); reprinted in the Penguin ed. of *Wives and Daughters*.　　55

Ernest A. Baker, *A History of the English Novel*, x (London 1924).　　55

F. R. Leavis, *The Great Tradition* (London, 1948).　　59

P. Swinden (ed.), *George Eliot, Middlemarch: A Casebook* (London, 1972) for reviews of *Middlemarch* quoted on this page and following.　　60

Amy Cruse, *The Victorians and their Books* (London, 1935).　　60n

Chapter 3: Detachment

Richard Stang, *The Theory of the Novel in England 1850–1870* (London, 1959).   62

Kenneth Graham, *English Criticism of the Novel 1865–1900* (London, 1965).   62

Edmond Duranty, *Réalisme* (Paris), July 1856–May 1857.   62

Emile Zola, *La Roman expérimental* (Paris, 1880).   62

——, *Les Romanciers naturalistes* (Paris, 1881).   62

Guy de Maupassant, Preface to *Pierre et Jean* (Paris, 1888).   62

M. A. Ward 'Recent Fiction in England and France', *Macmillan's Magazine*, L (Aug 1884).   63

N. H. Kennard, 'Gustave Flaubert and George Sand', *Nineteenth Century*, xx (1886).   63

Arabella Shore, 'Modern English Novelists', *Westminster Review*, cxxxiv (1890).   64

G. J. Becker, *Documents of Modern Literary Realism* (Princeton, 1963).   64

Harry Levin, *The Gates of Horn: A Study of Five French Realists* (New York, 1963).   64

Gustave Flaubert, *Œuvres complètes de Gustave Flaubert: Correspondance*, Nouvelle édition augmentée, ed. Conard (Paris, 1926–33).   64

——, *Correspondance Supplément*, ed. Dumesnil, Pommier et Digeon (Paris, 1954).   64

——, *Lettres inédites à Tourguéneff* (Monaco, 1946).   64

Gustave Flaubert and George Sand, *Correspondence entre Gustave Flaubert et George Sand*, ed. Lévy (Paris, 1904).   64

Saint-René Taillendier, 'Le Réalismépique dans le roman', *Revue des Deux Mondes*, XLIII, 15 Feb 1863.   65

A. Thorlby, *Gustave Flaubert and the Art of Realism* (London, 1956).   66

W. C. Frierson, 'The English Controversy over Realism in Fiction 1885–1895', *P.M.L.A.*, XLIII (June 1928).   66

D. Pacey, 'Flaubert and his Victorian Critics', *University of Toronto Studies*, Philological Series, xvi (1946).   66

Georges Dumesnil, *L'Époque réaliste et naturaliste* (Paris, 1946).   66

Erich Auerbach, *Mimesis: The Representation of Reality in Western Literature*, trans. Willard Trask (Princeton, 1953).   69

M. Bonwit, 'Gustave Flaubert et le Principe d'Impassibilité, *University of California Publications in Modern Philology*, XXXII (Berkeley, 1947–51). 71

Susan Sontag, *Against Interpretation* (New York, 1966). 72

Robert Scholes, *The Fabulators* (New York, 1967). 72

Alain Robbe-Grillet, *Pour un nouveau roman* (Paris, 1963). 73

Roland Barthes: see for p. 19. 74

Bruce Morrissette, *Les Romans de Robbe-Grillet* (Paris, 1963). 76

John Sturrock, *The French New Novel* (London, 1969). 76

R. A. Gettman, *Turgenev in England and America* (Urbana, Ill., 1941). 88

Eugène Melchior de Vogüé, *Le Roman Russe* (Paris, 1886). 88

'Ivan Serguievitch Tourgenieff', *London Quarterly Review*, LXIII (Oct 1884). 89

'Two Russian Realists', *London Quarterly Review*, LXX (Apr 1888). 89

George Moore, *Impressions and Opinions* (London, 1899). 89

D. Magarshack (ed.), *Turgenev's Literary Reminiscences and Autobiographical Fragments* (London, 1899). 90

E. Halperine-Kaminsky (ed.), *Tourgeneff and his French Critics* (London, 1898). 91

Ford Madox Ford, *Henry James* (London, 1914). 91

John Galsworthy, *Castles in Spain, and Other Screeds* (London, 1927). 91

R. H. Freeborn, *Turgenev, the Novelists's Novelist: A Study* (London, 1960). 92

Henry Gifford, *The Novel in Russia: From Pushkin to Pasternak* (London, 1964). 92

F. W. J. Hemmings, *The Russian Novel in France 1884–1914* (London, 1950). 92

Maurice Baring, *Landmarks in Russian Literature* (London, 1910). 95

Donald Davie (ed.), *Russian Literature and Modern English Fiction* (Chicago, 1965). 95

C. R. Decker, 'Victorian Comments on Russian Realism', *P.M.L.A.*, LII (1937). 95

Gilbert Phelps, *The Russian Novel in English Fiction* (London, 1956). 95

John Bayley, *Tolstoy and the Novel* (London, 1966). 96

Chapter 4: Registration

R. P. Blackmur (ed.), *The Art of the Novel* (New York, 1934).　101

Henry James, review of W. D. Howells's *A Foregone Conclusion*, in *Nation*, xx (Jan 1875).　101

——, 'Anthony Trollope', *Century Magazine*, xxvi (July 1883); reprinted in *Partial Portraits* (London, 1888).　101

——, 'The Art of Fiction', *Longman's Magazine*, iv (Sep 1884); reprinted in *Partial Portraits*.　101

——, review of Flaubert's *La Tentation de Saint Antoine*, in *Nation*, xviii (June 1874); reprinted in *Literary Reviews and Essays* (New York, 1957).　102

——, 'Gustave Flaubert', *Macmillan's Magazine*, lxvii (Mar 1893); reprinted in *Essays in London and Elsewhere* (London, 1893).　102

For Henry James's views on Turgenev, see his:　102

'Ivan Turgénieff', *Library of the World's Best Literature* xxv (New York, 1897); reprinted in *The Future of the Novel* (New York, 1956).

'Ivan Turgénieff', *Atlantic Monthly*, liii (Jan 1884); reprinted in *Partial Portraits*.

Review of *Terres Vierges*, in *Nation*, xxiv (Apr 1877); reprinted in *Literary Reviews and Essays*.

'Ivan Turgénieff', *North American Review* (Apr 1874); reprinted in *French Poets and Novelists* (London, 1878).

Henry James, 'Guy de Maupassant', *Fortnightly Review*, xlix (Mar 1888); reprinted in *Partial Portraits*.　102

——, Preface to *Madame Bovary* (London, 1902); reprinted in *Notes on Novelists* (London, 1914).　103

James Ashcroft Noble, review of *The Portrait of a Lady*, in *Academy*, xx (Nov 1881).　104

Review of *The Portrait of a Lady*, in *Blackwood's Edinburgh Magazine*, cxxxi (Mar 1882).　104

George Saintsbury, 'The Present State of the Novel', *Fortnightly Review*, xlii (Sep 1887); xliii (Jan 1888).　104

Henry James, review of *Middlemarch*, in *Galaxy*, xv (Mar 1873).　104

——, 'Daniel Deronda: A Conversation', *Atlantic Monthly*, xxxviii (Dec 1876); reprinted in *Partial Portraits*.　104

Henry James, Preface to Balzac's *The Two Young Brides* (London, 1902); reprinted in *Notes on Novelists*. 105

———, 'The Lesson of Balzac', *Atlantic Monthly*, xcvi (Aug 1905); reprinted in *The Question of Our Speech* (London, 1905). 105

W. D. Howells, 'Henry James Jnr.', *Century Magazine*, xxv (Nov 1882). 105

M. Fullerton, 'The Art of Henry James', *Quarterly Review*, ccxii (Apr 1910). 105

N. Friedman, 'Point of View in Fiction: The Development of a Critical Concept', *P.M.L.A.*, lxx (1955). 105

The *Academy* reviews of James's work from 1881 to 1905 in vols. xx, xxvi, li, lvi, lxvii. 106

Joseph Warren Beach, *The Method of Henry James* (New Haven, 1918). 107

J. I. M. Stewart, *Eight Modern Writers* (London, 1963). 107

F. O. Matthiessen and K. B. Murdock (eds.), *The Notebooks of Henry James* (New York, 1957). 108

Percy Lubbock, *The Craft of Fiction* (London, 1921). 108

Tony Tanner, *The Reign of Wonder: Naïvety and Reality in American Literature* (London, 1965). 109

Reginald Bliss [H. G. Wells], *Boon* (London, 1915). 112

Edith Wharton, 'The Criticism of Fiction', *Times Literary Supplement*, 4 May 1914. 115

John Bayley: see for p. 45n. 115

Maxwell Geismar, *Henry James and his Cult* (London, 1964). 117

Chapter 5: Time and Motion

Ford Madox Ford, *The English Novel* (London, 1929). 121

———, *Joseph Conrad: A Personal Remembrance* (London, 1924). 121

Frank MacShane, *The Life and Work of Ford Madox Ford* (London, 1965). 124

Guy de Maupassant: see for p. 62. 124

E. D. Sullivan, *Maupassant the Novelist* (Princeton, 1954). 124

Emile Zola: see for p. 62. 134

C. R. Decker, 'The Aesthetic Revolt against Naturalism', *P.M.L.A.*, liii (1938). 134

Storm Jameson, *The Georgian Novel and Mr Robinson* (London, 1929). 134

John Galsworthy: see for p. 91. 134

Virginia Woolf, *The Common Reader*, 1st series (London, 1925). 135

Arnold Bennett, 'Neo Impressionism and Literature', *New Age*, 8 Dec 1910; reprinted in *Books and Persons* (London 1917). 136

——, *The Author's Craft* (London, 1914). 137

Newman Flower (ed.), *The Journals of Arnold Bennett* (London, 1932). 137

James Hepburn (ed.), *The Letters of Arnold Bennett* (London, 1966). 137

George Moore, *Confessions of a Young Man* (London, 1888). 139

Arnold Bennett, 'Ivan Turgenev: An Enquiry', *Academy*, LVII (Nov 1899). 157

——, 'Tourgeniev and Dostoievsky', *New Age*, 31 Mar 1910; reprinted in *Books and Persons*. 157

Chapter 6: Growing Pains

'Balzac and his writings', *Westminster Review*, IV (July 1853) 158

Arnold Bennett, review of R. E. C. Lang's translation of *The Kiss, and Other Stories*, in *New Age*, 18 Mar 1909; reprinted in *Books and Persons*. 158

Arnold Bennett: see for p. 137. 158

Harry T. Moore (ed.), *The Collected Letters of D. H. Lawrence*, 2 vols. (London, 1962). 162

E. T. [Jessie Chambers], *D. H. Lawrence: A Personal Record* (London, 1935). 164

J. Middleton Murry, *Son of Woman* (London, 1931). 164

F. R. Leavis, *D. H. Lawrence, Novelist* (London, 1955). 169

J. I. M. Stewart: see for p. 107. 169

Raymond Williams, *Modern Tragedy* (London, 1966). 174

Bernard Bergonzi, *The Situation of the Novel* (London, 1971). 174

Walter Allen, *Tradition and Dream* (London, 1964). 183

Chapter 7: Plots

John Bayley: see for p. 45n.   203

Iris Murdoch, 'Against Dryness', *Encounter*, XVI (Jan 1961).   211

Stuart Hampshire, *Thought and Action* (London, 1959).   211

Christopher Ricks, 'One Little Liberal: *The Beginners* by Dan Jacobson', *New Statesman*, 3 June 1966.   214

Frank Kermode, 'The Prime of Miss Muriel Spark', *New Statesman*, 27 Sep 1963; reprinted in *Modern Essays* (London, 1971).   224

——, 'The Novel as Jerusalem: Muriel Spark's *The Mandelbaum Gate*', in *Modern Essays*.   224

——, 'The House of Fiction', *Partisan Review*, XXX, no. 1 (spring 1963).   231

Iris Murdoch, *The Sovereignty of Good* (London, 1971).   233

Malcolm Bradbury, 'Iris Murdoch's *Under the Net*', *Critical Quarterly*, IV, no. 2 (spring 1962).   237

John Passmore, *A Hundred Years of Philosophy* (London, 1957).   239

Ludwig Wittgenstein, *Tractatus Logico-Philosophicus*, trans. C. K. Ogden and F. P. Ramsey (London, 1922).   239

A. S. Byatt, *Degrees of Freedom* (London, 1965).   242

Ludwig Wittgenstein, *Philosophical Investigations*, trans. G. E. M. Anscombe (Oxford, 1953).   243

Ronald Bryden, 'Talking to Iris Murdoch', *The Listener*, LXXIX, 4 Apr 1968.   **249**

Index

Academy, 106
aevum, 10–11
apocalypse, 6–7
Aquinas, St Thomas, 10–11, 13, 64
Aristotle, 7
Auerbach, Erich, *Mimesis*, 69–70, 99
Austen, Jane, 115–16, 121, 169, 172, 173; *Emma*, 50–2, 77

Baker, Ernest, 55
Ballantyne, R. M., 182; *The Coral Island*, 24
Balzac, Honoré de, 75, 85, 105, 158; *La Cousine Bette*, 134
Baring, Maurice, *Landmarks in Russian Literature*, 95
Barth, John, 72, 87
Barthes, Roland, 19, 196; *Le degré Zéro de l'écriture*, 74–5, 87
Bayley, John, 45; *The Characters of Love*, 116–19, 174–5, 203–9, 212, 257–8; *Tolstoy and the Novel*, 96–8
Bazley, Frances, 182
Beach, Joseph Warren, 107
Beckett, Samuel, 21, 25
Bennett, Arnold, 46, 136, 158, 162, 163, 172, 204, 258; *Anna of the Five Towns*, 137, 162; *The Author's Craft*, 137, 157; *The Old Wives' Tale*, 56, 120, 137–148, 157, 159–60, 161, 174, 177, 210–11, 245
Bergonzi, Bernard, 174
Berkeley, Bishop, 21

Bernard, Claude, 134
Bichât, Xavier, 134
Blackwood's Edinburgh Magazine, 104
Boege, F. W., 37
Borges, Jorge Luis, 25
Brontë, Charlotte, 53
Broughton, Rhoda, 45
Brown, Ford Madox, 137
Bryden, Ronald, 249, 257
Bunyan, John, *The Pilgrim's Progress*, 17–18
Burke, Edmund, 207
Butt, John (and Tillotson, Kathleen), *Dickens at Work*, 32
Byatt, A. S., 242

Camus, Albert, *L'Etranger*, 19
Chambers, Jessie, 164
Chantepie, Mme Leroyer de, 64
Chaucer, Geoffrey, 17, 204, 205; 'The Knight's Tale', 201; *Troilus and Criseyde*, 202, 206
Chekhov, Anton, 158
Colet, Louise, 64
Collins, Wilkie, *The Woman in White*, 40
Collins, W. L., 60
Conrad, Joseph, 95, 121, 126, 172; *Lord Jim*, 218; *Nostromo*, 218; *Typhoon*, 181
Cruikshank, George, 40
Cruse, Amy, *The Victorians and their Books*, 60
'crystalline' novels, 212, 221

Daiches, David, 54

Dante, 15–16, 19, 20, 71

Daudet, Alphonse, 88, 90

Degas, Edgar, 137

Defoe, Daniel, 22–3; *Robinson Crusoe*, 24

Deism, 70

Dennis, Nigel, 49

Dicey, A. V., 60

Dickens, Charles, 27–42, 44, 45, 101, 102, 159, 162, 205, 216, 258; *All the Year Round*, 27; *Bleak House*, 27–32, 34, 35–7, 38–40, 42–7, 56–7, 258; *David Copperfield*, 32, 33–4, 34–5, 134, 146, 161; *Dombey and Son*, 30, 32, 37; *Great Expectations*, 25–6, 33, 38, 161; *Household Words*, 27; *Little Dorrit*, 33, 37 n., 41–2; *The Old Curiosity Shop*, 27; *Our Mutual Friend*, 37, 40

Dostoievsky, Fyodor, 95, 172

Dumas, Alexandre, *The Hunchback of Notre Dame*, 154

Duranty, Edmond, *Réalisme*, 62

Edinburgh Review, 60

Eliot, George, 21, 42–4, 46, 56–61, 63–4, 100, 104, 105, 162, 173; *Adam Bede*, 53; *Daniel Deronda*, 54, 59, 106; *Felix Holt the Radical*, 59; *Middlemarch*, 43, 52, 54, 57–60, 63, 106, 111–12, 214; *The Mill on the Floss*, 54, 56, 161; *Romola*, 104

Empson, William, *Some Versions of Pastoral*, 45 n.

Examiner, The, 60

Fielding, Henry, 100, 123

Flaubert, Gustave, 24, 64–72, 75, 78, 87, 88, 90, 91, 94, 102–3, 122–3, 133, 162, 173, 206, 222; *L'Education sentimentale*, 63, 67–8, 70–1, 92, 103, 123, 134, 139, 199; *Madame Bovary*, 63, 64, 65, 69–70, 75, 89–90, 91–2, 94, 99, 103, 123, 133–4, 139, 205;

La Tentation de Saint Antoine, 67, 102

Ford, Ford Madox, 46, 94; *The English Novel*, 121–2; *The Good Soldier*, 48, 78, 119, 124–33, 136, 158–9; *The Marsden Case*, 126; *Parade's End*, 205

Forster, E. M., *The Longest Journey*, 196; *A Passage to India*, 125–6; 'The Road from Colonus', 255

Fortnightly Review, 89, 104

Fry, Roger, 136

Galsworthy, John, 90, 136; *Castles in Spain*, 134; *The Man of Property*, 135

Garnett, Edward, 170, 178

Gaskell, Elizabeth, 42; *Cousin Phillis*, 55; *Wives and Daughters*, 49–53, 55, 77, 146

Gasset, Ortega y, 88

Geismar, Maxwell, 117

Gerhardi, William, 204

Gettman, R. A., 88

Gissing, George, 173

Godard, Jean Luc, 72

Gogol, Nikolai, 214

Golding, William, *The Inheritors*, 24–5; *Pincher Martin*, 24–5

Goncourt, Edmond and Jules de, 88, 90

Graham, Kenneth, 63

Greenwod, Frederick, 55

Gunn, Thom, 140

Hampshire, Stuart, *Thought and Action*, 211–12

Hardy, Thomas, *Two on a Tower*, 48

Harvey, W. J., 38

Hawthorne, Nathaniel, 208; *The Scarlet Letter*, 22

Homer, 205

Hopkins, Gerard Manley, 2

Howells, W. D., 105

Hugh of St Victor, 15

Hughes, Richard, 181–202, 258; *The Fox in the Attic*, 181, 182, 185, 187, 190–202; *A High Wind in Jamaica*, 181, 182–7, 190; *In Hazard*, 181, 184–5, 188–190, 194
Hume, David, 208
Huysmans, J. K., 78

Jacobson, Dan, *The Beginners*, 213–20, 221, 225; *A Dance in the Sun*, 214; *The Price of Diamonds*, 214
James, Henry, 60, 91, 100–19, 121, 122, 169, 173, 208, 233, 247; *The Ambassadors*, 106, 109; 'The Art of Ficton', 108; 'Daisy Miller', 109; *The Golden Bowl*, 106, 107, 109, 110, 114–19, 204, 247; *Notebooks*, 108, 114; *The Portrait of a Lady*, 100, 104, 106–7, 108, 109, 113, 114, 118, 257; *The Tragic Muse*, 109; *What Maisie Knew*, 106, 108, 109; *The Wings of the Dove*, 106, 107, 109, 110–13, 118
James, William, *Principles of Psychology*, 136
John, Augustus, 182
Johnson, B. S., *Travelling People*, 221; *Trawl*, 221
Johnson, Samuel, 21
Josipovici, Gabriel, *The World and the Book*, 10, 14–20, 21–6, 207–9, 222 n., 256
'journalistic' novels, 212, 213
Joyce, James, 205, 222; *A Portrait of the Artist as a Young Man*, 64, 70

Kafka, Franz, 'The Truth about Don Quixote', 20
Keats, John, 2
Kennard, N. H., 63
Kermode, Frank, 224, 230, 231–2, 244, 256; *The Sense of an Ending*, 5–13, 14, 15, 20–6, 207

Lafayette, Mme de, 121
Lawrence, D. H., 157, 160–81, 205; *Birds, Beasts and Flowers*, 180; 'The Captain's Doll', 179–80; *Lady Chatterley's Lover*, 179; *The Rainbow*, 169, 171, 175–8, 179, 180–1, 210; 'St. Mawr', 162, 169, 179–80; *Sons and Lovers*, 160–8, 174, 175, 178; *Women in Love*, 162, 165, 167, 172, 174–5, 178, 179
Leavis, F. R., 169; *The Great Tradition*, 59
Le Fanu, Sheridan, 223
Lerner, Laurence, 52
Locker-Lampson, Frederick, *My Confidences*, 45, 75
London Quarterly, 89
Longman's Magazine, 101
Lubbock, Percy, 90, 108–9

Macmillan's Magazine, 63
Mann, Thomas, *Death in Venice*, 19
Marinetti, Filippo, 170
Maupassant, Guy de, 67, 71, 90, 102; *Bel Ami*, 124; *Fort comme la mort*, 124–6, 128, 139; *Notre coeur*, 124; *Pierre et Jean*, 62, 124
McLeod, A. W., 162
Meredith, George, 173
Milton, John, 99
Monet, Claude, 137
Moore, Brian, 211; *An Answer from Limbo*, 120
Moore, George, 63, 89, 94; *Esther Waters*, 88, 137, 144; *The Lake*, 88
Murdoch, Iris, 82, 87, 118–19, 211–213, 221, 230–56, 257; 'Against Dryness', 211; *The Bell*, 234, 235, 245, 249; *Bruno's Dream*, 1–4, 12, 203, 249, 251; *A Fairly Honourable Defeat*, 237, 247–256, 257; *The Flight from the Enchanter*, 255; *The Italian Girl*, 247; *The Nice and the Good*,

Murdoch, Iris – *cont.*
248, 251; *A Severed Head*, 242;
The Time of the Angels, 249;
Under the Net, 233, 234, 236,
237–47; *The Unicorn*, 233, 245,
249; *An Unofficial Rose*, 233,
234, 235, 246–7
Myers, L. H., 205

Naipaul, V. S., 145, 204, 211, 258;
A House for Mr Biswas, 148–
157, 160, 214, 215, 219, 245;
The Mimic Men, 148, 154; *The
Mystic Masseur*, 154
Nation, The, 60, 63
Nerval, Gerard de, 1
New Age, 136, 158
New Statesman, 224
Nineteenth Century, 63
nouveau roman, 21, 72–88

O'Brien, Flann, *At Swim-Two-
Birds*, 25

Passmore, John, 239
peripeteia, 7–8, 224
Phiz, 40
Ponge, Francis, 2
Powell, Anthony, *The Music of
Time*, 213
Powys, J. C., 205
progression d'effet, 131–2
Proust, Marcel, 204, 205, 208

Queneau, Raymond, 237–8; *Zazie
dans le Métro*, 238

Rabelais, François, 17
Reade, Charles, *Griffith Gaunt*, 58
Resnais, Alain, *L'Année dernière à
Marienbad*, 72–4, 86; *Muriel*, 73
Revue des Deux Mondes, 88
Richardson, Samuel, 121
Ricks, Christopher, 214, 216
Robbe-Grillet, Alain, 21, 73–88,
221; *Dans le labyrinthe*, 19, 78,
82–5, 222; *Les Gommes*, 78, 82;
La Jalousie, 73, 76, 77, 78, 81,
82, 85; *Le Voyeur*, 78–82

roman d'analyse, 124
roman objectif, 124

Saintsbury, George, 104
Sand, George, 64, 67 n.
Sartre, Jean Paul, *La Nausée*, 62,
86, 88, 234
Scott, Sir Walter, 123
Shakespeare, William, 204, 205;
Love's Labour's Lost, 249;
Macbeth, 73–4; *Much Ado
About Nothing*, 250; *Othello*,
253–4, 255
Simon, Claude, 21
Snow, C. P., *Strangers and
Brothers*, 213
Sontag, Susan, *Against Interpreta-
tion*, 72–3, 87
Spark, Muriel, 221–30, 231, 256;
The Bachelors, 224; *The Ballad
of Peckham Rye*, 221; *The
Comforters*, 223–4, 229; 'A
Curtain Blown by the Breeze',
221–2, 223; 'The Go-Away
Bird', 222; *The Mandelbaum
Gate*, 221, 225–30; *Memento
Mori*, 204; 'Miss Pinkerton's
Apocalypse', 228; *Not to Disturb*,
196; 'The Portobello Road',
221; 'The Seraph and the
Zambesi', 222
Spectator, 60
Stendhal, 121, 204
Stephen, Leslie, 60
Sterne, Laurence, 22
Stevens, Wallace, 8, 11, 20
Stevenson, R. L., 182
Stewart, J. I. M., 108, 169, 178
Sullivan, E. D., 124–5
Swift, Jonathan, 22, 99

Tale of Genji, 205
Tanner, Tony, 109–10
Teresa, St, 57
Thackeray, Annie, 45
Thackeray, W. M., 42, 44, 123, 159,
208; *Vanity Fair*, 46–49, 50, 53,
94, 146

Tillotson, Kathleen, *see* Butt, John

Tolstoy, Leo, 95–9, 101, 102, 134, 172, 205, 208; *Anna Karenina*, 97, 174–5, 206, 215, 218; *War and Peace*, 98, 159, 200; *Youth*, 97

Trollope, Anthony, 33, 42, 44–6, 55, 59, 75

Turgenev, Ivan, 88–95, 96, 98, 113, 122–3, 134, 173, 214; *Fathers and Children*, 93–5, 214; *Literary Reminiscences*, 90; *A Nest of Gentlefolk*, 92, 93; *On the Eve*, 214; *Rudin*, 92, 93; *Smoke*, 89; *A Sportsman's Sketches*, 90

Vaihinger, Hans, *The Philosophy of As If*, 5, 11

Vogüé, Eugene Melchior de, *Le Roman Russe*, 88, 89

Ward, M. A., 63

Wells, H. G., 136; *Boon*, 112; 'The Grisly Folk', 24

West, Rebecca, *The Birds Fall Down*, 205

Westminster Review, 57, 64, 158

Wharton, Edith, 115

Williams, Raymond, 54, 174–5

Wilson, Angus, *The Middle Age of Mrs Eliot*, 213; *No Laughing Matter*, 223–4

Wittgenstein, Ludwig, *Philosophical Investigations*, 243; *Tractatus Logico-Philosophicus*, 234, 238–239, 241, 251

Woolf, Virgina, 135–6, 137, 159; *Mrs Dalloway*, 136

Wordsworth, William, 55

Zola, Émile, 69, 88, 134; *Le Roman expérimentale*, 62; *Les Romanciers naturalistes*, 62